the complete guide to

buying
property
in France

The masculine pronoun has been used throughout this book. This stems from the desire to avoid ugly and cumbersome language, and no discrimination, prejudice or bias is intended.

First published in Great Britain in 2003
Second edition 2004

Apart from any fair dealing for the purposes of research or private study, or criticism or review, as permitted under the Copyright, Designs and Patents Act 1988, this publication may only be reproduced, stored or transmitted, in any form or by any means, with the prior permission in writing of the publishers, or in the case of reprographic reproduction in accordance with the terms and licences issued by the CLA. Enquiries concerning reproduction outside these terms should be sent to the publishers at the undermentioned addresses:

Kogan Page Limited
120 Pentonville Road
London N1 9JN
United Kingdom
www.kogan-page.co.uk

Kogan Page US
22883 Quicksilver Drive
Sterling VA 20166–2012
USA

© Charles Davey, 2003, 2004

The right of Charles Davey to be identified as the author of this work has been asserted by him in accordance with the Copyright, Designs and Patents Act 1988.

The views expressed in this book are those of the author only. Except in respect of its own advertisement, Eurotunnel has not been involved in the writing or publication of this book and shall not be responsible for any matter arising therefrom.

British Library Cataloguing in Publication Data

A CIP record for this book is available from the British Library.

ISBN 0 7494 4261 1

Typeset by Saxon Graphics Ltd, Derby
Printed and bound in Great Britain by Cambrian Printers Ltd, Aberystwyth, Wales

the complete guide to

buying property in France

2ND EDITION

charles davey

London and Sterling, VA

Property Owners' Club

WH...TMENT

Not quite a property owner...
then call to discover our great
deals for **PROPERTY HUNTERS**

WHEN YOU CAN MAKE TWO?

When you've invested in a second home abroad, there's one other investment that really makes sense. For just £65* you can join our Property Owners' Club which gives you discounted crossings with Eurotunnel. Plus a lot of extras, too. Like reductions on fares for your family and friends, automatic membership of our Privilège Plus frequent traveller scheme and even the opportunity for free crossings for you. Spend a little time checking out the details on our website or call **0870 243 0892**. It's one of the best investments a property owner can make.

eurotunnel.com /2ndhome   EURO TUNNEL

ACCELERATE TO FRANCE IN 35 MINUTES   INSPIRING POSSIBILITIES

*Registration fee £30. Annual fee £35. Property Owners' Club terms and conditions apply and are available on request or at www.eurotunnel.com/2ndhome

Home comforts...house hunting is easier with Eurotunnel!

What better way to go house hunting abroad than in the comfort of your own car? Driving abroad has never been easier thanks to Eurotunnel. Just 35 minutes platform-to-platform, Eurotunnel is the fast, frequent and easy way to cross the Channel. It's a great way of getting to your destination fast, especially when hunting for your new home abroad.

Travelling with Eurotunnel is simplicity itself. Book online in three easy steps at **www.eurotunnel.com**. You can even **plan your route, pre-order** your cross-Channel shopping, and even arrange your **travel insurance** and **euro currency**, all from the comfort of home. Then sit back and think of France, safe in the knowledge that you're travelling with **the number one cross-Channel operator**, the choice of over 2.3 million motorists every year.

Eurotunnel – Fast, simple and reliable
Crossing time 35 minutes
From Folkestone, Kent to Calais/Coquelles, France
Website: **www.eurotunnel.com**
Telephone: 08705 35 35 35

The Eurotunnel system was designed with the motorist in mind with **its own dedicated exit** (junction 11a) off the M20 motorway in Kent. This brings you directly to **Check-In**, where your journey with Eurotunnel really begins. You'll need to arrive at least 30 minutes prior to departure, although you may want to give yourself a little longer if you want to spend time in the Passenger Terminal Building.

Here you can **take-a-break from driving** and grab a bite to eat at Pret-a-Manger, Burger King, or Little Chef, as well as making those last minute purchases for the journey ahead from high street favourites such as Dixons, Boots and WH Smith. There's also a **handy convenience store**.

Visit the AA travel information centre **for advice on motoring on the Continent**. There is also advice on driving conditions throughout Europe, as well as a route planning service. If it is hotel accommodation en route you're looking for, the **'Before u go @ eurotunnel'** shop can even arrange accommodation at Accor hotels throughout Europe, and arrange restaurant reservations from a selection of the best eateries in the Pas-de-Calais area.

From the Passenger Terminal Building it's just a short drive to the frontier controls and the platforms. The French authorities will actually check your passports before you board, so when you arrive in France, you can **drive straight off and onto the autoroute**. You may also be subject to a security search prior to boarding. From there, it's on to the allocation lanes, and then down to the platform for boarding.

The Eurotunnel Shuttles themselves are bright and airy and can carry up to 120 cars. Depending on the height of your vehicle, you'll be travelling on either a single or double deck carriage. With Eurotunnel, the journey is so quick that there's no need for shops or restaurants, but there are toilets and two radio stations that you can tune into in the car, Eurotunnel Pop (99.8FM) and Eurotunnel Kids (95.6FM). **Before you know it, you're in France!**

If you cross the Channel for business, then why not travel **Eurotunnel Club**. For just a £45 supplement each way you can use the dedicated Check-In lanes, take the next available departure, use the exclusive Club lounge and take advantage of priority boarding.

Following the introduction of the **Pets Travel Scheme,** your pets can now come too! Pets prefer Eurotunnel because they can stay with their owners throughout the journey. For more information on the scheme, visit www.defra.gov.uk

If your second home is where the heart is...
...join our Property Owners' Club!

If you buy a property on the Continent, you'll qualify to join the Eurotunnel **Property Owners' Club**. Specifically set up for those who own a property abroad, this special scheme offers members the opportunity to get the most out of their second home, value for money as well as maximum flexibility on travel across the Channel.

To become a member of the Property Owners' Club, there is an initial registration of just £30 and an annual membership of £35. This entitles you to buy between 5 and 50 discounted Long Stay and Short Stay tickets. Buy, for example, 10 Long Stay tickets, and you could **save in excess of £2000!***

In addition to these great savings, your friends and family can also benefit from discounted tickets, plus you become an automatic member of our **Privilège Plus** frequent traveller scheme which allows you to use the Club Check-In; reserved car parking at the Passenger Terminal Buildings and get a free hot drink!

You'll also receive Points every time you travel with Eurotunnel, and when you dine or shop at one of our partner outlets in the Passenger Terminal Buildings. And when you have enough Points, you can claim free Eurotunnel travel.

For more information on the Eurotunnel Property Owners' Club, or to request an application form including all terms and conditions, call the Property Owners' Club Customer Services on **0870 243 0892** or visit **www.eurotunnel.com/propertyowners**

Discovering the Continent with Eurotunnel
Don't leave home without a free copy of Eurotunnel's handy Discover Guides, featuring tips and information for cross-Channel motorists. The regions covered are Pas-de-Calais, Lille & the Nord, Champagne-Ardenne, Cities of Flanders and areas of Wartime Memories.
Call **08705 353535** to get your free copies.

*based on Red Plus 'Peak Time' car tariff – correct at the time of going to press.

Contents

Contents

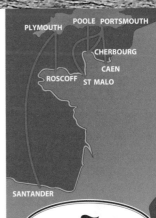

Preface

France is a beautiful country, with a breathtaking array of varied land-scapes and climate, and steeped in culture and history. With the advent of so many competitively priced airfares, the Channel Tunnel and the efficient and economic French rail network, more and more people are contemplating the purchase of a home in France. In 2003 there was a substantial increase in the number of Britons purchasing property in France and in 2004, the centenary of the *Entente Cordiale*, the trend appears set to continue.

It is all too easy, however, to fall into the trap of assuming that as France is a European country, the rules and regulations are the same as or similar to those in the United Kingdom. This is not the case. There are certain rules, regulations and practices that the prospective buyer should be aware of. Only by knowing and adhering to these can you be best protected against a purchase that could ultimately result in serious financial losses and possibly costly, lengthy and difficult court proceedings. The peaceful holiday or retirement home or, worse still, your principal residence, could turn into a veritable nightmare.

Anyone contemplating buying a house or home in France needs to have a basic knowledge of the process. I have endeavoured to give a precise step-by-step guide in understandable English for the prospective purchaser. I use the legal terminology in both English and French with a clear explanation of the meanings of terms used throughout the book to make the information here accessible to all.

As a practising barrister, I am familiar with advising clients after a disaster has occurred. It is my hope and intention to guide the prospective purchaser away from the pitfalls ahead so that this situation does not occur. To this end I have placed the emphasis very much on practical advice and guidance. As a fluent French speaker I have drawn on the experience not only of the English-speaking community, but also that of the French regarding their own housing market, as highlighted in various exposés that have appeared in the French media.

This book deals with the nitty-gritty of buying or renting a home in France, and provides practical advice on living in France. It is designed to guide you through the legal labyrinth of jargon, and provides the general information necessary for the prospective purchaser. It is not a book about French culture or history, or about the delights of living in France. Rather, this book concentrates on the important aspects of obtaining a home in France, on the practical issues pertinent to purchasing and renting a property, and settling in France. Where other books advise a particular course of action (such as renting before you buy), this book goes one step further by telling you how to do it, and how to get out of it!

This book aims to guide you through the main issues to help facilitate your acquisition of a house in France, and tells you how to make your home here, and how to avoid the mistakes that others have made.

Acknowledgements

My grateful thanks to everyone at Kogan Page who has helped bring this book to publication. I would especially like to express my appreciation to Jon Finch, Commissioning Editor, for his constructive comments and professional advice. Also, my thanks go to Michelle Clark, freelance copy-editor, most notably for her thorough cross-checking of references.

Lastly I would like to thank my wife Michaela, whom I have had the good fortune to have as my closest friend as well as my wife, without whose constant support and encouragement this book would never have been written.

Get this feeling.

See a lot more of France in a lot more style.

Rent a car with Europcar and experience a fantastic range of services and superb selection of vehicles. No matter what your travel needs, we will find a package to suit.

Call us now on **0870 607 5000** or log onto **www.europcar.co.uk**

Standard terms and conditions of rental apply.

Calais

Boulogne

Cherbourg

Picardy

Strasbourg

Caen

Metz

Normandy

Paris

Lorraine

Chartres

Seine

Nancy

Brittany

Rennes

Vosges

Orleans

Mulhouse

Nantes Loire

Burgundy

Bourges

Dijon

Poitiers

La Rochelle

Jura

ATLANTIC OCEAN

**Poitou-
Charentes**

Clermont-Ferrand

Lyon

Bordeaux

Rhône

Garonne

Alpes

Languedoc

Provence

Aquitaine

Nimes

Monaco

Toulouse

Marseille

Nice

Cannes

Carcassonne

Montpellier

Toulon

Perpignan

MEDITERRANEAN SEA

1 Choosing your location

Once you have decided to move to France or buy a holiday or retirement home in France, the next decision is to choose an area. There is a wide diversity and considerable care is required before coming to a decision. Although property prices are generally much lower than in the UK (Paris and the Riviera excepted), the costs of purchasing are high, and when you come to sell you will find that estate agents' fees are generally far higher than at home. Not surprisingly, the French do not buy and sell their homes as frequently as the British. I strongly recommend that you rent first to avoid making expensive and time-consuming mistakes. Tenants have far more security than in the UK. You will not be obliged to leave after six months, as is so often the case at home. You can take your time getting to know your area at your leisure and, indeed, visit other areas within easy reach before making a decision that can affect your life for many years to come.

In deciding where to start, it is a good idea to list the factors that are important to you. These are likely to include many of the following.

Climate

France is divided into four climatic regions. The hottest is obviously the Mediterranean climate, stretching along the entire southern coastline with hot summers and mild winters. The temperature in October is often above 20°C and it is not unknown to be able to eat outside in December.

Most of France, including the Atlantic and Channel coasts, is categorized as Oceanic. The sea warms the land in winter and cools it down in summer. Accordingly, the climate is mild and the temperature differences between summer and winter are relatively modest. In Nantes, for

The Climates of France

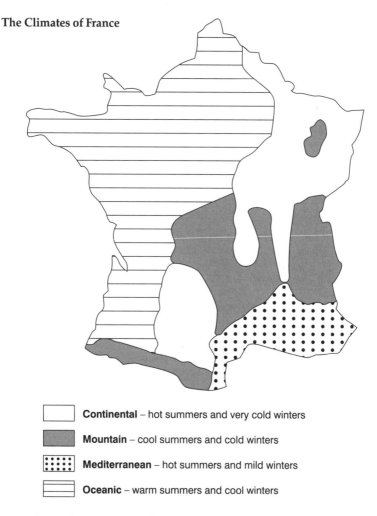

Continental – hot summers and very cold winters

Mountain – cool summers and cold winters

Mediterranean – hot summers and mild winters

Oceanic – warm summers and cool winters

example, on the west coast, the average temperature in the coldest month of January is 6°C, while the average for August is 18°C.

Most of eastern France, stretching from the area from the German and Swiss borders south to Grenoble and west to the Massif Central, has either a Continental or a Mountain climate. The Continental climate is characterized by hot summers and cold winters.

A Mountain climate, unsurprisingly, is very cold in winter and cool in summer. France has five mountain ranges: the Vosges, Jura and Alps on its

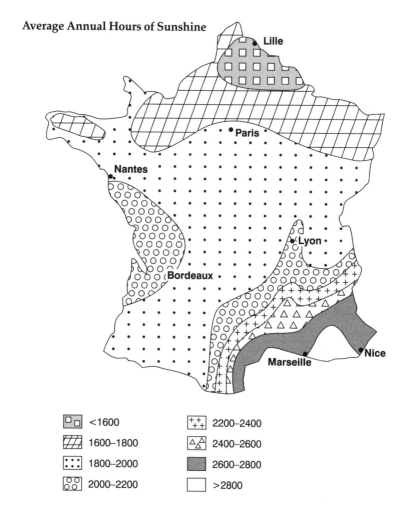

Average Annual Hours of Sunshine

Legend:

□□ <1600	+++ 2200–2400
/// 1600–1800	△△ 2400–2600
::: 1800–2000	▓ 2600–2800
○○ 2000–2200	□ >2800

eastern borders with Germany, Switzerland and Italy, the Massif Central between the centre of France and its southern coast and the Pyrenees on the border with Spain. The north and west parts of France are comparatively flat, although there are some exceptions, such as the Massif Armorican in Brittany and parts of Normandy (often called la Suisse Normande owing to its similarity to the Swiss landscape).

As to rainfall, this is heaviest in the mountain areas, in much of Brittany, much of the northern coast and the Atlantic coast from

Bordeaux southwards. The area of the least rainfall is a band that crosses France from Nantes, along the Loire and then up to Paris. Having said that, however, I spent one rain-drenched summer in the Loire Valley.

The highest levels of sunshine are obviously in the south, from Lyon down, but reasonably high levels are to be found on the Atlantic coast, from Nantes to Bordeaux. Some French refer to the Loire as a dividing line, claiming that it is much colder and wetter to the north than to the south. This is often borne out on the forecasters' weather maps.

As important as geographical location is, ensure that the property you buy – in particular any balconies, terraces and gardens – face south.

Property prices and the cost of living

By far the most expensive areas are Paris and Île de France and the Côte d'Azur. The discrepancy is so marked that these are the only two of the 22 regions where the average cost of buying an apartment is above the national average, with apartment prices in all other regions being below the national average. As to house prices, only four regions are significantly above the national average – Paris and Île de France, Côte d'Azur, Alsace and Corsica. The greatest rate of increase of house prices in the last five or six years or so has been in Corsica, Aquitaine and Basse Normandie, Nord/Pas de Calais, and the Côte d'Azur. The cost of living generally is much higher in Île de France (especially Paris) and the Côte d'Azur, and lower in the country areas.

There are so many different factors that determine property prices that it is unwise to overgeneralize about different regions. Much depends on a property's exact location within a region, its proximity to local facilities and communication routes, its condition and the views – to mention only some of them. Even the condition of the neighbouring property may have a very significant effect on the price of the property for sale. It is safe to say, however, that the cheapest properties are those in rural areas, particularly the least populated such as in Limousin, while coastal areas tend to be among the most expensive.

The areas most favoured by the British are:

▌ Pas de Calais, especially the coast from Montreuil to Cap Blanc Nez;
▌ Normandy, especially the coast between Le Havre and Caen;
▌ Brittany, especially the milder northern coast;

- Vendée, especially the coast;
- Indre-Loire and Loire et Cher, especially around Tours;
- Aquitaine (though the department of Landes is less popular), as well as the neighbouring department of Lot;
- Languedoc-Roussillon, in particular Le Gard;
- Provence, in particular Vaucluse, Bouche du Rhône and Les Alpes Maritimes;
- Burgundy and the Vosges in the central and western areas of France.

The following is only a very general indication as to what you might be able to purchase in different price ranges up to £450,000 (as at 2004):

Up to £22,000	an unrestored farmhouse in the remoter parts of France, such as Auvergne and Limousin.
Up to £33,000	building plots in many areas; an unrestored cottage in Brittany or parts of Normandy.
Up to £55,000	a three-bedroom house requiring substantial renovation in Charente-Maritime; a studio apartment in a small resort in the French Alps; a three- to four-bedroom country house requiring renovation in Brittany; a farmhouse requiring extensive renovation in parts of Aquitaine; a habitable one-bedroom bungalow, loft and outbuilding suitable for conversion in the Loire Valley; a new one-bedroom apartment in a coastal resort on the Vendée coast; a one-bedroom apartment in a coastal town in Languedoc.
Up to £90,000	a three- to four-bedroom habitable country house in Brittany; a four-bedroom farmhouse set in its own land with central heating in a small village an hour from Calais; a two-bedroom classical-style property in good condition with large attic for conversion and large outbuilding in the Loire Valley; a nearly new bungalow with sizeable garden, or a three- or four-bedroom townhouse in good order in a pretty village, both in the Loire Valley; a new one-bedroom, possibly two-bedroom, apartment in the coastal resort of Honfleur in Normandy; a newly built two-bedroom apartment in a coastal resort in Charente-Maritime; a new two-bedroom apartment in a coastal town in Languedoc; a new two-bedroom house in a coastal area of Gironde.

Up to £110,000   a two-bedroom apartment in a small resort in the French Alps; a three- or four-bedroom apartment, or a three-bedroom house requiring some work on the Brittany coast; a four-bedroom house of character in good condition, with a workshop, in Brittany between Rennes and St Malo; a two-bedroom cottage-style house with a small amount of land in the southern Dordogne (the northern Dordogne is slightly cheaper); a spacious two-bedroom flat in good condition in the old town of Nice; a four-bedroom house with loft suitable for conversion with established gardens in the Loire Valley; a new three-bedroom apartment in a coastal town in the Languedoc; a new three-bedroom house in a coastal area of the Gironde.

Up to £165,000   a new four-bedroom, two-bathroom chalet in a small resort in the French Alps (fairly remote); a four-bedroom house with a pool in the southern Dordogne; a renovated farmhouse in the Dordogne; a restored barn with three to four bedrooms and 2 hectares of land in the Lot et Garonne; a five-bedroom traditional property on the banks of the river Loire suitable for B&B, with a large outbuilding; a six-bedroom classical-style property ideal for B&B in a small town in the Loire Valley; a new four-bedroom property in the Gironde; a luxurious three-, possibly four-bedroom new apartment in Honfleur in Normandy; an attractive three-bedroom apartment in the centre of Montpellier.

Up to £220,000   a four-bedroom chalet on the edge of a sizeable resort in the French Alps suitable for a whole year's occupation or for a rental income between 5 and 10 per cent of your outlay in the letting seasons (winter ten to twelve weeks, summer six to eight weeks); a four-bedroom house in excellent condition in a pretty coastal village between Boulogne and Le Touquet, half an hour's drive from the Channel Tunnel; a three-bedroom house in good condition, with swimming pool and attractive garden, near St Malo and excellent golf course; a classical four-bedroom property in excellent condition, with tennis court, on the edge of a small town in the Loire Valley; a three-bedroom apartment with balcony 50 metres from the beach in a resort just outside of Cannes; a large four- or five-bedroom house in good condition in a town in Vaucluse; a four-bedroom renovated farmhouse with excellent views of the Pyrenees in Haute Garonne.

Up to £330,000   a three-bedroom property in a small private development with shared pool and good views in the centre of Mandelieu (Alpes Maritimes); a four-bedroom house with independent studio attached, large garden, pool and good views in the hills on the borders of the Var and Alpes Maritimes; a very large fully renovated five-bedroom property with substantial land, pool and stables, near a small village in the countryside outside Montpellier.

Up to £450,000   a renovated manorial château ten minutes from the northern Brittany coast; a substantial villa in good condition in many areas of Provence; a superb villa with four bedrooms and pool in Mougins in Alpes Maritimes.

Employment

How secure is your employment? If you may at some point need to obtain employment, you should note that jobs are often filled, even in many larger companies, via *'le piston'* – that is, it's not what you know, but who you know. Traditionally no non-French person could be a *fonctionnaire* (civil servant) or undertake certain professions. This has started to change in recent years. Certainly employment prospects will be greatly enhanced if you are within commuting distance of Paris, where there are far more employment opportunities than in other parts of the country. Many Britons find employment via the English-speaking *piston*, including contacts established within the various British and English-speaking groups and associations.

Crime

Crime, including violent crime, is particularly prevalent in Paris and the Côte d'Azur and insurance premiums are accordingly higher. Remote houses in these regions are the most vulnerable. This is less true of rural village properties – a stranger will find their presence noted by the locals, and this discourages theft and break-ins.

Noise and pollution

Properties adjacent to motorways, airports and industrial areas tend to be cheaper for obvious reasons. Do not assume that life in the countryside is necessarily peaceful. Watch out for motorway and TGV routes – both those already constructed and those planned. Nearby church bells can shatter the quiet of a Sunday morning, not to mention the presence of a cockerel, even some distance away (or even a peacock), keen to provide an early wake-up call every morning of every week of every year, with reminders during the day. In rural France, it is common for many families to keep their own hens (and cockerel). Indeed, they have also been known to disturb town-dwellers.

Tourists

France is the most popular European tourist destination. Remember that some areas that are quiet in low season are overrun by tourists in the summer. You may find yourself having to join them on grid-locked roads that resemble overflowing car parks, stifling in the heat. Some property owners in the Côte d'Azur, for example, rent out their properties over the summer, charging rentals many times their monthly mortgage payments. This easily finances their own holidays to less hectic and less stifling holiday resorts! Equally, some parts of tourist areas have the appearance of ghost towns or villages for much of the year.

The presence of tourists also attracts criminals who regard tourists as a soft target, especially in severe traffic jams. *Le vol à la portière* is a common occurrence – two thieves on a motorbike draw up to your car, one dismounts and opens the door, grabbing anything he can, often threatening with a knife. Within seconds he has disappeared on the revving motorbike, leaving the car driver helpless to pursue him. The answer is to always keep the doors locked and to change to French registration plates immediately (and ultimately to get a left-hand-drive car).

Education

If your children are of school age, you may wish to send them to an English/American school or an international school. There are a limited number of such schools, with most choice being available in the Île de France, and the Côte d'Azur. These schools are expensive (up to £10,000 per child per year).

There are a small number of international state schools. If you wish to send your children to a private French school, there are numerous Catholic schools available, but relatively few private non-Catholic schools. With Protestants making up only 2 per cent of the population of France, there are very few Protestant schools. A list (of only eight) can be obtained from the *Fédération Protestante de France* (tel: 01 44 53 47 00). The list includes schools in Toulouse, Mâcon and Aix en Provence, but many stop at the end of primary school. Further details of schools for each region are set out in Chapter 2 and Appendix 1.

Proximity of facilities

If you are old or suffer from bad health you should avoid remote areas and consider settling not too far from centres of medical care. On the other hand, living in the countryside will probably enable you to rent or purchase a larger property and enjoy living without the restrictions imposed on occupants of apartment blocks. You do, however, need to bear in mind the advantages of having shops, restaurants and other facilities around the corner.

The local population

Inhabitants of different regions have different reputations. Generalizations are dangerous and, in any event, invariably subject to exceptions. According to many French, people from the Côte d'Azur are considered to be among the most unfriendly, although this has not been my personal experience. The people from Burgundy are noted for their friendliness, and the Bretons are noted for their celtic warmth. The Parisians are said to regard most of their compatriots as less educated and refined than themselves, especially southerners.

The most important ingredient in settling in any area of France is your own determination to learn to speak French well and to participate in the local community. Unfortunately many foreigners (including, for example, Britons and other Europeans working at the European space agency in Toulouse or in parts of the Côte d'Azur, the Dordogne and northern France) tend to live together in foreign enclaves.

On the other hand, some Britons have proved that integration and/or active participation is possible. One village in Normandy boasts a British mayor and in Aquitaine British residents in some areas have taken the lead in forming pressure groups to fight local environmental issues. The last municipal elections saw 16 Britons elected to local councils.

Transport links to the UK

Even if you prefer to live in the countryside, you may wish to be within easy reach of the UK, Paris and major cities. The proximity of an airport with low-cost flights home and to other destinations can be important. easyJet, Go (now part of easyJet), Ryanair, Buzz, Flybe and BMI Baby have flights to destinations throughout France, including to 26 destinations direct from London. Nice (France's second-busiest airport) is particularly well served with low-cost flights to London Luton, London Gatwick, London Stansted, Bristol, East Midlands, Leeds/Bradford, Liverpool, Paris, Geneva and Zurich, Stockholm, Copenhagen and Amsterdam. The TGV (*train à grande vitesse*) makes a huge difference to journey times. The extension into Lorraine and Alsace will reduce the journey time from Strasbourg to Paris from 4 hours to 2 hours 30 minutes.

I have listed most major air links with UK airports for each region in Chapter 2, although the lists are not exhaustive. Connecting flights to many cities are also available via Brussels, Paris, Amsterdam and Clermont-Ferrand. You will also find the addresses and Web sites of various useful motoring organizations in Appendix 1.

Availability of English-speaking contacts

You may wish to socialize with other English speakers. If you do, there are numerous British and English-speaking contact organizations, especially in the Paris region, the Côte d'Azur and Aquitaine. Details can be obtained from the *Association France–Grand-Bretagne* (see Appendix 1). Here you will also find some of the more hospitable anglophiles among your French hosts. The Royal British Legion and the Royal Air Force Association have various branches. There are also quite a few English-speaking churches of all denominations. The Anglican Church in particular has several churches in Paris and the Île de France, nine along the Côte d'Azur, as well as others including in Normandy, Lyon, Grenoble, Bordeaux, Toulouse, Biarritz and Pau. Some areas have sports clubs, women's groups, Conservative and Labour associations, Scottish associations, amateur dramatic and choral groups.

British/Irish/American goods and services

There are English-language schools, libraries and bookshops at various locations in France, including Paris, Aix en Provence, Nice, Lille, Marseille, Lyon, Bordeaux and Toulouse. There is a nationwide English-language newspaper, *The News*, and also several local English newspapers and magazines (including four publications in the Riviera as well as others in Paris, Aix en Provence and Aquitaine) and English radio stations in Paris and on the Riviera. Barclays Bank has an extensive network of branches throughout France and the Abbey National also has several branches, as does La Banque Woolwich (now owned by Crédit Immobilier de France).

There are various English (and French) grocers selling British, American and Irish food and other products, and many English (and Irish) pubs scattered throughout France. Not surprisingly these are concentrated in Paris, Aquitaine and the Riviera. Various companies deliver British groceries and other products, such as *Life's Little Luxuries* (tel: 0190 561 1499, Web site www.lifeslittleluxuries.co.uk), Expat Direct (tel: 0797 480 7557, Web site www.expatdirect.co.uk) and Expat Essentials (tel: 020 8400 1527, Web site www.expatessentials.co.uk). The English Panier in Champagne de Belair will deliver British groceries, ethnic and oriental products, and fresh, chilled and frozen foods (tel: 05 53 03 21 97, e-mail sales@theenglishpanier.com). They have a standard charge of about 15 euros for deliveries of up to 30 kilometres anywhere in mainland France. The Web site www.americansinfrance.net has details of goods and services of particular interest to Americans.

Flooding

The last few years have witnessed dramatic scenes of severe flood damage, with some parts being declared disaster areas by the central government. Historically, much of France has been prone to flooding since records began, but the problem is undeniably becoming more serious, with 2002 seeing some parts hit for the first time.

The areas most at risk are in the south (excluding Aquitaine) where, during the summer, the heat, sea and mountains together give rise to short-lived but severe storms, often resulting in flash floods. In the autumn and winter, cold air passing over the southern mountains meets the build-up of hot, humid air coming from the Mediterranean and the resultant rainfall can last several days, causing severe flooding as rivers overflow. The south of France is not unique – this problem is shared with Spain, parts of Italy and also Greece.

Below, I have identified the areas most at risk. Do not be put off these regions, especially if you have set your heart on one of them. Often it is only part of the region that is at risk. You should, however, be extremely prudent about where you buy in these regions. Avoid low-lying areas and make as many enquiries as you can as to any past flooding.

The South

Languedoc-Roussillon is the region that has taken the brunt of recent flooding, in particular the Gard, Hérault and Lozère. In September and November 2002, flash floods in these areas caused at least 20 deaths and thousands were forced out of their homes into temporary shelter. Nîmes was particularly badly hit (as it was in 1988, 1999 and 2001) and so was Montpellier (as it was in 1979). Collias (near Uzès), Blauzac and Sommières also suffered extensive damage. The town of Alès (40,000 people) was cut off from the rest of the world, without road, rail, phone or mobile contact, for 48 hours. December 2003 saw serious flooding in Mérault (especially Maugio, just outside Montpellier) and in Gard (Nîmes was without fresh water for four days after a reservoir was flooded). The communes most at risk in the region and in Vaucluse in Provence have been identified in a study by the university of Savoie. This is accessible (in French) on the Internet by searching for 'Inondations Univ Savoie'.

Rhône-Alpes suffered from the torrential rains and violent storms that struck the south of France generally in September 2002. They caused extensive damage here, most notably in Drôme, Ardèche and Rhône (especially near Lyon). Ardèche also suffered from floods in December 2003.

Parts of the region of Provence were also hit in September 2002, particularly Vaucluse and Bouche du Rhône. In December 2003 there was again significant flooding in Vaucluse and Bouche du Rhône (notably at Arles). Marseilles was also hit.

The North-east

In Picardy, the department of the Somme, especially around Amiens, has been subject to very serious flooding, including in the autumn of 2002. Parts of the departments of Oise and Aisne were flooded in January 2003.

In the Champagne-Ardenne, parts of the Ardennes have experienced flooding.

The East

In Bourgogne, the area between Dijon and Mâcon near the river Sâone suffered from flooding in 2002.

In February 1997 in Lorraine, floods struck an area on the borders between Luxembourg, France and Germany, with the areas between Metz and Thionville and between Metz and Nancy suffering damage as the river Moselle rose.

In Franche-Comté in the first three weeks of March 2001, the city of Besançon in the department of Doubs in eastern France had 25 cm of rain, exceeding the previous record of 21 cm in 1914.

The North and West

December 2000 and January 2001 saw some areas of both Normandy and Brittany having levels of rainfall three times the average for the season, with resultant flooding as river levels reached 5 metres above their seasonal norm. Some coastal towns were under record levels of water, including Caen in Normandy, and in Brittany, Redon, Quimper, Quimperole and Lorient (on the west coast).

Two months later, in March 2001, hundreds of people were evacuated in Brittany and Normandy as rivers burst their banks and some towns were submerged under 1.5 metres of water.

In December 2003 the Loire Valley also suffered from flooding, especially the area between Orléans and Angers.

Paris and the Île de France

In March 2001, sightseeing tours on the Seine were cancelled as the embankment roads flooded. Some parts of the Île de la Cité were under water.

Termites

Termites have been a serious problem in the south-west of France from at least the eighteenth century. In the last 25 years, however, they have spread north-east and in the early 1990s the infestations had also occurred in 15 quartiers in Paris – no doubt a major reason behind an investigation and report on the problem by the French Senate in 1996. These developments only serve to underline the importance of having a full survey carried out before purchasing.

The report by the Senate is accessible by carrying out a *recherche* for *termites* on the Senate's Web site www.senat.fr, then clicking on the first entry 'Rapport No. 184: Lutte contre les termites'. Appendix 2 (at the end of the document) contains a list of the 32 communes that are members of an association against termites and other insects. This list at least serves to identify some of the areas where you should pay particular attention to this problem. Of the 32 communes, all bar three (Paris, the coastal holiday resort of La Baule and a small commune just outside Le Mans) were in the west (south of the river Loire), south-west or south. The 32 communes included Angoulême, Arles, Avignon, Biarritz, Bordeaux, Cognac, Marseille, Nantes, Paris, Perpignan and Toulouse. None of the communes are in the Alpes-Maritimes.

Drought damage

There are a substantial number of properties throughout France that have been built on clay (*argile*). During the drought of 2003 cracks appeared in the clay in several regions, causing structural damage to many homes. The worst hit areas were in Paris and the far North-east. The departments concerned are: Nord (59), Yvelines (78), Seine et Marne (77), Essonne (91) and Indre et Loire (37), and also just north of Fre'jus in the Var (83). If you are contemplating purchasing, or have already purchased, a property constructed on clay, there are steps that can be taken to avoid damage occurring. The costs of preventive work are far less that the costs of repairs and reconstruction following drought damage. Information can be obtained from the Centre Scientifique et Technique de Bâtiments (CSTB), 4 Ardu Recteur, Poincaré 75782 (tel: 01 40 50 28 28), website www.cstb.fr.

Other hazards of nature

Some parts of France are prone to forest fires, including in particular Le Var, where seven people lost their lives and 21,000 hectares of forest were destroyed in the summer of 2003. The Côte d'Azur is an earthquake zone and, according to some analysts, the next earthquake is overdue. Others claim that it could be another 200 years before disaster hits the region. For several years, however, regulations have been in force to strengthen new apartment blocks to reduce the risk of collapse and serious damage occurring should an earthquake strike.

2 The regions

France is divided administratively into 22 regions and 95 departments (each with a name and numbered in roughly alphabetical order). Below are short descriptions of the regions, taken from north to south, west to east and their important characteristics. All regions and major towns have tourist boards willing to send you publications in English and/or French. Most *mairies* and tourist offices also have Web sites that are relatively easy to find. *Accueil des Villes Françaises* is well worth contacting. This is a voluntary association designed to assist French citizens and foreigners who have moved to a new area. There are branches in most towns. The association's Web site is: www.avf-accueil.com.

Regions of France

THE DEPARTMENTS

Alsace
67 Bas Rhin
68 Haut Rhin

Aquitaine
24 Dordogne
33 Gironde
40 Landes
47 Lot et Garonne
64 Pyrénées Atlantiques

Auvergne
03 Allier
15 Cantal
43 Haute Loire
63 Puy de Dôme

Bourgogne
21 Côte d'Or
58 Nièvre
71 Saône et Loire
89 Yonne

Bretagne
22 Côtes d'Armor
29 Finistère
35 Île et Vilaine
56 Morbihan

Centre
18 Cher
28 Eure et Loir
36 Indre
37 Indre et Loire
41 Loir et Cher
45 Loiret

Champagne-Ardennes
08 Ardennes
10 Aube
51 Marne
52 Haute Marne

Corse
20A Corse du Sud
20B Haute Corse

Franche-Comté
25 Doubs
39 Jura
70 Haute Saône
90 Territoire de Belfont

Île de France
75 Ville de Paris
77 Seine et Marne
78 Yvelines
91 Essonne
92 Hauts de Seine
93 Seine-Saint-Denis
94 Val de Marne
95 Val d'Oise

Languedoc-Roussillon
11 Aude
30 Gard
34 Hérault
48 Lozère
66 Pyrénées Orientales

Limousin
19 Corrèze
23 Creuse
87 Haute Vienne

Lorraine
54 Meurthe et Moselle
55 Meuse
57 Moselle
88 Vosges

Midi-Pyrénées
09 Ariège
12 Aveyron
31 Haute Garonne
32 Gers
46 Lot
65 Hautes Pyrénées
81 Tarn
82 Tarn et Garonne

Nord-Pas de Calais
59 Nord
62 Pas de Calais

Basse Normandie
14 Calvados
50 Manche
61 Orne

Haute Normandie
27 Eure
76 Seine Maritime

Pays de la Loire
44 Loire Atlantique
49 Maine et Loire
53 Mayenne
72 Sarthe
85 Vendée

Picardie
02 Aisne
60 Oise
80 Somme

Poitou-Charentes
16 Charente
17 Charente Maritime
79 Deux Sèvres
86 Vienne

Provence-Alpes-Côte
d'Azur
04 Alpes de Haute
    Provence
05 Hautes Alpes
06 Alpes Maritimes
13 Bouche du Rhône
83 Var
84 Vaucluse

Rhône-Alpes
01 Ain
07 Ardèche
26 Drôme
38 Isère
42 Loire
69 Rhône
73 Savoie
74 Haute Savoie

The Departments of France

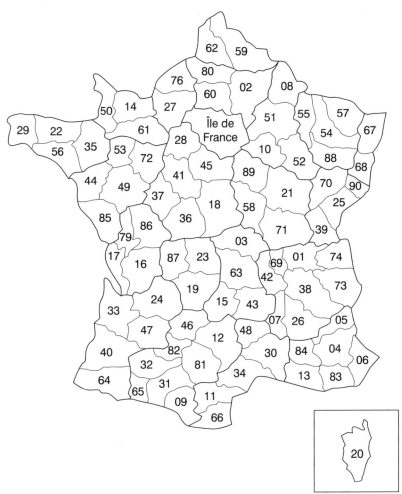

Nord-Pas de Calais

The region, often referred to as the gateway to France, consists of two departments: Le Nord (59) and the Pas de Calais (62). It borders on Belgium.

By far the largest city is Lille, France's fourth-largest city, with a population of nearly one million, and a total of five universities. Lille and the surrounding areas constitute a major conurbation that witnessed the start of industrialization in France during the nineteenth century. The area remains heavily industrialized, despite many factory closures. The other main towns of the region, all much smaller, are Calais (an English possession from 1347 until 1558), Boulogne sur Mer, Arras, Dunkerque and Valenciennes.

The region has seen the creation of numerous jobs in the information technology and communication industries, especially in the new town of Villeneuve d'Ascq. A Eurotechnology Park is planned. There are various multimedia businesses based in Valenciennes, where Toyota has recently located.

The Opal Coast offers an unspoilt varied coastline including cliffs, long wide sandy beaches and dunes, small sheltered bays (for example, between Cap Gris Nez and Blanc Nez and Boulogne), and several seaside resorts. Le Touqet in particular, but also Hardelot and Wimereux, attract many summer visitors from Paris, Lille and Belgium. These resorts first became popular with the British aristocracy towards the end of the nineteenth century and it is they who were responsible for the construction of many of the buildings, golf courses, tennis courts and even a cricket ground.

The region boasts many good golf courses, museum attractions, several fortified towns and five nature parks. Sailing, speed sailing, sand yachting and horse-riding are all popular. There is a famous nautical and sea world centre in Boulogne.

The climate is fresh. Winters are cold with frequent rain and fog, while summers are similar to those in southern England. The people are reputed to be friendly and welcoming, and know how to enjoy themselves.

Property prices are relatively low. Traditionally a favourite location for the British, the region has bypassed a steep rise in property prices following the opening of the Channel Tunnel, probably because many would-be British housebuyers are now more inclined to venture further afield.

Just outside Calais you will find a huge shopping mall – Le Cité, including a Carrefour where the prices are particularly attractive.

British and English-speaking contacts

There is an active British Community Association with regular newsletters and a British Cultural Centre in Lille (tel: 03 20 54 22 79), which includes an English library with over 6000 books, language cassettes, newspapers, journals and so on. There are church services in English in Lille (including a Sunday school and Brownies, tel: 03 28 52 66 36), Arras, Calais and Boulogne sur Mer. There is an 'English-speaking' retirement home at Fort-Mahon Plage (one hour from Calais; Web site www.jardins-de-cybele.tm.fr, tel: 04 66 81 12 22).

The *Ecole Active Bilingue Jeannine Manuel*, situated just outside Lille at 418 bis rue Albert Bailly, 59700 Marcq en Baroeul (tel: 03 20 90 65 50), is a fee-paying day and boarding secondary school up to the baccalaureate.

Calais remains the top destination for Britons shopping in France, especially Le Cité (or City Europe), which in addition to the huge Carrefour supermarket, houses a Darty electrical store and a Tesco wine store. Well over 50 per cent of Carrefour's sales are to Britons, and you will find many items catering for the British market. See Web sites www.calais.cci/fr and www.calais-bargains.com.

Further details of the various English-speaking associations, lists of translators and interpreters and so on can be obtained from the British Consulate in Lille (see Appendix 1).

UK travel links

Air
Biggin Hill–Le Touqet (Lov'air)
Birmingham–Lille (via Paris)

Train

Eurotunnel (via M20 south of Folkestone to Calais) 35 minutes
London–Lille 2 hours

There are Motorail services to Avignon, Brive, Narbonne, Nice and Toulouse.

Ports

Dover–Calais (P&O, Hoverspeed)
Dover–Dunkirk (Norfolkline)
Newhaven–Dieppe, in Seine Maritime (Hoverspeed)

Other travel information

Eurostar

Lille is a Eurostar station and a major point of connection with destinations throughout Europe.

TGV

Paris–Lille more than 20 TGVs per day (1 hour)
Paris–Arras more than 10 TGVs per day (50 minutes)
Paris–Dunkirk 7 TGVs per day (1 hour 30 minutes)

Other trains

Lille–Brussels 40 minutes
Lille–Amsterdam 3 hours 30 minutes

By car (where possible by motorway)

Lille–Paris 2 hours 20 minutes
Lille–Calais 1 hour 10 minutes

International airport

Lille-Lesquin

Normandy

Normandy is often divided into *La Haute Normandie* (consisting of the departments of Eure (27) and Seine Maritime (76)) and *La Basse Normandie* (consisting of Calvados (14), Manche (50) and Orne (61)). Their landscapes are very different, with *La Basse Normandie* to the west being much more rugged and similar to neighbouring Brittany than to *La Haute Normandie*, and the area to the south of Caen being known as *La Suisse Normande*.

Normandy boasts beautiful countryside (referred to as *le bocage*), a mild, humid climate similar to southern England, but with slightly warmer summers, and attractive half-timbered buildings. Farming and fishing play an important role in the region's economy.

The main towns are Bayeux, Caen (destroyed during World War II), Alençon, Rouen, Le Havre, Cherbourg, Lisieux, Dieppe and Evreux. There are many seaside resorts along the nearly 400 miles of coastline, especially on the *Côte Fleuri*, including Cabourg, Houlgate, Deauville, Trouville and Honfleur. Other famous tourist attractions include Bayeux, the D-Day beaches, the museum for peace at Caen, Monet's garden at Giverny, Château Gaillard and Mont St Michel. Gastronomically, Normandy is of course noted for its cider, calvados, apple tarts and cheeses.

Despite supplying France with much of its agricultural produce, only 5 per cent of the population of the region is employed in agriculture, with 30 per cent employed in industry and 55 per cent in the tertiary sector. The industry around Caen is noted for its electrical products, whereas *Basse Normandie* has various chemical plants and oil refineries. The region has a number of nuclear power stations. About half of France's maritime traffic passes through the ports of Le Havre and Dieppe.

Owing to its proximity to the capital, many people commute between Haute Normandie and Paris, especially those who are in a position to carry out much of their work from home. Property prices are also higher around the fashionable coastal resorts of Deauville, Honfleur and Trouville where Parisian and other weekend visitors have helped push up prices. Much better bargains are to be had further inland.

You should exercise extreme caution if you are contemplating a purchase in the eastern part of Normandy. The area is rich in chalk deposits and has been heavily mined over many years. Underground there is a labyrinth of tunnels and caves. For the most part they are unmapped and, as most have been sealed up, there is little trace of the mines on the surface. Rainwater has attacked the walls and roofs of these tunnels, leading to dramatic cases of subsidence and expensive, largely uninsured, damage to many homes and businesses.

British and English-speaking contacts

The *Association France–Grande-Bretagne* is very active in the university town of Caen (tel: 02 31 73 18 80) and there is also an English-speaking group on the western side of the Cherbourg peninsula that can be contacted via the Association. There is an English shop and tea shop (Dolly's English shop) in the centre of Caen (tel: 02 31 94 03 29) where you can buy fish and chips and an English breakfast, and there is an Irish bar by the port. There is an Adventure Park near Saint Gatier de bois.

In the department of Orne (61) you will find The English Bookshop at Domfront, 30 minutes drive south of Flers (tel: 02 33 37 13 020, The Rugby Tavern in Taillebois (junction D43/D15 tel: 02 33 66 80 27) and an English brewery in Joué du Bois (i.e. Brewery, tel: 02 33 37 77 26). There is also an English run vegetarian restaurant near Vimoutiers (tel: 02 33 36 95 84).

There are Anglican Churches in Caen (tel: 02 31 73 18 80), Rouen and Coutances.

In the small village of Saint Cénéri le Gerei you will even find an English-born *Maire* – Ken Tatham.

For those living in the south-west of Normandy, the city of Rennes is only a drive away. Here you will find a number of services and facilities catering for English speakers, including English-language films, an English lending library, a bilingual primary school and an international lycée (see under Brittany).

There is an English language website providing information for British inhabitants of Normandy (and indeed in the rest of North Western France): www.ukgrapevine.monsite.wanadoo.fr.

UK travel links

Ports

Newhaven–Dieppe (Hoverspeed, Transmanche)
Portsmouth–Cherbourg (P&O)
Portsmouth–Le Havre (P&O)
Poole–Cherbourg (Brittany Ferries, Condor)
Portsmouth–Caen (Brittany Ferries)
Rosslare–Cherbourg (Irish Ferries)

From 2004, P&O will be operating a catamaran ferry service from Portsmouth to Caen with a journey time of 3 hours 30 minutes (compared to a conventional ferry crossing of 6 hours).

Air

London Gatwick–Le Havre (British European, Air France, Brit Air)
London City–Le Havre (Air France, Brit Air)

Other travel information

Train

Paris–Rouen 1 hour 30 minutes
Paris–Caen 2 hours
Paris–Cherbourg 3 hours 30 minutes

TGV

The area is not served by the TGV, although Rennes (in Brittany and south of St Michel) is on the TGV network and a special bus serves Mont St Michel from Rennes station.

By car

Paris–Caen 2 hours 30 minutes
Pairs–Rouen 1 hour 30 minutes
Paris–Cherbourg 4 hours

Picardy

The region contains the departments of Aisne (02), Oise (60) and Somme (80). The main towns are Amiens, Beauvais, Abbeville, Noyon, Laon, Compagne, St Quentin, Soissons and Château Thierry. The region has been the site of many battles throughout history, most notably those of World War I. Parts of the region have been badly affected by flooding in recent years, in particular near the Somme around Amiens (including in the autumn of 2002) and parts of Oise and Aisne (including in January 2003). The region is not a popular destination for British and other foreign purchasers and property prices are low, although this is changing in the Oise, the department closest to Paris. The tourist attractions include the magnificent cathedrals at Amiens, Beauvais and Laon.

British and English-speaking contacts

In Chantilly, there is an association for English-speaking parents. Classes in English are organized and a GCSE examination centre is available. Contact ARPEC at BP 60302 Chantilly.

UK travel links

Air

Paris Beauvais (in the department of Oise) to Glasgow, Dublin and Shannon operated by Ryanair and to Birmingham by TravelLite.

Other travel information

Paris–Amiens 1 hour 45 minutes by train

By road, the A1 links Paris and Lille

Paris and Île de France

The region covers the departments of Ville de Paris (75), Hauts de Seine (92), Essonne (91), Seine et Marne (77), Seine-Saint-Denis (93), Val d'Oise (95), Val de Marne (94) and Yvelines (78). Besides Paris, the main towns are Montes La Jolie, Pontoise, Creil, St Denis, Meaux, Melun and St Germain.

Hosts of books are in print describing the vibrant, romantic city of Paris, a bustling city of over 9.5 million inhabitants. Its public transport system is one of the best in the world. Compared to London, travelling around the city on the metro or using the bus network is a joy. Despite the efficiency of the public transport system, however, the capital is dogged with problems of car pollution that from time to time necessitate restrictions on car use within the city. Pollution is the explanation offered by experts for Parisian men having the lowest sperm counts in a survey covering the inhabitants of the main cities of western Europe.

The departments around Paris are relatively unspoiled and have retained much of their natural beauty and charm. The cost of living in central Paris is extremely high. A majority of Parisians still rent, preferring to own a home in the country or on the coast. Those living in the outskirts are far more inclined to buy there, but properties are still much more expensive than further afield, especially near the RER with its easy rail access to Paris.

In Paris itself, the bustling Latin Quarter (3rd and 6th arrondissements) appeals to many. The 10th to 15th arrondissements are less expensive than the most fashionable areas but are worth considering. Outside Paris, Versailles and St Germain are particularly popular.

British and English-speaking contacts

There are many British and English-speaking community associations and groups in Paris and throughout the Île de France. A list of over 60 is published by the British Community Committee, which is available free of charge from the British Consulate and the *Association France–Grande-Bretagne* (see Appendix 1). Americans in France also has a considerable range of information and guidance (Americansinfrance.com).

There are British, Irish and Canadian cultural centres, a British hospital, an American hospital and several churches, including Anglican churches in the centre of Paris (St Michael's Church, 5 rue d'Aguesseau, 75008 Paris, tel: 01 47 42 70 88), Chantilly, Fontainebleau, Maisons Lafitte and Versailles. In Paris itself, there is an American Episcopalian Church, a Scots Kirk, an English-speaking Roman Catholic church and the American Church. Some of these churches are particularly lively and sociable and provide a lunch after the Sunday service. Practical help and advice is sometimes available with job and accommodation offers advertised on church noticeboards. Some of the churches periodically produce booklets setting out practical advice and contact information.

The numerous societies and organizations include the British Rugby Club of Paris, Thoiry Cricket Club, the Standard Athletic Club, The Oxford Society, the Cambridge Society of Paris, the Welsh Society of Paris and a Caledonian Society. There are several theatre and amateur dramatic groups and various charities, some designed to assist Britons who find themselves in financial or other difficulties. There is an American Women's Group in Paris and an Association of American Wives of Europeans (see their Web site at www.newcomersclub.com/fr.html). WICE is a non-profit educational and cultural association with about 1000 members among the various English-speaking nationalities in and around Paris. It organizes continuing education courses and offers a range of other support services and resources. See their Web site at www.wice-paris.org/about_wice.html.

There are numerous language schools to assist in beginning or perfecting your knowledge of the French language and culture, most notably the *Alliance Française*. Importantly there are several international schools, private and state-sponsored, as well as British and American schools, including the American School of Paris, the British School of Paris (with an entirely British curriculum, philosophy and style) and an American Catholic School (Marymount at Neuilly sur Seine) and several Montessori schools. There is also an American University of Paris.

There are a number of English-language libraries in Paris (including at the various cultural centres). There is also an English Language Library for the Blind (tel: 01 42 93 47 57 – see Appendix 1). The English language book-shops include Village Voice, 6 rue Princesse, 75006 Paris (tel: 01 46 33 36 47).

There is an association of English-speaking parents based at Chantilly, to the north of Paris, that organizes a number of activities for children from English-speaking families (see under Picardie).

English newspapers include *Fusac, France–USA Contacts* and *The Free Voice*. An English radio station, *Radio in English*, began broadcasting in 2003 at 95.2 MHz FM. The Web site is www.radioinenglish.com.

UK travel links

Direct flights to Paris (primarily to Charles de Gaulle) from London Heathrow (BMI and Flybe), London Gatwick (BA), London Luton (easyJet), London City (Air France and Flybe), Aberdeen (Air France, Flybe and BA), Belfast (easyJet) Birmingham (Air France), Bristol (Air France and Flybe), Cardiff (BMI), East Midlands (BMI), Edinburgh (Air France, Flybe and BA), Glasgow (BMI), Leeds/Bradford (BMI and Flybe), Liverpool (easyJet), Manchester (BA and Flybe), Newcastle (easyJet), Southampton (Air France and Flybe). Also flights from Dublin and Cork operated by Aer Lingus.

In addition, there are flights from Glasgow, Dublin and Shannon into Paris Beauvais airport operated by Ryanair and from Birmingham to Paris Beauvais operated by TravelLite.

Champagne-Ardennes

Famous for its production of champagne, this region stretches from Île de France in the west, northwards and eastwards to the Belgian border and in a south-easterly direction to Franche-Comté. It consists of the departments of Ardennes (08), Aube (10), Marne (51) and Haute Marne (52). The region's capital is the cathedral city of Reims with a population of just over 200,000. The other principal towns are Troyes, Charleville-Mézières, Reims, Chaumont, Châlons en Champagne and Langres.

Five rivers flow through the region – the Seine, Meuse, Aisne, Marne and Aube – and parts of the Ardennes have suffered from floods in recent years.

However, the landscape is rich in variety, with deep gorges, wide rivers and vast wooded areas, especially the forests of Ardennes on the Belgian border, noted for their ramparts and fortified castles, not to mention its wine-growing areas. At Sedan is the largest fortified castle in Europe.

Taken as a whole, this region has one of the least expensive property markets in France. That said, prices in the areas nearer to Brussels and Paris are well above average for the region. There are relatively few foreign house purchasers in the region, despite the low cost of housing.

The climate is often cloudy and humid. It is seldom very cold, save in the higher areas of the Ardennes. The production of champagne (about 250 million bottles a year, half of which are for export) is concentrated in the area between Châlons en Champagne, Epernay and Reims. The industry employs about 5000 people, rising to 40,000 during the grape-picking season.

This is also a popular region for tourists – and not merely those sampling the delights of the various vineyards. Water sports, hiking, hot-air ballooning, horse-riding and cycling (on mountain bikes) are all much in evidence. Le parc de Bel Val Bois des Dames contains bison, wild boar and other wildlife. There are large lakes (including the largest artificial lake in Europe) and many regional parks.

The education authority in Reims provides special facilities for English-speaking pupils aged from 8 to 19 to assist their integration into the French education system. The school, Classes Internationales de l'Academie de Reims, also has a boarding facility (tel: 03 26 68 60 00).

UK travel links

Air

There is a small airport at Reims.

Train

Paris–Reims 1 hour 30 minutes
Paris–Châlons en Champagne 2 hours 15 minutes
A TGV link is planned, but is still some way off

By car

Reims is 1 hour 30 minutes from Paris on the A4 motorway.

Lorraine and the Vosges

Consisting of the departments of Moselle (57), Meuse (55), Meurthe et Moselle (54) and Vosges (88), this region is noted for the rich variety of its landscape and its natural beauty. It boasts three regional natural parks, rugged peaks, an extensive network of waterways, many lakes and huge forests.

Besides the region's capital, Metz, the main population centres are at Bar le Duc, Briey, Nancy, Verdun and Epinal. To the north, the region borders on Belgium, Luxembourg and Germany – the last having controlled the region during much of its history, leaving a Germanic presence very much in evidence.

Although nearly 90 per cent of the region is dedicated to agriculture, the 1980s and 1990s saw the region suffer considerably owing to the decline of the traditional industries of mining and steel manufacturing that had ensured its prosperity in the past. Other industries have now established themselves, most notably the manufacture of cars, electrical goods, machinery, paper and plastics. More recently, economic growth has been centred in the area formed by Longwy-Nancy-Sarreguimes and around Metz, Thionville and Epinal. Lorraine remains famous for its Moselle wines and its quiche.

The region welcomes nearly 6 million tourists a year, including many on business. Others are attracted by the winter sports – most notably at Bresse and Gérardmer, the thermal resorts, the 700 km of navigable waterways or the numerous golf courses. Despite its industrialized past and manufacturing present, the region, including its medieval towns and villages, has remained largely unspoiled.

Property prices here remain well below the national average, but have failed to attract many foreign buyers.

UK travel links

Air

London Gatwick–Metz-Nancy-Lorraine (Air France via Clermont-Ferrand)
See also the UK travel links for Alsace (below).

Other travel information

Train

Paris–Nancy 3 hours
Paris–Metz 3 hours
The opening of a TGV is expected in 2006.

By car

Paris–Metz 3 hours by the A4 motorway

Alsace

Situated between the Vosges to the west and the Rhine to the east, the small region of Alsace is made up of the two departments of Bas Rhin (67) and Haut Rhin (68). The main towns are Strasbourg, Colmar, Haguenau and Mulhouse. On the border with Germany, and for much of its history under Germanic control, the population and customs of Alsace share many of the characteristics of France's neighbour. German is spoken by many.

The main city, Strasbourg, houses the European Parliament. If you visit Strasbourg while the parliament is sitting, you may have accommodation problems. The Council of Europe and the European Court are also both based here. The Cathedral at Strasbourg is stunning. Around its square there are several hidden restaurants in which you can sample excellent food.

Alsace boasts some beautiful and unspoiled landscapes. It is a rich and efficient farmland region, famous for its wines and beers (over 50 per cent of French beer is produced here) and numerous excellent restaurants. It has many picturesque villages, as well as dense forests and rolling hills frequented by long-distance skiers during the winter. Despite this landscape, Alsace is the third most industrialized region in France, with the industry being centred around Strasbourg and Mulhouse. Colmar is noted more for its cultural centres. The region is not yet free of the after-effects of World War II – more unexploded grenades and bombs are discovered here than in the whole of the rest of France.

The climate in this region is definitely Continental, with cold winters and hot summers. Spring arrives late and autumn early.

Property prices are among the highest in France (it is the fourth most expensive region of France per square metre). Unlike other parts of France, the rural areas are not suffering from depopulation. The area is host to many international fairs and 10 million visitors per year.

The Lycée-Collège International des Pontonniers in Strasbourg provides a co-educational day school for 3- to 18-year-olds and has a British section (tel: 03 88 37 15 25).

English-speaking contacts

Americans in Alsace (Strasbourg) can be contacted by e-mail at Americans_InAlsace@hotmail.com. There is an English-language bookshop in Strasbourg (The Bookworm, 3 rue de Pâques, tel: 03 88 32 26 99).

UK travel links

Air

Strasbourg International Airport is 15 km to the south-west of the city. Three other major airports are within less than 2 hours' drive: Zurich, Frankfurt and L'Euro-Airport Basel-Mulhouse-Friborg, 25 km to the south-east of Mulhouse.

London Gatwick–Strasbourg (Air France, Flybe and Brit Air)
London Gatwick–Strasbourg (Air France via Clermont-Ferrand)
London Heathrow–Basel-Mulhouse (BA, Swissair)
London Gatwick–Basel-Mulhouse (Air France via Clermont-Ferrand)
London Heathrow–Zurich (BA, Swissair)
London Gatwick–Zurich (easyJet, Air Seychelles)
London Luton–Zurich (easyJet)
Birmingham–Zurich (Swissair)
Edinburgh–Zurich (BA)
Birmingham–Strasbourg (via Brussels, Frankfurt or Paris)

Dublin–Basel-Mulhouse (Swissair)
Dublin–Zurich (Aer Lingus, Swissair)

Other travel information

Train

Paris–Strasbourg 4 hours
Paris–Mulhouse 4 hours
Strasbourg–Mulhouse 50 minutes

The arrival of the TGV is eagerly awaited. This will cut the train journey time from Paris by 1½ hours to 2 hours 30 minutes.

By car

Paris–Strasbourg 4 hours 30 minutes
Paris–Mulhouse 5 hours

Brittany

This westernmost region of France, a peninsula jutting out into the Atlantic Ocean, consists of the four departments of Côtes d'Armor (22), Finistère (meaning 'the end of the world', 29), Île et Vilaine (35) and Morbihan (56). Besides the capital and university city of Rennes, the principal towns are Fougères, St Brieuc, Brest, Quimper, Lorient, Vannes and St Malo. Modern communications, agriculture, tourism and, in recent years, industry have brought prosperity to parts of Brittany that were once renowned for their poverty.

The region has its own unique character. The Bretons, their language and culture are distinctly Celtic and they share far more with the Irish, Welsh and Cornish than with fellow Frenchmen, not least their tales of fantasies and legends. Breton is spoken in much of Finistère, Morbihan and the west of Côtes d'Armor. It is similar to Welsh and has a very different structure and sound to French. In 1992, it was estimated that the language was the mother tongue of just under 300,000 inhabitants in the area to the west of a line between St Brieuc to the north and Vannes to the south, with a total of 500,000 speaking the language well. Successive French administrations have sought to outlaw the language (estimated to have been spoken by about 1.4 million in 1914). Schoolchildren found speaking Breton had a wooden cross or a clog placed around their necks. Offenders were ridiculed and insulted and were given cleaning duties or received corporal punishment.

In the post-war period, there has been a renewed interest in the Breton language. Tele Breizh began broadcasting programs for children in Breton about three years ago and there are now several Breton radio stations and newspapers as well as a number of adult education courses in the language. If you are intending to place your children in a French school beware. Although the language is spoken by a smaller proportion of the population than is the case for Welsh in Wales, some Breton schoolchildren are being educated in the language – an added complication that you will probably wish to avoid.

Brittany's 1,200 km of coastline offers hidden coves, sandy beaches, cliff faces and quiet harbours, such as those at Cournaille, Port Aven and Douarnenez in Finistère. The most popular coastal resorts are those of Dinard, Perros-Guierec and La Baule. The last, actually just south of Brittany and in the Pays de la Loire (Western Loire), was featured daily on French television throughout one summer. The beaches look wonderful, with room to breathe and kick a football around, which is in complete contrast to the cramped beaches along the Côte d'Azur. The north-west coast of Brittany is rockier and wilder than the region's south coast. Away from the coast, the region is unspoiled and scenic, including the Massif Armorican, the mountainous central area. Dotted along the coasts are many islands and about a dozen of these are linked to the mainland by ferry services. The Île de Sein – a tiny island off the coast of Finistère – was once described by de Gaulle as representing a quarter of France. Addressing the recruits to the small Free French navy in 1945, he discovered that of the 600 who had answered his appeal to sailors to join him in England, 150 were from the Île de Sein.

Over 3 million French and 700,000 foreigners take their holiday in Finistère alone.The people of Brittany are among the most friendly and welcoming. The region is particularly popular with British tourists, and many have purchased a holiday home and some have settled. The ports of Roscoff and St Malo provide convenient access back to the UK, not to mention the ports further east along the coast in Normandy and beyond. It is estimated that there are more than 20,000 Britons living in the region.

Brittany has many local festivals, some of them attended by fellow Celts from overseas, including from as far away as the United States, Canada and Australia. Some have settled here and there are some Irish pubs, such as the Tara in the Brest docklands, not to mention the Ty Elise in Plouyé run by a friendly Welshman.

Tourist attractions include the standing stones at Carnac, the castles and fortresses at Josselin, Vitré, Fourgères and Combourg, the medieval town of Dinan, the regional parc d'Armorique and St Malo.

The climate is warm in summer, but in the mild winters it can be very rainy, with Brest competing with Cherbourg for the title of the wettest town in France. The northern coast benefits from the Gulf Stream and accordingly is warmer than elsewhere in the region. There is little snow in Brittany, save in the hinterland where the climate is more Continental.

Brittany is France's premier food-growing and livestock area, accounting for 50 per cent of French pork, 54 per cent of beef, over 40 per cent of poultry and 20 per cent of milk. Fishing is also of major importance, with 45 per cent of the French catch being landed in Brittany.

There is some industry in the region, including the automobile industry and naval construction, with industry centred around Brest, Lannion and Rennes. Brest was almost razed to the ground in 1945 and seems dominated by concrete apartment blocks. It remains a naval and military base.

Property prices along the coast are relatively expensive, particularly around the more popular towns of Quimper, Bénodet, St Malo, Dinard and Dinan. As with other coastal regions, the cost of accommodation is cheaper inland.

In parts of Brittany, the water is classed as unfit to drink owing to the presence of high levels of nitrogen and pesticides caused by the dumping of effluent by industrial pig and chicken breeders and also by arable farmers. Environmental groups are presently pursuing legal actions against the main culprits.

British and English-speaking contacts

There is an association of British residents, the *ABC du Résident en Bretagne*, based around Baud. Contact the president Graham Jefferies, c/o AXA Insurance BP 24 56150 Baud, tel: 02 97 51 02 60 or 02 97 39 77 17, e-mail graham@bir.fr.

There are Anglican churches in Dinard, Nantes, Guerlesquin, Pontivy and Ploermel. The information about services, practical help and pastoral care for the anglophone community in Brittany is coordinated under the umbrella of Christ Church (tel: 02 97 39 77 17).

The Franco-American Institute, at 7 quai Châteaubriand, Rennes (tel: 02 99 79 20 57) has an English-language lending library and a range of cultural and social activities, including a Cine Club with English films shown weekly. There are also English-language films in Brest, Dinard, Rennes, Quimper, St Malo and at about 10 other locations (see www.brittany-angloinfo.com). In Rennes there is also a bilingual primary school attended by French and foreign children (Ecole Jean Moulin, tel: 02 99 54 57 04) and a lycée with an Anglo-American section (tel: 02 99 54 44 43).

There are a number of bookshops and newsagents selling English-language books and newspapers, including La Louve in Callac (tel: 02 96 45 50 40), La Plume d'Or in Loudeac (02 96 66 08 26), La Maison de Presse in Concarneau (02 98 97 00 95) and Presse du Cabestin in St Malo (02 99 40 94 61).

British food produce is available from La Crème Anglaise, Place de l'Eglise, Seglien in Morbihan (tel: 02 97 28 02 03), and at market stalls in Pontivy and Josselin all in Morbihan (02 97 93 56 03). British clothing brands are available from Ascott, 12 rue de Mene, Vannes in Morbihan (tel: 02 97 54 29 59). Shops specialising in clothes for babies and children include Bebe 9, 12 rue de Cadelac, Loudeac, Côtes d'Armor (tel: 02 96 28 02 61) and New Baby, 4 rue de Verdun, Fougeres, Ille et Vilaine (tel: 02 99 99 00 04).

There are British/Irish pubs in St Malo, St Marcan, Port de Plaisance in Vannes, Lorient, Buleon, Port Augan, Malguenac, Seglien, Vannes, Huelgoat, Concarneau, Kerandouaron (near Rostrenen) and Loudeac.

The Angloinfo Web site www.brittany-angloinfo.com is of particular interest to English-speakers as it is the Grapevine website covering the north west of France: www.ukgrapevine.monsite.wanadoo.fr. Other useful Web site for the region is www.annuaire-emeraude.com.

UK travel links

Air

London Gatwick–Brest (Air France, Brit Air)
London Stansted–Brest (Ryanair)
London Stansted–Dinard (Ryanair)
London Gatwick–Rennes (Air France via Clermont-Ferrand)

There are also flights into Nantes International Airport (just to the south of Brittany) from London Gatwick (Air France, Brit Air, BA, Flybe) and to Birmingham (via Brussels).

Ports

Poole–St Malo (Condor Ferries)
Portsmouth–St Malo (Brittany Ferries)
Weymouth (via Guernsey)–St Malo (Condor Ferries)
Plymouth–Roscoff (Brittany Ferries)
Rosslare–Roscoff (Irish Ferries)
Cork–Roscoff (Brittany Ferries)

Other transport information

TGV

Paris–Rennes 2 hours
Paris–Brest 4 hours
Paris–Quimper 4 hours

By car

Paris–Rennes 3 hours 30 minutes by motorway.

Air

There are several flights daily to Paris from Brest, Lannion, Lorient, Quimper and Rennes.

Les Pays de la Loire (Western Loire)

Made up of the five departments of Loire Atlantique (44), Maine et Loire (49), Mayenne (53), Sarthe (72) and Vendée (85), the region was a main trade route from the fall of the Roman Empire until the nineteenth century and is dotted with strategically sited castles, such as Brissac, Clisson, Goulaine, Guérande Le Lude, Montmirail, Serrant and Tiffauges, to name only a few. It is a region steeped in history, with many sites of interest, including troglodyte caves at Rochemenier, the Puy de Fou medieval theme park, medieval towns and villages, cathedrals (including Nantes) and abbeys (most notably that at Fontrevaud) and Roman remains.

Apart from its capital at Nantes, which has a population of nearly 500,000 and is France's seventh largest city, the principal towns of Western Loire are Angers, St Nazaire and Le Mans. The region's universities are at Nantes, Le Mans and Angers. In surveys carried out in 2002 and 2003, the magazine *Le Point*, using a set of seven indicators, declared Nantes to be the best of the 100 largest towns and cities in France in which to live.

The 160 km of Atlantic coastline stretches from the beautiful long beaches (8 km in all) at La Baule, just north of the mouth of the Loire at St Nazaire, almost to La Rochelle. This peaceful region – France's second most important agriculturally – is flat and wooded in the west, but has cultivated fields and intermittent undulating hills in the east. It is a favourite location for cycling enthusiasts and boasts a good number of golf courses. Tourism is most heavily concentrated in the coastal areas near the beaches at La Baule, Le Croisic, Pouliguen and Pornic. The climate is mild with hot summers.

Industrially, this region is France's fourth most important, with an emphasis on the exploitation of agricultural and food products, as well as shipbuilding, the large Renault factory at Le Mans and a growing high-tech sector. The region is also a major centre for fishing.

Property is fairly reasonably priced, with house prices generally being just below the national average. Coastal locations, especially in La Vendée and around La Baule, are more expensive than elsewhere in the region.

British and English-speaking contacts

There are Anglican churches or services at Pay de Serre and La Merlatière, both in the Vendée (tel: 02 51 62 96 32).

For those living in many locations in Mayenne (53) the city of Rennes is only a drive away. Here there are a number of services and facilities of interest to the English-speaking communities, including English-language films, an English lending library, a bilingual primary school and a lycée with an Anglo-American section (see under Brittany). There is an English pub in Herce in Mayenne (53), the King Dick tel: 02 43 00 28 86. It has a garden to the rear.

There is an English Web-site for residents in north western France (including les Pays de la Loire at: www.ukgrapevine.monsite.wanadoo.fr.

UK travel links

Air

London Gatwick–Nantes (Air France, Brit Air, BA, Flybe. Also Air France via Clermont-Ferrand)
London Gatwick–Angers (Air France via Clermont-Ferrand 3½ hours)
Birmingham–Nantes (via Brussels or Paris)

Other travel information

TGV

Paris–Nantes 2 hours
Paris–Angers 1 hour 30 minutes
Paris–Le Mans 1 hour

By car

Paris–Nantes 3 hours 40 minutes by motorway
Paris–Le Mans 2 hours by motorway

Centre – the Loire Valley

This region consists of the six departments of Cher (18), Eure et Loire (28), Indre (36), Indre et Loire (37), Loir et Cher (41) and Loiret (45). It is host to 1200 km of France's longest river, the Loire, as it makes its way towards the Atlantic coast at St Nazaire in neighbouring Pays de la Loire. The principal towns are Chartres, Orléans, Blois, Tours, Bourges and Châteauroux.

Steeped in history and culture, the Loire Valley boasts numerous medieval villages, towns and cities, such as the magnificent ancient capital at Bourges, imposing cathedrals at Chartres and Bourges and magical châteaux (150 in all), such as the impressive Chenonceaux, Amboise, Cheveny and Azay le Rideau. The châteaux date from the early sixteenth century. They were constructed on Italian lines by the kings and nobles returning from the Italian wars who had been impressed with the luxury of the great Italian châteaux. The area around Orléans is closely associated with Joan of Arc, who, some time after her death at the hands of the English, became St Joan. Orléans is a former capital of France.

Besides its numerous châteaux, the Loire Valley is noted for its many wines, including Vouvray and Sancerre. Recent years have seen tremendous growth in the populations of Chartres, Orléans and Tours. The region is known for its four nuclear power stations along the banks of the Loire, its production of cereal crops, its pharmaceutical industry and tourism. Much of the region is flat, so if you want a rugged mountainous landscape, this is not for you. The area between Orléans and Angers suffered from flooding in December 2003.

The region is popular for holiday homes and so property prices tend to be above the national average, especially in Chartres and around Tours.

UK travel links

Air

London Stansted–Tours (Ryanair)

Train

London–Lille-Tours 4½ hours

Other travel information

Train

Paris–Chartres 40 minutes to 1 hour
Paris–Orléans 1 hour

The region is linked by motorway to Paris, Lyon, Bordeaux, Clermont-Ferrand, Rennes and Nantes. Tours is 2 hours 20 minutes by car from Paris. There is a small airport at Orléans.

Bourgogne (Burgundy)

The region is noted above all for some of the finest wines in the world. Situated between Paris and Lyon, it consists of the departments of Côte d'Or (21), Nièvre (58), Saône et Loire (71) and Yonne (89). Besides the region's capital Dijon, the principal towns are Autun, Auxerre, Beaune, Chalon sur Saône, La Charité sur Loire, Fontenay, Mâcon, Nevers, Paray le Monial, Sens, Vézelay.

This is a serene, fertile land of rolling hills, forests, vineyards and over a thousand kilometres of navigable but sleepy canals and rivers. There is very little industry. The era of industrialization left the region rather untouched. Further back in time, however, Burgundy was very much more centre-stage. It has a rich colourful past, including during the Hundred Years War (1337–1453) when the dukes of Burgundy allied themselves with the English against the kings of France. Historical buildings abound, including feudal fortresses, Renaissance châteaux and many famous abbeys (most notably those at Cluny, Citeaux, Fontenay and Vézelay).

The people of Burgundy are noted for their warm hospitality, but, despite this, it has not been a popular area of settlement for foreign property buyers. The climate can be quite cold in winter, while the summers are rather hot and sometimes rainy. Autumn, the season of grape picking, tends to be mild. The area between Mâcon and Lyon to the south has been subjected to flooding in recent years when the River Saône has burst its banks after heavy rainfall.

Three million tourists visit the region each year, attracted by the region's cultural past and its wine (Chablis is produced at Yvonne and Saône is the home of Beaujolais). Other attractions include fishing, the natural regional park at Morvan, with its lakes and rivers offering various water sports, and the waterways dotted with pleasure boats based at the 11 ports in the region. This area is not known for its golf courses. Farmhouse holidays are popular.

Property prices are relatively high thanks in part to demand from Parisians for second homes here. As yet, there has been little foreign interest in the area, but this is thought by some to be about to change.

UK travel links

London Gatwick–Dijon (Air France via Clermont-Ferrand)

Other travel information

TGV

Paris–Dijon 1 hour 40 minutes

The TGV also extends to Chalon sur Saône, which connects to Lille (and thence to London).

By car

Dijon–Paris about 3 hours by motorway

Franche-Comté

Franche-Comté borders on Switzerland and is made up of the departments of Doubs (25), Jura (39), Haute Saône (70) and the Territoire de Belfort (90). The principal towns are Belfort, Besançon, Dole, Lons le Saunier, Luxeuil les Bains, Montbéliard, Pontarlier, St Claude and Vesoul.

Between the Vosges to the north and the Jura to the south, Franche-Comté boasts stunning mountain areas, thick pine forests and rolling farmland. Though not greatly frequented by foreign tourists, the landscape of Franche-Comté has an almost magical quality very similar to that of neighbouring Switzerland.

The area is noted for its abundant wildlife, including wild boar, foxes, badgers and all sorts of birds, and winter sport attractions.

Property prices are a little lower than the national average, but to date the region has not attracted many foreign purchasers. The region is a tourist attraction, especially for hiking, horse-riding, cycling (mountain bikes), fishing and long-distance skiing. The region boasts over 80 lakes.

There are various industries present in the region, including the automobile industry.

UK travel links

The international airports at Geneva and Basel-Mulhouse are not far away. From Geneva, there are flights to London (Heathrow, Gatwick, Stansted, Luton and City airports), Birmingham, East Midlands and Dublin. For further details, see under Rhône-Alpes later in this chapter. There are also flights to Basel-Mulhouse from London Heathrow (BA, Swissair), London Stansted (easyJet), Liverpool (easyJet) and Dublin (Swissair). The western side of the region is also served by the airport at Dijon (see under Bourgogne, above).

Other travel information

TGV

Paris–Besançon 2 hours 40 minutes
Paris–Dole 2 hours

Other trains

Paris–Vesoul 3 hours 15 minutes

By car

There is a fast motorway from Besançon to Dijon.
There is small airport at Dole-Tavaux.

Poitou-Charentes

Poitou-Charentes consists of the departments of Charente (16), Charente Maritime (17), Deux Sèvres (79) and Vienne (86). It is situated between the Loire and the Gironde, and between the Atlantic and the beginnings of the Massif Central. The main towns are La Rochelle, Angoulême, Niort, Poitiers and Royan.

This is the sunniest region in the west of France. With very little industry, it is also one of the most peaceful and unspoiled areas of France. The Atlantic coastline is characterized by sandy beaches and romantic islands, to which man has added marinas and some stunning golf courses to aid one's enjoyment of the long hot summers and mild winters. The most notable seaside resorts are those of La Rochelle, the beautiful Île de Ré and Île d'Oleron (both joined to the mainland by bridges), Royan and Brouage. For tourists, La Rochelle is a must, although do not expect to drive around the town, as cars are forbidden and transport is by cycle. Inland, the landscape is somewhat monotonously flat. The Futuroscope, near Poitiers, is one of the nation's major attractions, with over 2 million visitors annually (down on the 3 million of some years ago and not breaking even).

Poitou-Charentes is a popular destination for the expatriate British, especially between Angoulême and Royan. Taken as a whole, property prices are significantly lower than the national average and than in neighbouring Dordogne. However, this hides large differences between the coastal and inland areas, with properties in the former being very much more expensive than those in the latter.

Vienne and its capital and university city Poitiers are growth areas, whereas the rural areas of Deux-Sèvres and Charente have declining populations. Information technology and communication systems are the most important growth areas. New businesses benefit from a support package. The climate is mild with frequent but not heavy rainfall. It seldom snows or freezes.

The region has many historical attractions, including the ruins of five medieval castles at Chauvigny, 'Sleeping Beauty's Castle' at La Roche-

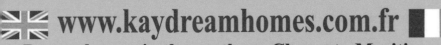

Courbon, 600 Roman monuments and numerous museums, including maritime museums. La Rochelle was a centre of Protestantism until the revocation of the Edict of Nantes in 1685 (in 1598, the Edict had granted religious toleration to Protestants). Thousands were murdered or persecuted and many more fled the country. Protestants today make up only 2 per cent of the population of France.

British and English-speaking contacts

There are Anglican churches in Civray, St Leger, Le Grand Madieu, Magné, Chasseneuil sur Providence, Cognac, Chasseneuil sur Bonnieure and Linzay. There is a Gilbert and Sullivan society in Jonzac (in the south of Charente-Maritime).

There are Best of British grocery stores (also selling some books) in Civray in Vienne (86) and Confolens in Charente (16) tel: 05 45 85 49 63.

In Angoulême a new shop has recently opened selling British groceries and books (tel: 05 45 37 58 70, Web site www.auxilesbritanniques.fr). British groceries are also available from the Cockleshell in the town centre of Ruffec (tel: 05 45 85 93 55, Web site www.thecockleshell.com), and a Best of British grocery store is to open in Nantes in 2004 (tel: 04 32 60 17 75). There are a number of British and Irish pubs in Charente, including at Aubeterre-sur-Dronne, Châteauneuf-sur-Charente, Jarnac, Paizay Naudoin, Bonnes and Angoulême, and also in Poitiers.

There is a British run golf course, Le Golf Aubeterre at St Severin (tel: 05 45 98 55 13). English books are also available from Librairie Claire de Plumes in Ruffec (tel: 05 45 31 37 84).

UK travel links

London Gatwick–La Rochelle (Air France via Clermont-Ferrand)
London Stansted–La Rochelle (Ryanair)
Southampton – La Rochelle (Flybe)
London Stansted–Poitiers (Buzz)
London Gatwick–Poitiers (Air France via Clermont-Ferrand)
Birmingham–Poitiers (via Paris)

London Gatwick–Angoulême (Air France via Clermont-Ferrand)
London Gatwick–Nantes (Air France, Brit Air, BA, Flybe)
Birmingham–Nantes (via Brussels or Paris)
London Gatwick–Angers (Air France via Clermont-Ferrand 3½ hours)

Other travel information

The A10 connects Bordeaux to the south with Saintes and Poitiers, and to the north with Tours, Orléans and Paris. The TGV Atlantique that links Bordeaux and Paris serves Poitiers, Angoulême, Niort and La Rochelle. The Futuroscope has its own TGV station and is only 1 hour 30 minutes from Paris. There is also a direct link from Angoulême and the Futuroscope at Poitiers to Lille.

Limousin

The region is made up of three departments – Corrèze (19), Creuse (23) and Haute Vienne (87). The principal towns are Limoges, Gueret, Tulle, Aubusson, Ussel, Brive la Gaillarde and Rochechouart.

The region is mainly farmland (primarily grazing for cows, sheep and pigs) and is sparsely populated, with a falling birth rate and, consequently, an ageing population. The varied landscape includes the valleys of the Dordogne and the Creuse, the Monédières Mountains and Lake Vassivière.

Opportunities for outdoor sports abound, particularly water sports, rambling, cycling and fishing. On the cultural front, there are châteaux and historic monuments to visit, and a contemporary art centre in Meymac. Limoges is famous for its pottery.

The cost of property per square metre is lower here than anywhere else in France – under two-thirds of the national average and well under half that of the Riviera. The area has not attracted foreign property buyers. The climate is milder than in neighbouring Auvergne.

There is now a Best of British grocery store in Brive in Corrèze (19) tel: 05 55 25 09 54.

UK travel links

London Stansted–Limoges (Ryanair)
Southampton – Limoges (Flybe)

Much of the eastern side of the region is accessible via the airport at Clermont-Ferrand (see Auvergne below)
There is a Motorail service from Calais to Brive.

Other travel information

Train

Paris–Limoges 3 hours
A TGV Paris-Orléans-Limoges-Brive-Toulouse route is planned.

By car

The A20 motorway passes near to Limoges.

Auvergne

The Auvergne consists of the departments of Allier (03), Cantal (15), Haute Loire (43) and Puy de Dôme (63). The main towns are Moulins, Clermont-Ferrand, Aurillac, Le Puy en Velay, Thiers, Issoire and Riom and the spa town of Vichy.

The region, in the highlands of the Massif Central, boasts some of the most dramatic scenery in the hexagon (as the French affectionately refer to their homeland), including gorges, lakes, geysers, rivers and large expanses of forest. Like its neighbour Limousin, it is totally unspoiled and sparsely populated, with a falling birth rate and ageing population.

Property prices are low (although not as low as for Limousin). Besides the extinct volcanoes and the *Parc Régional des Volcans d'Auvergne*, there are also numerous activities for the sporting enthusiast – cycling, horse-riding, water sports, hang-gliding, hot-air ballooning and skiing in the Massif Central during the extremely cold winter. Summers are very hot. There is abundant wildlife, including falcons, owls and otters, and over 50 châteaux dotted over the region. Do not miss Vulcania, a recently created park devoted to the explanation and demonstration of volcanic activity.

Clermont-Ferrand is an industrial centre, housing Michelin and the printing press for La Banque de France, along with various other manufacturing businesses. Aurillac is a commercial centre.

British and English-speaking contacts

There are relatively few English speakers living in Auvergne. However, with air links now between Clermont-Ferrand and London this may be set to change.

UK travel links

London Gatwick–Clermont-Ferrand (Air France, Flybe)
London Stansted–Clermont-Ferrand (Flybe)
London City–Clermont-Ferrand

Other travel information

Airport

There are direct flights from Clermont-Ferrand to 22 French cities and also Amsterdam, Brussels, Geneva, London, Milan and Turin.

Train

Paris–Clermont-Ferrand 4 hours

By car

Paris–Clermont-Ferrand 3 hours by motorway
Lyon–Clermont-Ferrand 1 hour

Rhône-Alpes

Rhône-Alpes, bordering on Italy and Switzerland, boasts some of the most breathtaking mountain scenery in France, with the Massif Central to the west, the river Rhône as it makes its way from the Swiss mountains to the Mediterranean, and the Alps to the east. It is the second-largest region of France, geographically the size of Belgium and with a population of about 5 million.

There are eight departments – Ain (01), Ardèche (07), Drôme (26), Isère (38), Loire (42), Rhône (69), Savoie (73) and Haute Savoie (74). The region's capital is Lyon, now France's second-largest city, with a population of just over 1 million. It is the gastronomic centre of France. The region's second city is Grenoble, with a population of about 400,000. The other major towns are Aix les Bains, Albertville, Annecy, Bourg en Bresse, St Etienne, Vienne, St Chamond, Romans sur Isère, Valence, Montélimar, Chamonix-Mont Blanc and Chambéry.

There has been considerable migration into the region, especially around Lyon and Grenoble (the population of Lyon has trebled in the last 20 years and that of Grenoble has more than doubled) as well as St Etienne. Grenoble is noted for its high-tech industries. Lyon, Grenoble and St Etienne are all university centres.

The Rhône is a dominating influence in the centre region. It is a major route for traffic between the north and south, as are the railway line and A7 motorway that accompany the river along its journey to the south coast. The Rhône Valley is also one of France's chief industrialized areas. Despite the areas of industrialization around Lyon and along the corridor between Grenoble and Geneva, the region remains one of the most scenic in France, with thick heavily wooded forests.

The possibilities for leisure pursuits and holiday activities are endless, including white-water rafting, canoeing, climbing, hiking and biking. To the east are some of the world's most prestigious ski resorts, including Chamonix and Meribel. Indeed, there are a total of about 70 ski stations in the region accessible via Grenoble, Chambéry and Annecy.

On average, Rhône-Alpes is the fifth most expensive region for property prices of France's 22 regions. However, there is a wide diversity of prices within the region, with property near the Alps being more highly priced.

As to climate, the Rhône Valley is definitely Continental, being very hot in the summer and very cold in the winter. However, from about Valence southwards, this gives way to the Mediterranean climate of hot summers and mild winters. The areas to the east (the Massif Central) and the west (the Alps) have very cold winters accompanied by cool summers.

British and English-speaking contacts

There are Anglican churches in Lyon, Grenoble, Annecy and Evian, and a Roman Catholic Mass once a week in English in Lyon.

There are several British and English-speaking associations in the region, especially around Lyon, Grenoble and St Etienne. These include the *Association France–Grande-Bretagne* (in Lyon contact Karine Robinson, tel: 04 78 28 41 81), a parents and young children's group in Lyon (contact Sarah Delorne, tel: 04 72 67 91 51), branches of the Royal British Legion and RAF Association, a Robert Burns Club (in Lyon contact Mary Wigley, tel: 04 78 43 05 05) and a Scottish country dancing group. Further details of these and other associations are available from the British Consulate in Lyon (see Appendix 1). There is an American Club of Lyon (BP 6039, 69411 Lyon, Cedex 06 France).

The Lycée Collège International Ferney-Voltaire, 14 km from Geneva, offers fee-paying co-educational schooling following the UK national curriculum in part (tel: 04 50 40 00 00). In Grenoble, there is an international state co-educational day school (for children aged from 11 to 18), the Cité-Scolaire Internationale Stendhal (tel: 04 76 54 83 83). There is also the Cité-Scolaire Internationale de Lyon (tel: 04 78 69 60 06) and the Lycée Multilingue de Lyon. The latter is a private international school offering bilingual education for children aged from 3 to 18 (tel: 04 78 23 22 63). There are English-language bookshops in Grenoble (including Glenat) and Lyon (including Decitre, 29 place Bellecour, Lyon, tel: 04 26 68 00 12, and Discovery, 31 Quai Victor Auganeur, Lyon, tel: 04 78 62 76 58, e-mail: discoveryshop@wanadoo.fr). British food and drink items are also sold at Discovery. There is an Irish pub in Lyon (Jonny Walsh's).

A practical guide to living in Lyon has been published (in English), entitled *Breaking the Ice*; there is also a similar guide to living in Grenoble (contact the Association France–Grande-Bretagne for details – see above).

UK travel links

Lyon

London Heathrow (British European, Air France, BA)
London Gatwick (Air France via Clermont-Ferrand)
London Stansted (easyJet, European Airways)
Birmingham (BA)
Belfast (charter flights)
Dublin (Aer Lingus)

Geneva

London Heathrow (BA and Swissair)
London Gatwick (easyJet, BA, Air 2000, My Travel, Monarch, Britannia)
London Luton (easyJet)
London Stansted (Ryanair, Inghams, Crystal, First Choice Ski, Thomson Ski)
London City (Swiss Air)
Aberdeen (BMI)
Cardiff (BMI)
East Midlands (easyJet)
Guernsey (Flybe)
Jersey (Flybe)
Leeds/Bradford (Jet2)
Liverpool (easyJet)
Manchester (BMI)
Southampton (Flybe)
Teeside (BMI)
Dublin (Swiss Air, Aer Lingus)

St Etienne

London Stansted (Ryanair)

Other flights

Bournemouth–Chambéry (winter only)
London Gatwick–Annecy
Southampton–Chambéry (Flybe)

Other travel information

The region is extremely well served by the rail network, with over 250 stations and good links to many French cities, including Lille.

Train

Paris–Lyon 2 hours by TGV
Paris–Annecy 3 hours 40 minutes
Paris–Grenoble 3 hours
Paris–St Etienne under 2 hours 45 minutes

By car

Paris–Lyon 4 hours 15 minutes
Paris–Annecy over 5 hours

Aquitaine

The region consists of five departments – Dordogne (24), Gironde (33), Landes (40), Lot et Garonne (47) and Pyrénées Atlantiques (64).

Its main population centre is Bordeaux, France's fifth-largest city, with a population that has increased rapidly over the last 20 years to 700,000. The other main towns, all far smaller than Bordeaux, are Agen, Bayonne, Bergerac, Biarritz, Dax, Mont de Basan, Pau, Périgueux and Sarlat.

The region is very much agricultural, with over 8 per cent of its population still employed in this sector. Here you will find tranquillity and a temperate climate with hot, dry summers and mild, rainy winters. There are various seaside resorts along the Atlantic coastline, including Biarritz, Arcachon and Cap Ferrat.

Bordeaux is a very prosperous city. Historically deriving its wealth from the region's wine production, the city is a favourite centre for conventions and exhibitions and has also seen the development of high-tech industries. Bordeaux has good road and rail access and is an ideal location for doing business with the Iberian peninsula.

Aquitaine has been a jewel over which the English and French have quarrelled for many years. The region was under English rule for much of the Middle Ages, was devastated during the Hundred Years War and was eventually returned to French control in 1472. The Dordogne is particularly scenic, especially around Sarlat and Rocamadour, and is famous for its *bastides*, which are fortified hilltop towns.

Like parts of the region's coast, the Dordogne is a favourite tourist and settlement area for the British. There are said to be tens of thousands of British spread across the Dordogne and the neighbouring department of Lot et Garonne. There is a significant British community around the town of Eymet, for example.

Property prices are highest in the Dordogne and have been significantly influenced by foreign purchasers over a period of more than 20 years. Prices are highest near the river and somewhat lower in Lot et Garonne (though still high compared to other rural areas of France). You will find more reasonably priced bargains in Gironde, and particularly in Pyrénées Atlantiques and Landes, the latter being well known for its dunes and pine forests extending over an area of a million hectares.

Sporting activities include surfing and windsurfing (with surfing conditions said to be the best in Europe), hiking and kayak inland, sailing on the many lakes, sea and freshwater fishing and playing golf on some fine courses around Bordeaux (but not in the Dordogne and Lot et Garonne). Other tourist attractions include the spa at Dax, the many Roman chapels, the numerous prehistoric sites in Périgord, Rouffignac, the cave at Lascaux, the Basque country and the Pyrenees.

British and English-speaking contacts

There are Anglican churches/services in Bordeaux, Biarritz, Pau, Chancelade (Périgueux), Floirac, Chapdeuil, Limeul, Monteton and Riberac.

There is an international school in Bordeaux, the Bordeaux International School, which is a private school that bases its education on the UK national curriculum (tel: 05 57 87 02 11, Web site: www.bordeaux-intl-school.com). The Collège Cheverus and the Lycée François Magendie both have international sections catering for foreign children (tel: 05 56 48 57 00). There is an examination centre for the University of Cambridge Examination Board, and also a British Council in Bordeaux (tel: 05 57 57 19 52).

There are English bookshops in Bordeaux (Bradleys and Librarie Valery) and English films are shown at various cinemas in the region, including Bordeaux and Castillones (south of Bergerac). There are also English shops selling groceries, gifts and other goods from the United Kingdom, including The English Shop in Eymet (south of Bergerac, tel: 05 53 23 79 39) and The Tea Cosy in Bordeaux. Best of British grocery stores have a branch in Périgueux (tel: 05 53 08 13 03). There are English video libraries including at Meilhan-sur-Garonne. There are branches of Barclays Bank in Bordeaux and Biarritz, and a branch of the Body Shop in Bordeaux.

There are cricket clubs (including at Eymet, and also at La Brede, tel: 05 56 26 25 98), women's groups, Conservative and Labour associations, a branch of the Royal Navy Association, and a Scottish association. There is a Bordeaux British Community Association (Web site: www.bordeauxbritish.com), and the WISE (Welsh, Irish, Scottish and English) Sporting and Cultural Association, which meets in the Connemara Irish Pub (tel: 05 56 52 82 57).

The many native English speakers providing services in the region include architects, surveyors, builders, painters and decorators. You will also find a selection of British and Irish pubs, hotels and restaurants, mostly in Bordeaux, but also several in the Dordogne and at Pau and Périgueux. Details of these and many other associations in Bordeaux, the Dordogne and elsewhere in the region that may be of interest to British residents are available from the British Consulate in Bordeaux: information can also be found in *Aquitaine News* distributed free of charge with copies of *The News* (see Appendix 1).

UK travel links

Bordeaux

London Gatwick (BA and Air France via Clermont-Ferrand)
Birmingham (BA)

Bristol (Flybe)
East Midlands (BMI)
Manchester (BMI)
Dublin (Air France)

Biarritz

London Gatwick (Air France via Clermont-Ferrand)
London Stansted (Ryanair)
Birmingham (via Paris)

Bergerac

London Stansted (Ryanair)
Bristol (Flybe)
Southampton (Flybe)

Pau

London Stansted (Ryanair)
Birmingham (via Paris)

Ports

The port of Santander in northern Spain has a ferry service from Plymouth operated by Brittany Ferries.

Other travel information

Air

There are small airports at Pau and Agen.

TGV

Paris–Bordeaux 3 hours
Angoulême is served by the TGV.

The TEV is to be extended with a section from Tours to Bordeaux to be completed by 2014, giving a Paris–Bordeaux journey time of 2 hours 10 minutes.

Other trains

Paris–Pau 8 hours

By car

The 560-km journey from Bordeaux to Paris should take about 5½ hours by motorway.

Midi-Pyrénées

This is the largest region of France, but the most sparsely populated. It consists of the eight departments of Ariège (09), Aveyron (12), Haute Garonne (31), Gers (32), Lot (46), Hautes Pyrénées (65), Tarn (81) and Tarn et Garonne (82), all bar Hautes Pyrénées taking their name from one or more of the main rivers flowing through the region.

About 40 per cent of the population of the region lives in the department of Haute Garonne. The department's capital, and that of the region, is Toulouse, with a population of 650,000, making it France's sixth-largest city. The other principal towns are Albi (known for its medieval character), Castre, Foix, Lourdes, Millau, Montauban and Tarbes.

Notable tourist attractions include Lourdes, one of the world's most visited pilgrimage sites with over 6 million visitors per year. There are also about three dozen different ski resorts in the Pyrenees, including Superbagnères and Mourtis, and thermal baths at St Lary-Soulan, Luz-Ardiden and Gourette. Generally the ski resorts here are cheaper than their Alpine counterparts. Other attractions include the gorges of the Aveyron and of the Tarn, numerous grottoes and the national park of the Pyrenees. The Massif Central is a favoured haunt for potholers.

Average property prices remain below the national average, although the rate of increase in the price of property has been consistently greater than the national average over the last six years, and in some areas prices are substantially above the region's average. This is a very popular region for holidays and second homes and, in some parts, particularly in Lot, the proportion of such homes is approaching 50 per cent and prices here are among the highest for this region.

The climate here is somewhat variable. Summers are very hot and winters very cold. Autumn can be sunny but rainy.

The area is well known for its aeronautical industry in Toulouse. Companies from various European nations are located here, including Lucas Aerospace. There has been growth in the high-tech industry in the region.

British and English-speaking contacts

There are Anglican churches/services in Toulouse, Cahors and Cornbarrieu.

There is an international school and a Lycée Polyvalent International in Colomiers with a British section (tel: 05 61 15 94 94).

There is also an Anglo-American library in Toulouse and an English library at the university (tel: 05 61 50 40 92). There are English bookshops in Toulouse and Montcuq in the Lot (see Appendix 1). In Foix (1 hour south of Toulouse) Simply British sells British groceries and a wide range of books, DVDs and videos (tel: 05 61 64 98 89, e-mail simplybritfoix@aol.com). There are a number of British/Irish pubs in Toulouse.

There are cricket clubs, women's groups and Conservative and Labour associations. The many English-run services in the region include architects, surveyors, builders, painters and decorators, as well as British and Irish pubs and hotels and restaurants, mostly in Toulouse. Details of these and many other associations in Toulouse and elsewhere in the region that may be of interest to British residents are available from the British Consulate in Bordeaux. For the association Americans in Toulouse visit their Web site at www.newcomersclub.com/fr.html. There is a branch of Barclays Bank in Toulouse, and the British International Network may be contacted on tel: 06 89 50 77 76.

UK travel links

Toulouse

London Heathrow (Air France, British European)
London Gatwick (Air 2000, BA, Britannia, Flybe, My Travel, easyJet)

London Stansted (European Air Charter, Crystal, JMC, Panorama Ski, Neilson Ski, Airtours Ski, Thomson Ski)
Aberdeen (BMI)
Belfast (charter flights)
Birmingham (BA, Flybe)
Bristol (Flybe)
Cardiff (BMI Baby)
East Midlands (BMI Baby)
Edinburgh (Flybe)
Glasgow (Flybe)
Guernsey (Flybe)
Jersey (Flybe)
Southampton (Flybe)
Dublin (Aer Lingus)

Lourdes

London Luton

Rodez

London Stansted (Ryanair)

Other travel information

TGV

Paris–Toulouse 5 hours 15 minutes

Toulouse is also served by Lille Europe and there is a Motorail service from Calais to Toulouse.

By car

Paris–Toulouse 700 km and 7 hours by motorway
Bordeaux–Toulouse 242 km and 2 hours 15 minutes by motorway

Languedoc-Roussillon

The region consists of the five departments of Aude (11), Gard (30), Hérault (34), Lozère (48) and Pyrénées-Orientales (66).

The region's capital and cultural centre is the university town of Montpellier. The other principal towns are Perpignan, Béziers, Alès, the Roman city of Nîmes (with its well-preserved arena), the medieval city of Carcassonne, Narbonne and Mende.

The departments of Aude, Gard, Hérault and Lozère have taken the brunt of France's flood damage in recent years (see the earlier discussion on this subject in Chapter 1), with Nîmes being very badly hit in 1988 and 2002 and the area around Narbonne suffering a similar fate in 1999. Notwithstanding the severity of the problem, many areas in these departments have remained relatively untouched by the floods.

Languedoc-Roussillon, or Le Midi, is celebrated for its tranquillity, beauty and romance, with its mixture of French and neighbouring Catalan and Spanish traditions and culture. The red and yellow flags are those of the Catalans and of Aragon. Bullfighting is a popular spectator sport in this region, especially in Nîmes.

On the coast, you will find 200 km of sandy beaches from the Camargue to the border with Spain, 25 ports (including the delightful port of Collioure), thousands of small craft and some of France's favourite locations for sailing, watersports, big-game fishing and scuba-diving. Inland to the north is the Massif Central and to the south is the Pyrénées. The more mountainous areas provide ideal locations for walking, horse-riding, camping and mountain biking, with skiing closer to the Spanish border, including at the thermal resort of Ax-les-Thermes.

This is one of the largest wine-growing regions in Europe. Most of the region is primarily agricultural, with 15 per cent of its population still employed in this sector. Around 80 per cent of the population, though, is concentrated in the urban areas that border the coast, especially in Le Gard and Le Hérault, with Montpellier being a growth area for information technology. Well over half of the people who live in this region have moved here from elsewhere in France and Europe.

The region is visited by 14 million tourists annually. Besides the many sports and leisure resources, its attractions include the Cévennes national park (the largest in France), the 240 km of the Canal du Midi and the medieval town of Carcassonne (the most important medieval town in Europe). Also of particular note are the abbeys of Saint Gilles and Canigou and the fortified cathedral at Béziers. 'L'homme de Tautevel' is famous with all French schoolchildren. His remains – an incomplete skull along with teeth – are the oldest human remains found in France. They were discovered in the Caune de l'Arago – a cave near Tautevel, about 20 km from Perpignan.

On the coast, the climate is very hot and dry in summer and mild in winter. Inland it can be very cold during the winter. The weather can be rainy in spring and autumn.

The cost of living and property prices contrast markedly with the Riviera, where the average property price per square metre is well over 50 per cent higher than here. There is, nevertheless, a substantial foreign presence in this region, with the average property price hiding substantial variations. Not surprisingly, property prices (in both regions) are higher near the coast, especially in the more fashionable ports, and nearer to the present and future planned routes of the TGV. A number of new resorts have been constructed along the Côte Vermillion in recent years, including at Port Leucate, Cap d'Agde, Gruissan and La Grande Motte. Many people still prefer the more traditional and attractive homes, even if it means looking further away from the coast.

British and English-speaking contacts

In Montpellier, there is an English bookshop, La Maison de Cambridge, branches of the Franco-Scottish Association and the British Cultural Association, a Scottish dancing association and a cricket club.

There is a private international school (from nursery to sixth form) ten minutes from Montpellier in Baillargues (Ecole Privée Bilingue Internationale, tel: 04 67 70 78 44 and e-mail jml.ebi@wanadoo.fr).

There is a home-delivery service for British groceries covering Pyrénées-Orientales and Aude (tel: Au goût anglais on 04 68 83 38 54) and a Best of British grocery store, which also sells DVDs, videos, cards, etc. For those living near Béziers it may be worthwhile contacting britsaroundbezier@group.msn.com in 2004 (tel: 04 68 26 55 13).

UK travel links

London Stansted–Perpignan (Ryanair)
London Gatwick–Perpignan (Air France via Clermont-Ferrand)
London Stansted–Montpellier (Ryanair)
London Gatwick–Montpellier (BA, plus Air France via Clermont-Ferrand)
London Stansted–Carcassonne (Ryanair)
London Stansted–Nîmes (Ryanair)
Birmingham–Montpellier (via Paris)

Other travel information

Air

There is a small airport at Mende.

TGV

Paris–Montpellier 4 hours 30 minutes (10 trains daily, including a sleeper)
Paris–Nîmes 4 hours (7 trains daily, including a sleeper)

The TGV (6 a day) also connects Paris to Béziers, Perpignan and Narbonne, with journey times of about 5 hours to all these destinations. It is planned to extend the TGV to Barcelona. Arles also is served by the TGV. Montpellier has a direct link with Lille Europe and there is a Motorail link from Calais to Narbonne.

Train

Marseille–Montpellier 2 hours

By car

Paris–Perpignan 8 hours by motorway

Provence (excluding Alpes Maritimes)

Bounded by the Mediterranean to the south, the Rhône to the east and the Alps to the north and east, this region is famed for its romance and climate. It is known, too, for its fashionable coastal resorts (most notably St Tropez), cuisine, the aromas of its rich vegetation and sleepy hilltop villages set in an often rugged landscape.

It consists of the six departments of Alpes de Haute Provence (04), Hautes Alpes (05), Bouche du Rhône (13), Var (83), Vaucluse (84) and Alpes Maritimes (06). Some information relating to Var is also included under the section for the Côte d'Azur, devoted primarily to the Alpes Maritimes.

The capital of Provence is Marseille – France's third-largest city just after Lyon, with a population of around 1 million. Marseille is the country's largest Mediterranean port, with a substantial volume of traffic, most notably to North America, the Arab world, the Far East and, naturally, Corsica. The other principal cities and towns are Arles, Avignon, Carpentras, Gap, Sisteron, Dignes les Bains, Aix en Provence and, of course, Toulon (France's eighth-largest city, with a population nearing 450,000). The region's industry is concentrated in the Bouche du Rhône.

Tourist attractions include La Camargue, with its stunning nature reserve, lagoons, white horses, flamingos and bullfights, the Gorges du Verdun, Avignon and its papal palace for many years the heart of the Catholic Church, the Roman remains at Arles and Orange, and the national nature-park in Hautes Alpes.

You will find much of the region wild. Shooting is a popular pastime, including of wild boar (*sanglier*) that are known to come searching for food and can do substantial damage to gardens and fences, especially in the Var.

In recent years, some areas of Vaucluse have suffered from significant flooding.

Property prices are, not surprisingly, more expensive around the fashionable resorts and near the population centres of Marseille and Toulon, but bargains are to be found inland.

Property Investments Provence

We are a dynamic international team
who will help you to find and purchase
your ideal property in Provence

Property Investments Provence is an international estate agent located in Aix en Provence, with partner offices in England, Germany and Holland. Our experienced, multilingual staff will help to reduce the stress of purchasing a property in a foreign country. In addition to our own selection of properties for sale, situated in the most attractive areas between Montpellier and the Côte d'Azur, we work together with over 100 French Agents to carry out well targeted property searches for our clients.

Contact Ilia Kalogroulis

4 rue des Sauriers
13510 EGUILLES (AIX EN PROVENCE), FRANCE
Telephone: +44 (0)4 4292 5155
Fax: +44 (0)1 7372 4210
info@propertiesprovence.com
www.propertiesprovence.com

British and English-speaking contacts

In the Var, there is an English-language newspaper, the *Var Village Voice* (tel: 04 94 04 49 60). There are English bookshops in Villcroze, Draguignan (Heidi's, tel: 04 94 67 55 50) and Fayence (Castle Bookshop, tel: 04 94 84 72 00). Nearby at Lorgues British foodstuffs are available at de Bragance, which also boasts a tea and coffee shop (tel: 04 94 84 04 16). In and around Marseille *Torrefaction Noailles* – a chain of over a dozen confectionery and coffee shops – has recently held a promotion of British foods that it may stock on a permanent basis (see www.noailles.com). There are branches of the Best of British grocery store in Aix-en-Provence (tel: 04 42 26 47 99) and St Remy (04 32 62 88 49). In Aix en Provence Paradox International (tel: 04 42 26 47 99) sells English books. There are Anglican churches in Marseille and St Raphael, and branches of the Association France–Grande-Bretagne in Marseille, Toulon and La Garde. There are branches of the Royal British Legion in Marseille and the RAF Association in La Croix and Valmar. There is a cricket club in the Var at Entrecasteaux (tel: 04 94 04 74 56). There are a number of British/Irish pubs in the Var, including at St Tropez. You will find a Yorkshire welcome at Les Arbousiers restaurant on the shore of Lac de Saint Cassien (10 minutes off the A8 at exit 39 – see under Côte d'Azur – Alpes Maritimes).

Schools in Aix en Provence include the British American Institute (tel: 04 42 27 24 23), the Ecole Val Saint André (tel: 04 42 27 14 47) and also a Protestant (French) school for 3- to 18-year-olds. In nearby Luynes there is the Lycée International Général et Technologique Luynes (tel: 04 42 60 86 00), the bilingual primary school CIPEC (tel: 04 42 60 84 25) and the International Billingual School of Provence, a primary and secondary school (tel: 04 42 24 03 40).

There is also an English library in Aix kept by the Anglo-American Group of Provence (tel: 04 42 26 91 84). The library has 10,000 books (including many children's books). The annual membership is 32 euros for an individual and 40 euros for a family. In Vaucluse there is an English library (The Beaumont Library) at Malaucene (tel: 04 90 65 25 60).

Further details of these and other groups and organizations are available from the British Consulate in Marseille.

In Marseille you will find branches of the Body Shop, Virgin Megastore, Burberrys and Ad hoc Books (8 rue Pisconçon, tel: 04 91 33 51 92), which has a selection of English books, mainly fiction. There is also a branch of the Body Shop at Aix. There is an Irish bar in St Tropez, and a branch of the Woolwich at St Raphael.

UK travel links

Marseille

London Gatwick (BA, easyJet, plus Air France via Clermont-Ferrand)
Birmingham (Maersk)
Coventry (Thomsonfly)

Toulon

London Gatwick (BA, EB Airways, plus Air France via Clermont-Ferrand)

Also London Gatwick–Avignon (via Orly – 3 hours), Birmingham–Avignon (via Paris), Birmingham–St Tropez (via Zurich).

The Var is accessible via Nice Airport, France's second-busiest airport, with many flights from the UK (see under Alpes Maritimes below).

Other travel information

TGV

With the Channel Tunnel and the recent arrival of the TGV, Marseille is now just under 7 hours from Waterloo by train. There is a Eurostar connection to Avignon during the summer months and a Motorail service to Avignon. The arrival of the TGV has cut the train journey time to Paris to 4 hours.

Air

There is a small airport at St Tropez. In the height of summer, the journey from Nice to St Tropez could involve your day slipping between your fingers in stationary traffic. The journey by air is not cheap (about 210 euros), but has the advantage of being a stress-free and scenic 25 minutes.

By car

Paris–Marseilles 7 hours

Côte d'Azur – Alpes Maritimes

The Côte d'Azur, in the south-east corner of France at its border with Italy, is France's sunniest region. Despite its small geographical size, this area of France inevitably takes up more space in this chapter than any other. The principal towns of the Alpes Maritimes are the department's capital Nice (with a population of 350,000, France's tenth-largest city), Antibes and Cannes on the coast, and France's perfume capital Grasse inland. Technically, the Côte d'Azur includes both the Alpes Martimes and the Var, but for convenience this section deals almost exclusively with the Alpes Martimes. For additional material on the Var, see under Provence (previous entry).

The Alpes Maritimes is the most popular destination for British expatriates, as well as expatriates of other English-speaking and European countries. As a result, there are more facilities here for the English community than anywhere else outside Paris (and possibly more than in Paris itself). It is also a popular holiday destination (an estimated 2 million Britons visited the region in 2003). There are a huge range of leisure activities, especially from April through to October, and, of course, skiing in the Alps during the winter.

The early development of the Côte d'Azur as a tourist area in the nineteenth century owes much to the British. They became a major influence in this area and are responsible for the construction of many of the older hotels and, of course, the Promenade des Anglais along Nice's seafront. It was they who termed the area 'the Riviera', although how far the Riviera extends along the coast is a matter of dispute. It starts at the Italian border and continues beyond Cannes at least as far as the border between the Alpes Maritimes and the Var.

The area continues to attract numerous migrants from other regions of France and Europe – particularly the retired. Foreign buyers are targeted by numerous estate agents, many of them English-speakers from Britain and elsewhere. The Italians are also numerous, with the Italian border being very close by. In addition, there are smaller but still substantial numbers of Germans and Scandinavians (there is a local German newspaper). Recent years have also seen a significant influx of wealthy Russians. All this activity has resulted in a steep rise in property prices at the upper end of the market in some areas and a boost to the select clothing boutiques in Cannes and Nice (the Russians, according to one proprietor interviewed on French news, never ask the price). The region – especially Cannes and the independent principality of Monaco – still attracts the rich and famous, not least during Cannes' film festival in May (www.festival-cannes.fr).

The Côte d'Azur has attracted a good number of foreign businesses, especially high-tech companies, around the vast business park of Sophia Antipolis. A government-sponsored international state school (the International School of Sophia Antipolis) was created some time ago to cater for the children of the employees of these businesses.

For many years, the region has also been home to many poorer economic migrants from Algeria, Italy, Spain and Portugal, despite the area's relatively high rate of unemployment. Nevertheless, there is a labour shortage in some sectors during the summer months and hotels and restaurants have severe problems recruiting staff, primarily because of poor salary levels.

The Côte d'Azur remains a bastion of the Right. In the first round of the 2002 presidential elections, Jean Le Pen came out on top in both Alpes Maritimes and the Var with, respectively, nearly 26 and 23.5 per cent of the votes cast. Support for Le Pen was most marked in the inland areas (the *arrière pays*). Since the recent extension of the right to vote in local elections to all EU citizens, there is now a sizeable English-speaking vote. One of the first English councillors is Sue Dunnachie, who sits on the council in Mougins and is responsible for tourism, communications, education and highways.

Corruption is said to be more common here then elsewhere in France. In 2002, a Nice judge was charged with allegedly taking a bribe for granting bail to a suspect. The public prosecutor in Nice is presently campaigning against the alleged influence of freemasonry among the local judges.

The region is the sunniest and hottest in France, benefiting from its own microclimate. With 3000 hours of sunshine per year, temperatures in the summer are often above 30°C and in September, and even October, often over 20°C. Winters (January and February) are mild. Some people claim to have had Christmas dinner outside. When it rains, the rain is often heavy and areas bordering the seafront between Cannes and Mandelieu can be flooded, although the Côte d'Azur has not suffered anywhere near the same extent of flood damage suffered in Languedoc-Roussillon or in northern France. A major influence in the winter is the mistral, which can bring winds of up to 100 km per hour. The noise is eerie and property damage, especially to windows, can be serious.

This region is also an earthquake zone. Several hundred people died in 1887 in an earthquake that hit the stretch between Nice and Menton, and there have been several tremors in the three years prior to the publication of this book. According to seismologists, another is due within the next 200 years. The area from the Italian border towards Cannes is subject to different classifications according to the risk of earthquake damage and, since 1994, much new building work, particularly apartment blocks, has been subjected to additional building regulations. These regulations, however, are not always followed to the letter. The risk does not seem to have had any impact on the housing market. In the various French and English publications I have seen that discuss a move to this area, the subject rarely gets a mention.

The area covering the Provence-Alpes-Côte d'Azur department has the highest average house prices in the whole of France. Within that area, the Côte d'Azur is the most expensive and a small flat in Cannes can cost the same price as a substantial property elsewhere in France. On the other hand, properties in and around Monaco make prices elsewhere on the Riviera seem very reasonable indeed. Cash transactions are still very much part of business on the Riviera, with many property deals being partly settled in this manner. Suitably located property has huge letting potential and, in July, August and early September, many permanent local French and foreign residents let out their homes. The income they receive pays for their holidays elsewhere in France, with money left over.

Being one of the world's most popular and prestigious holiday resorts has its drawbacks. Besides being expensive, the Côte d'Azur is very crowded throughout the summer (the road along the seafront of Cannes can resemble a sweltering car park at times). Public transport leaves much to be desired, although that is set to change in Nice, where a tramway is planned for the city. The project is likely to take four to five years to complete and, in the short term, will cause major disruption to the busiest areas of the city.

The region also attracts crime. Keep your car doors locked at all times, especially in stationary or slow-moving traffic. Otherwise, you may have your car door opened and any valuables seized. The offender(s), very determined and sometimes armed with a knife or other weapon, speeds off on a motorbike, leaving you stuck in traffic and unable to pursue.

A feature of recent years is the arrival of beggars from Eastern Europe, notably Romanians, Bosnians and Poles. Some of them are, or purport to be, quite seriously handicapped. Most of them are thought to be controlled by Mafia types, to whom they have to hand over their takings.

Tourist attractions include hilltop towns and villages, such as Vence and St Paul, and Marineland with its huge whale pool, dolphin and seal shows, shark tunnel and other marine life. Cannes is famous for its many festivals, but especially the Cannes Film Festival in May, when the eyes of the world are on the La Croisette (a favourite seafront photograph location for the stars during the Festival).

Nice is famous for its long promenade, the Promenade des Anglais, and the delights of sampling *Bouillabaisse* (a fish soup with a difference) in the restaurants in old Nice.

Antibes, like Cannes, is a favourite mooring ground and has a wide variety of services for the yachting industry. These include the purchase, sale, lease or hire of a wide range of vessels, the recruiting of crew and the provision of all sorts of supplies to yachts, including British and American foodstuffs from Geoffrey's of London and, more recently, Carrefour.

Beach resorts include Théoule sur Mer (the French winner of a European award for tourism), Juan les Pins, Menton, St Jean Cap Ferrat and Port Grimaud. Pollution can be a problem and some of the beaches are not too clean (not that the UK record in this area is anything to boast about). The bacterial and chemical pollutants can cause stomach or ear infections or various types of rash. After a swim you should wash down under one of the many showers provided on the beach. The cleanest beaches are reputed to be those of Cap d'Ail in Alpes Maritimes and Grimaud, Ste Maxime and Hyères in the Var. Avoid swimming after it has been raining, as pollution levels are at their highest at these times.

British and English-speaking contacts

The following is merely a brief summary of the facilities, help and assistance available in the region for British and other English-speaking nationalities (see Appendix 1 and www.angloinfo.com for further contact details).

English newspapers and journals

The Riviera Reporter, *The Riviera Times*, *The Riviera Gazette*, *Connections Côte d'Azur* and in the Var, the *Var Village Voice*. There is also an English *Yellow Pages* for the Côte d'Azur and an English information Web site at www.angloinfo.com.

English-language radio stations

Radio Riviera in Monaco (with BBC World Service News). Also Radio International, The Breeze, and Radio Caroline South.

Community and advice associations

These include the British Association, with branches in Cannes, Menton, Monaco and Nice. Adapt in France, in Sophia Antipolis, was set up by a friendly woman from Brittany to help foreigners adapt to the area. It has a resource centre as well as a total of 15 practical workshops ranging from banking services to Social Security, to creating a company.

Social groups

These include the British Association, the *Association France–Grande-Bretagne* and the Auld Alliance (a club for Scots) in Nice, the Commonwealth Club, the Australian Club, the Canadian Club of Monaco, the South African Club and the Anglo-American Group of Provence.

Amateur dramatics groups include the Riviera Amateur Dramatic Association, Monaco Drama Group and Red Pear Theatre Company in Antibes.

Dance and music groups include a Scottish dance group in Monaco, Country Music Association, an English choir, English Chamber Choir and Cathedral Singers.

Servicemen's groups include the Royal British Legion, Navy League and Royal Air Force Association.

Sports groups include cricket clubs (Monaco, tel: 04 93 77 11 86; Cabris, tel: 04 93 70 27 23), Sailing for Singles and an English boules club.

Other groups include Monaco Bookworms, an English-speaking MENSA group, Oxbridge Set (Oxford, Cambrige and Trinity College, Dublin), and 30-Something.

Anglican churches

These can be found in Nice, Sophia Antipolis, Menton, Monaco, Beaulieu and there is the Holy Trinity in Cannes (tel: 04 93 94 04 56). There is also a Christian Fellowship group (not Anglican) in Sophia Antipolis, International Baptist churches in Cannes and St Paul and a bilingual International Evangelical church in Nice.

International schools

These include the Mougins School (offering a British-based education), the International School of Nice (with more American and European influences and offering the international baccalaureate), the ABC School in Nice, the International School of Sophia Antipolis (a state school with an anglophone section) and the International School of Monaco. There are also two private French schools under the same management, Le Pain d'Epice in Nice and Le Pain de Sucre in Cagnes sur Mer, purporting to offer a bilingual primary education. There is a Montessori school, Les Pouces Verts, in Mouans Sartoux. For further information visit www.angloinfo.com.

Libraries

These can be found in Nice, Vence and Monaco (the Princess Grace Irish Library) and there is a modest library in the Anglican church in Cannes.

Bookshops

There are bookshops stocking English books in Nice (Cat's Whiskers, tel: 04 93 80 02 66), Cannes (Cannes English Bookshop, tel: 04 93 99 40 08), Antibes (Antibes Books, tel: 04 93 34 74 11) and Monaco (Scruples, tel: 03 77 93 50 43 52) and The English Book Centre in Valbonne (tel: 04 93 12 21 42).

There is a second-hand bookshop, Sunnybank Books, in Mandelieu that is raising funds for an Anglo-American convalescent home, following the closure of Sunnybank Hospital (tel: 04 94 76 17 05).

British, Irish and American food and other products

These are sold by Geoffrey's of London (also selling cards and hiring English videos, tel: 04 92 90 66 40) and EuroBrits (tel: 06 14 56 07 37), both in Antibes. Selections of British products are also available in Supermarché Champion in Antibes, the Shopi Supermarché in Roquefort les Pins, Alimentation de la Famille (rue François Guisol) in Nice, Cap 3000 in St Laurent du Var and the Best of British and the E-mail Café both in the old town of Nice.

British shops

There are branches of the Virgin Megastore and the Body Shop in Nice, where there is also a branch of the Dutch store C & A.

Irish and English pubs and restaurants

Monaco, Nice, Cannes, Mondelieu, Valbonne and Antibes all have such venues. There is a Star 'n Bars American bar in Monaco, and an Australian bar in Nice. There is a fish-and-chip shop (Flo's) in Antibes, run by a French woman. On the shore of Lac de Saint Cassien (10 minutes off the A8 at exit 39) you will find the restaurant Les Arbousiers (tel: 04 93 60 67 89), with a blazing fire on winter evenings, jazz nights on alternate Saturdays and fish-and-chip suppers on Fridays. In summer you can swim in the lake or hire a pedal boat – a refreshing break from the stifling heat of the crowded coast. For an English Sunday lunch, it is worth visiting Le Relais des Coches, in Tourrettes sur Loup (tel: 04 93 24 30 24).

British and American banks

In Monaco there are branches of Barclays, Citibank, American Express Bank and Lloyds TSB, in Nice Abbey National, Barclays and Woolwich, in Antibes Barclays and Woolwich, in Cannes Abbey National, Barclays and Woolwich and in Cagnes-sur-Mer Barclays.

English dentists

Helen Giacommi practises in Cagnes-sur-Mer (04 93 22 92 77) and Robert Hempleman in Cannes (04 93 38 10 83).

Other contacts

In addition, there are British, Irish, American and Australian people running a whole range of businesses aimed primarily at the English-speaking community. These services include security and gardening, the supply of satellite dishes, insurance and financial advice, estate agencies, property management and letting agencies, computer repairs, house removals, building and property maintenance, hairdressing and piano tuning. The region also has an Alcoholics Anonymous. For further information, see the English *Yellow Pages* and www.angloinfo.com.

A substantial number of English-speakers find employment in the areas of security, building and maintenance, gardening, childcare and as domestic staff and crew members on yachts, often for British or American employers.

UK travel links

Nice

London Heathrow (BA, BMI)
London Luton (easyJet)
London Gatwick (easyJet, BA)
London Stansted (easyJet)
Birmingham (BA)
Belfast (easyJet)
Bristol (Air France)
Coventry (Thomsonfly)
East Midlands (BMI)
Edinburgh (BMI)
Glasgow (BMI)
Leeds/Bradford
Liverpool (easyJet)
Manchester (BA)
Newcastle (easyJet)
Teeside (BMI)

Other travel information

Train

With the Channel Tunnel and the arrival of the TGV, Nice is now a mere 9½ hours from Waterloo by train.

By car

Calais–Nice 10 hours 40 minutes by motorway
Paris–Nice 8 hours 20 minutes by motorway

Other transport information

Air

Nice is one of the best-connected locations in France, with direct flights to many locations within France and internationally. There are about 80 flights daily to Paris and cheap flights are available to a range of other destinations, including Geneva, Amsterdam, Copenhagen, Stockholm and Hanover.

There are also flights from Nice to the small airports at St Tropez, Cannes-Mandelieu and Monaco.

La Corse

Situated in the Gulf of Genoa, 160 km from the French Riviera, 84 km from the Italian coast and just 14 km from the Italian island of Sardinia, this stunning Mediterranean island (often named *Île de la Beauté*) has been repeatedly pillaged and invaded throughout its history. During the Middle Ages and the Renaissance, Corsica was under Italian domination. Since 1768, it has remained under French control.

Corsica has a population of about 250,000 and is divided into two departments – Corse du Sud (20A) and Haute Corse (20B). The two main towns are Ajaccio (the capital of Corsica and birthplace of Napoleon) and Bastia, the largest port and town on the island. The other principal towns (all coastal) are Bonifacio, Calvi and Porto Vecchio.

The island boasts 1000 km of coastline, much of it rocky, but also offering plenty of golden sandy beaches, especially on the western coast. The island prides itself on the fact that, unlike the neighbouring Côte d'Azur, the coastline is unspoilt and undeveloped. This is in no small part due to the restrictions imposed on developers and the requirement that new property must blend in with the existing landscape.

Inland, most of the island is mountainous (it has over 20 peaks above 2000 m), with a stark, primitive beauty. It is sparsely populated and, in large part, covered with vast forests.

The island grows a considerable volume of agricultural produce, notably wine, citrus fruits (oranges, lemons, mandarins) and peaches, apricots, pears and cherries.

Corsica has a strong sense of its own cultural identity and more independence than most regions, although not sufficient to satisfy the minority who support the independence movement. There have been a number of attacks on the more opulent holiday homes, primarily those belonging to French people.

There are few job opportunities on the island. There is a university, but this has a limited range of courses available. In some schools, the local Corsican language is taught.

Tourism is the island's main industry. Sporting and leisure opportunities abound, including sailing, surfing, kayaking, kite-surfing, windsurfing, deep-sea diving, rock climbing, canoeing, hiking, rafting, waterskiing, fishing and skiing during the winter season. A mountain railway will take you to some of these and delight you with stunning views during its winding journey. There are some museums, particularly in Ajaccio, with the emphasis very much on the history of the Napoleonic era.

As you would expect, the climate is hot in the summer and mild (often very windy, too) in winter. Property prices are quite high, partly because of the demand from the French and Italians, but also because of the difficulty of finding a property to purchase. The sale and purchase of property is much more complicated than on the mainland and it can take years rather than months to complete a transfer. Property is often in the joint ownership of several members of the same family, some of whom have long left the island. Their consent for the sale is required and they may prove difficult or impossible to trace. The problem is not limited to houses – it applies to plots of land as well. Building is not straightforward as the island has retained its beauty by imposing strict regulations on where you can build and what materials you must use.

UK travel links

Birmingham–Calvi (via Munich)
London Gatwick–Bastia (charter flights during the summer)

There is also an airport at Ajaccio with summer charter flights.

Other travel information

Corsica – via its ports at Bastia, Ajaccio and Propriano – can be reached by boat from Marseille, Toulon and Nice in France and Savone and Livourne in Italy. The journey from the French mainland takes 10 hours on the slow boat and 5 hours on the NGV.

Air France has flights to Calvi, Ajaccio and Bastia from Paris, Lyon, Marseille and Nice. The landing at Ajaccio is said to be hair-raising owing to the short landing strip and the proximity of the mountains.

3 Renting a home in France

Reasons to rent

Purchasing a property in France is a serious business. While property prices are generally lower than in the UK (notable exceptions being Paris and the Côte d'Azur), acquisition costs are much higher. Similarly, costs when you come to sell are also appreciably more. Choosing the wrong property or the wrong location will be an expensive mistake. Once you have purchased, you may not be able to sell and purchase elsewhere for some considerable time. Accordingly, you should give serious consideration to renting a property before you buy. Even if you know the area where you intend to purchase well, living somewhere is naturally very different from the occasional holiday, particularly if your holidays have all been during the summer months.

Renting, whether furnished (*meublé*) or unfurnished (*non meublé*), will give you the time to look around, consider your options and decide if the area does indeed fit your requirements after all. It will, however, also involve you in a greater outlay than in the UK, in particular estate agents' commission and a deposit equal to *two* months' rent (that the landlord has two months after your departure to refund).

In deciding whether to rent or buy you will need to consider:

▌ whether or not you have sufficient finances to cover the initial outlay of purchasing and can afford the monthly instalments;

▌ the size of the property you require – it is likely that you will be able to afford to rent a larger property than you will be able to buy and in the short to medium term this may suit your plans better than buying;

▌ the rental market – in some areas, such as Paris and the Côte d'Azur, the rental property market can be very limited, with far greater choice being available to those able to purchase their own home;

- whether or not the size of your family is likely to change over the following years;
- your job security and the availability of insurance for loss of employment;
- your age – it is obviously preferable to purchase prior to age 45 in order to be able to pay off your mortgage before retirement;
- whether your job is likely to require you to move or not and to what extent your employers will cover relocation costs;
- the likely rate of growth in the value of property in your chosen location – the value of a flat in Cannes is likely to rise faster than the value of a house in the remoter parts of France, for example;
- how much time you have available to carry out your research – the purchase of a property inevitably calls for more expenditure of time than does choosing a property to rent;
- whether you wish to tie up the capital required for the purchase of your property – a 100 per cent mortgage is seldom available and most lenders will not exceed 80 per cent of the purchase price;
- any implications for your tax position;
- your wishes in relation to the passing of property purchased on your death.

I would strongly recommend that anyone moving to France should rent initially, if only for a period of a year or so. It enables you to familiarize yourself with the locality and the various amenities (or lack of them) and the vagaries of the weather. It allows you the opportunity to get to know an area and some of the local population. Far better to read in the local paper about protests about a planned new road or nuclear power station while you are renting, than after you have sunk your hard-earned savings into what turns out to be a living nightmare.

I would also strongly recommend that you do not enter into a rental agreement before arriving at your destination in France. Instead, book two weeks or so in short-term or holiday accommodation.

If you are intending to rent for only a year or less, then do give consideration to a furnished letting.

Finding a home to rent

The small ads

In addition to the local and regional newspapers, each department has a free publication containing numerous advertisements, including houses for sale and rent. Each paper is known simply by the relevant department number. In the Alpes Maritimes, for example, the publication is known as *Le 06* (le zéro six). There are also often different editions for the main population centres within the department.

When answering these advertisements, take precautions. Ask as many questions as you can over the telephone before embarking on what may prove to be a totally wasted visit. You may be responding to an advertisement by an agent who is advertising an attractive, but non-existent property merely to persuade readers to ring in. Often they will not supply any information by post, are reluctant to discuss details over the telephone and insist on you attending their offices. In fact, they merely arrange appointments for you to be taken around properties by the proprietor. They charge you a (one-off) fee for doing this (about £100). This is payable in advance before you view a single property and is non-refundable. They promise to arrange for you to visit at least one property. Over the telephone you will be told that they do have a property on their books that fits your requirements and others that are likely to become available in the near future, but, in practice, when you come to view the property it may be totally inappropriate.

A useful publication is *Particular à Particular*. This contains huge numbers of advertisements by owners seeking to sell or rent direct without an agent. Published weekly, it covers the whole of France and costs about £2. It consists mostly of properties for sale, but includes a significant number of properties for rent, including in and around Paris and the Côte d'Azur. It also has a Web site at www.pap.fr with an English version. Two other Web sites that include properties to rent and which both have English versions are www.fnaim.fr and www.seloger.com.

Estate agencies (*agences immobilières*)

Often helpful, but more expensive than in the UK. They usually take a fee (*les honoraires*) from both the proprietor and the tenant, who pay about a month's rent each. Some rental agreements entitle the estate agent to a further fee on any renewal of the rental agreement, a rather nasty surprise to receive if you decide to extend your lease after three years! Do not accept this and have them bar this from the agreement.

Les notaires

Notaires are lawyers responsible for the transfer of property and perform some of the traditional roles of the English solicitor. They frequently have or know of properties available for rent. If you intend to rent in a rural location, the local *notaires* can be particularly useful.

Les administrateurs de biens

These are organizations that manage blocks of flats. As 45 per cent of the French live in apartments, there are many such businesses. In addition to managing, they also act as agents for those wishing to let (or sell) their apartments. You will find a list in the *Yellow Pages* (*Pages Jaunes*).

The Mairie (town hall)

Mairies keep lists of properties available for rental in the local area. The staff can be of assistance, but how much tends to vary considerably. Some French citizens believe that foreigners receive 'special treatment' and are given priority over local French people.

Visiting the property

Never go without a suitable tape measure. Properties are usually advertised as being so many metres square. If the property does not measure up to the advertisement, then use this as a negotiating tool.

Insist on visiting the property at least twice, preferably on different days of the week, at different times and, if possible, in different weather conditions. Watch out for any red and white signs on nearby properties '*Chantier – Interdit*', which means 'Work site, no entry'. These signs are normally attached to the wall of any property a month or two before any renovation works are going to start.

The protection afforded by French law

The rental market is subject to regulation by French law, which protects, in particular, the tenant's right to stay in the property and, in some cases, the level of rent. Where there is a conflict between the written rental agreement and French law, the law prevails.

Furnished lettings (*locations meublées*), seasonal lettings (*locations saison-nières*) and second residences (*résidences secondaires*) are not protected by this legislation. Unless stated to the contrary, this chapter deals with unfurnished, non-seasonal lettings, although much of the practical advice is pertinent also to furnished and seasonal lettings.

In relation to seasonal lettings, landlords had until 1 May 2004 to install safety measures (see the section on 'Pool safety' in Chapter 9).

The rental agreement

Read this carefully! Consider having it checked over by a *notaire*. Agreements can be oral, but you are entitled to a copy of a written contract confirming the tenancy and setting out the terms. The agreement should include the names of the proprietor (*le propriétaire*, referred to in the contract as *le bailleur*) and the tenant (*le locataire*), the date the tenancy commences and its length. It must also give a description of the property, including the number of rooms (*pièces*), level of rent, amount of the deposit and purpose for which the property is being let. You should insist on a written contract (*un contrat de bail*). If circumstances make this impossible, you can ask for this after moving into the property. There is a model letter at the end of this chapter.

French law forbids certain restrictions on tenants, including clauses that:

▌ forbid the tenant to work from home (see below);
▌ require payments by direct debit or direct from a tenant's salary;
▌ forbid the keeping of a pet (clauses outlawing pit bulls and other dangerous breeds of dogs have been upheld, however);
▌ require the tenant to take out a policy of insurance with a particular insurance company;
▌ permit the proprietor alone to estimate the sums due from the tenant in relation to any repairs required to the property to rectify any damage caused.

Married couples

The law provides that a tenancy contract signed by one spouse automatically renders the other spouse a tenant also, even if the marriage took place after the property was let.

The rent

Le loyer (rent) is normally payable from the first day of each month. Agreements normally contain a provision for automatic annual increases in the rent on each anniversary of the contract. Increases are tied in to the figure published by INSEE (pronounced 'incie'), the Institut National de Statistiques et des Etudes, for the cost of construction.

The deposit

Called la caution or le dépôt de guarantie, the deposit cannot be more than two months' rent (not counting any service charges) and cannot be increased during the period of the agreement. It is payable on the signing of the rental agreement. The proprietor may be prepared to give you more time to pay this – for example, taking half on moving into the property and half a month later. In any event, ask for a receipt (un reçu).

You may be entitled to financial assistance to pay the deposit. This is available to people under 30 years old who are in salaried employment or looking for employment, salaried employees moving for work reasons and students in receipt of a state bourse (grant). The Avance Loca-Pass can cover up to the whole of the deposit. Assistance, in the form of the Guarantie Loca-Pass, is also available where a landlord is insisting that the tenant provide a guarantor for the rent throughout the tenancy, in addition to the caution. The administration of this assistance is not centralized. However, the name of the relevant organization in your area can be obtained by contacting the umbrella organization UESL (Union d'Economie Sociale pour le Logement) in Paris (tel: 01 44 85 81 00, Web site www.uesl.fr) or by enquiring of one of the organizations listed below under the heading Resolving disputes.

The deposit is kept by the proprietor as a guarantee of the condition of the property and the other risks taken by him or her in letting the property. At the end of the rental, the deposit should be returned to the tenant. No interest is payable to the tenant. The proprietor is entitled to deduct his or her costs of rectifying any damage to the property and any unpaid rent. He or she is allowed up to two months to repay the deposit. If he or she keeps it for longer than two months, he or she is liable to pay interest on the sums withheld. If the proprietor fails to repay the deposit, you will need to write to him or her requesting its return. You should send a *lettre recommandée avec avis de réception* (a letter sent by recorded delivery followed by a confirmation sent to you by the post office that the letter has arrived). This may well have the desired result. If not, then, once you have heard back from the post office that the letter arrived at its destination and after you have given the proprietor eight days from the date of the delivery in which to respond, you can institute proceedings. It is now time to consider obtaining some legal advice (see below under the heading Resolving disputes).

You are not required to pay a *caution* if you pay your rent on a three-monthly basis. A tenant is entitled, however, to demand that he or she pay the rent on a monthly basis.

The estate agent's commission

This is usually two months' rent, with the landlord and tenant each paying half.

The length of the tenancy

Where the property is unfurnished, it must be let for a minimum of either six or three years. The minimum period is six years if the proprietor is a 'personne morale' – that is, a bank, insurance company or other company (*société*). This is reduced to a minimum of three years if the proprietor is an individual (*un particulier*) or a *Société Civile Immobilière*, in which case its name should include the letters SCI.

The tenant is not obliged to stay the full three or six years, but he has a right to stay for the entire period. The proprietor cannot compel him to leave before the end of the agreement except on limited grounds (primarily non-payment of rent and causing damage to the property).

In certain circumstances, the proprietor is entitled to insist on a shorter rental period, but even then it must be for at least a year. To do this, he has to identify a specific family or work reason for requiring the property back at the end of the period. Examples include a planned marriage or because he wishes the property to be occupied by one of his children or because he works abroad and wishes to return to the property. The proprietor must state the reason *before* the agreement is signed. In addition, the proprietor must, at least two months before the end of the tenancy, confirm to the tenant by recorded delivery that the anticipated event is still to take place (for example, his return from abroad to live in the property). If the proprietor fails to do this, the tenancy proceeds as a three-year tenancy.

Renewal of the tenancy – *le renouvellement*

A tenant is entitled to renew the tenancy of an unfurnished letting for a further period of the same length (three or six years). The landlord cannot refuse to renew the tenancy unless:

■ he is selling the property, in which case the tenant has the right of first refusal;
■ he wishes to live in it;
■ there is good cause for refusing, such as persistent problems with payment of rent.

If nothing has been said before the end of the tenancy and neither party has given notice to end the tenancy, then the agreement is automatically extended for the same length as the original tenancy.

The charges

Consumption of water, use of any collective heating supply (as in a block of flats), maintenance and minor repairs to the common parts, such as the lift, stairs and so on are all payable by the tenant. If the proprietor incurs any expenditure on behalf of the tenant, he has to make available to the tenant proof of the expenditure that has been incurred. Usually, where service charges are payable, an account is submitted once a year. The tenant can ask for proof and can also challenge the expenditure, but should do so *within one month* of receiving the account.

Maintenance of the property

This is the tenant's responsibility. His liability extends to minor repairs as well as maintenance in order to prevent the property falling into disrepair. This covers replacing broken windows and broken keys, paintwork, bleeding of radiators, and replacement of bulbs, fuses and light fittings.

The proprietor, on the other hand, remains responsible for more substantial works of maintenance, such as repointing of walls, replacing shutters and windows, and the hot water heater, and things to do with the structure of the building. A tenant is not, however, entitled to take out a lease of a property in a poor condition and then require the landlord to put it into a better state of repair than it was in at the start of the tenancy.

Improvements to the property

The tenant does not need permission to carry out minor works, such as the fitting of a carpet. However, he is not entitled to carry out any substantial work or make holes in walls, for example, without the written consent of the proprietor and under the supervision of an architect appointed by him.

The proprietor's right to carry out works

You are not entitled to object to any work that the proprietor wishes to carry out, whether it be to maintain or improve the property. If the works render the property uninhabitable, however, then the tenant is entitled to withdraw from the tenancy agreement. Most agreements contain provisions that stipulate that the tenant has to put up with such works without compensation.

If peace and quiet are important to you (especially if you are at home during working hours!) it would be wise to obtain the proprietor's confirmation that no works of improvement will be carried out during the tenancy save with your agreement.

The right to work at home

Since 1998, a tenant of property that is exclusively for use as a home (*un bail à usage exclusif d'habitation*) is entitled to carry out a commercial or professional activity *provided*:

▌ he does not receive clients or merchandise at the property;

▌ the property is his or her principal residence.

Slightly different rules apply to childminding.

If you are intending to rent a flat, then you will still need to check the rules governing occupation of the flats. These may restrict the tenant's right to carry on a commercial activity, as they would do if the proprietor were to live in the apartment.

A tenant can, in certain circumstances, have a letterbox specifically to receive business post.

Your obligation to insure

You are obliged to ensure that a policy of insurance is in force from the moment that you are in possession of the keys. Your insurer should give you an *attestation* to confirm that cover is in force. Agreements usually contain a provision allowing the proprietor to withdraw from the agreement if no insurance is in force.

Fixing the level of rent

A proprietor is only free to fix the level of rent if the property:

▌ is new;

▌ is being let for the first time, providing it meets various minimum quality standards;

▌ has been renovated within the preceding six months and at a cost at least equal to a year's rent when the property was last let.

Where the proprietor is not free to fix the rent, then rent levels are fixed by agreement, failing which the proprietor must apply to the *Tribunal d'Instance*.

If a proprietor wishes to increase the rent at the end of a tenancy, he can only do so if the rent is clearly too low. In this case, the proprietor must send a registered letter to the tenant six months before the end of the tenancy with the proposals for the new rent and enclose details of other similar properties in the neighbourhood (six if in Paris, Lyon or Marseille and three if elsewhere) to justify the increase. If the tenant does not agree to the proprietor's proposal, the proprietor has to apply to the local *Commission de Conciliation* and, if no agreement is reached, he then has to apply to the *Tribunal d'Instance*.

Subletting

A tenant cannot sublet an apartment without the prior written consent of the proprietor. Even If you are given permission to sublet, you remain liable to pay any rent not paid by your sub-tenant.

If you are offered a sub-tenancy, you should ensure that the proprietor's written consent has been obtained or, preferably, enter into an agreement directly with him. If you do not and the proprietor becomes entitled to end the tenancy he has granted to your landlord, you may well be left high and dry.

Giving notice to leave

A tenant of an unfurnished letting is entitled to give notice (*le congé*) at *any* time during the currency of the three- or six-year tenancy, providing, that is, he gives the correct notice. Generally, three months' notice is required and no reason or justification is necessary. The three months does not begin to run until the next payment date. Accordingly, if the rent is due on the first day of each month and you wish to leave at the end of August, you should ensure that notice is given (and received) before the end of May. If the notice is not received until the 1 June, then the three-month period does not begin to run until the end of June and you will be liable to pay the rent for September.

The notice period is, however, reduced to one month in the following circumstances:

■ change or loss of job or the obtaining of a new job after losing an existing employment;
■ if the tenant is more than 60 years old and his move is justified by the person's state of health;
■ when the tenant's income falls below a certain level.

The notice should be sent to the landlord by *lettre recommandée avec avis de réception*. If you are claiming to be entitled to give a month's notice because of a change in your employment, you will need to include photo-copies of documentation that confirms this (otherwise the notice period, and your liability to pay, will be extended to three months).

I have included a model letter at the end of the chapter giving notice, together with a translation. If you are relying on an entitlement to give one month's notice, you will need to add in a paragraph, for example:

J'ai été licencié par mon employeur, ce qui me permet de bénéficier d'une réduction du délai de préavis à un mois. Veuillez trouvez ci-joint une copie d'une lettre de mon employeur.

I have been made redundant by my employer, which entitles me to benefit from a reduction in the period of notice required to one month. I enclose a copy of a letter from my employer.

If you wish to leave before the expiry of the notice period, you can attempt to find a new tenant to take over the tenancy, failing which you remain liable for the rent and looking after the property.

Notice to leave given by the landlord

A proprietor can only give notice at the end of a tenancy and, even then, only for three motives:

- the property is to be occupied by himself or a close relative – essentially his partner or their parents or children;
- he or she wishes to sell the property;
- for misconduct by the tenant – non-payment of rent, nuisance, failure to insure, unauthorized subletting.

The proprietor must give the tenant at least six months' notice before the end of the tenancy by recorded letter or by using a *huissier* (bailiff). The letter must give details of the reason for the notice being given. If the proprietor intends to sell, he or she must indicate the price and conditions of the sale and offer the property to the tenant, who has the right of first refusal.

Before you move in

It is essential that an *état des lieux* is completed before you move in. This document records the condition of the property at the start of the tenancy. It is vital if you wish to reduce the risks of a nasty surprise when you come to leave. If this is not completed, a tenant is deemed to have received the house or apartment in a good state and is obliged to hand it back in a good state!

An *état des lieux* is often completed by a *huissier de justice*. He or she attends at the property with the proprietor and tenant, preferably prior to your furniture arriving. I recommend that you attend the property beforehand, armed with the draft in this book, and form your own view as to what you wish the *huissier* to record – he or she may be open to persuasion. Check that the cooker and any machines included in the letting are in working order.

The cost of instructing a *huissier* (about 235–305 euros) is shared equally between the proprietor and the tenant. The *huissier* should be contacted as early as possible.

Huissiers vary in the thoroughness with which they carry out this routine task. As is apparent from the draft at the end of this chapter, they stipulate in a very general way the condition of various items in the property, indicating whether they are in a good, average or bad state. You should ask the *huissier* to note any particular defect present, such as a cracked tile.

You do not have to employ a *huissier*. The estate agent instructed by the proprietor may be prepared to do it. Alternatively, you could simply go through the document yourself with the proprietor in the hope that you can reach agreement. You may wish to use a whole page per room rather than just three or four lines.

I suggest that you use a carbon to make two copies or each make your own copy. Ensure that they are identical before both signing them. If only one copy is completed and signed, insist on providing the photocopy yourself. If you give the only copy to the landlord, you may cause yourself considerable problems if he loses it or otherwise fails to supply you with your copy. Remember, without the *état des lieux*, the law presumes that the property was in a good state and you are obliged to hand it back in the same condition.

I strongly recommend that, on moving in, you take a video of the property, paying attention to any particular defects, and post this to yourself by recorded delivery so that you can prove the date that the video was taken. Do not open it unless some dispute arises at the end of the tenancy, in which case open it in front of some third party, such as a *notaire* or *avocat,* who can vouch for the fact that the envelope was previously unopened.

When you come to leave

A further *état des lieux* should be completed and a comparison made with the previous *état des lieux* to determine the extent of any damage caused during your occupation. I recommend, whether or not a *huissier* is employed, that you make a video of the premises before leaving. In the middle of the recording, video a news item on the television or that day's newspaper, so you can prove that it was not taken earlier.

Resolving disputes

In the event of a disagreement with the proprietor (for example, he is refusing to repair a faulty hot water supply or carry out other works for which he is responsible, or is refusing to repay the deposit), you should seek advice. Obviously, instructing an *avocat* can be expensive and may be out of proportion to the financial value of the dispute. There are, however, various agencies that provide free advice, including those that represent tenants' rights. At the back of the *Yellow Pages* you should find various contact addresses and numbers (perhaps under the heading *Vos Démarches Administratives* or *Logement*). Two agencies that provide advice and assistance are *La Direction Départementale de l'Equipement* (DDE) and *L'Association Départementale pour l'Information sur le Logement* (ADIL) – the address and telephone number of the latter should also be in the *White Pages* under ADIL (that is, under its initials) in the section for your locality. You can also try the *Association des Comités de Défense des Locataires* (ACDL) at 11 rue de Bellefond, 75009 Paris (tel: 01 48 74 94 84).

Litigation can be avoided by trying the conciliation procedure (*la conciliation judiciaire*). This route is entirely optional and free. It may result in the resolution of your dispute. To invoke the procedure, you write to *Le Greffe du Tribunal d'Instance*, setting out the basis of the dispute (courts are listed under *Tribunaux* in the *Yellow Pages*). The parties will be called to present their arguments to the judge, who will then give his or her opinion. The judge's decision is not of itself binding, but may result in an agreement being reached between the parties. If so, that agreement can be given binding force, just as if it were a decision of the court.

If no agreement is reached, then you will have to commence proceedings. There are several different courts in France, depending on the nature of the dispute. The relevant court here is the *Tribunal d'Instance*. This court deals with most civil claims up to the value of about 8000 euros.

As in the UK, a proprietor wishing to evict a tenant who is not paying the rent is only entitled to do so after completing various procedures and seeking an order of the court. First of all, the proprietor must arrange for a *huissier* to deliver a request for payment. A tenant then has two months to put matters in order. If he does not, then the proprietor must bring his claim before the court. The judge hearing the matter can then either order a tenant's eviction or give him time to pay the arrears of rent (as well as the costs of the proceedings).

As in the UK, the emphasis is on protecting the occupation of the tenant, providing he comes up with reasonable proposals to clear the arrears. Even if the tribunal grants an order in the landlord's favour for the eviction of the tenant, the eviction cannot be carried out between 1 November and 15 March.

Representation

You do not have to instruct an *avocat*. A person can represent himself or be represented by a spouse, partner or relative. This includes a relative by marriage and relatives up to twice removed. The representative should go armed with a letter of authorization (see the example at the end of this chapter) and identification papers for both himself and the person he is representing.

ETAT DES LIEUX

NOM DU LOCATAIRE:

NOM DU PROPRIETAIRE:

ADRESSE DU LOGEMENT:

DATE D'ENTRÉE:

| 1 = très bon | 2 = bon | 3 = passable | 4 = mauvais |

pièce	peinture plafond viterie	sol portes fenêtres stores	electricité	rangements	plomberie sanitaires	serrurerie
Séjour						
Cuisine						
Chambre 1						
Chambre 2						
Chambre 3						
Salle de bain						
Toilettes						
Entrée						
Cave						
Garage						

Les constatations ci-dessus sur l'état du logement sont reconnues exactes par les parties.

(Signed)

Le locataire   *Le proprietaire*

ETAT DES LIEUX

NAME OF TENANT:

NAME OF PROPRIETOR:

ADDRESS OF PROPERTY:

DATE OF MOVING IN:

| 1 = very good | 2 = good | 3 = passable | 4 = poor |

room	paintwork ceiling window-panes	floor doors windows blinds	electricity	cupboards/ storage units	plumbing toilet installations	locks ironwork
Living room						
Kitchen						
Bedroom 1						
Bedroom 2						
Bedroom 3						
Bathroom						
Toilet						
Hall/ entrance way						
Cellar						
Garage						

The above record on the state of the premises is acknowledged by the parties to be accurate.

Signed

The tenants   The proprietor

REQUEST FOR A WRITTEN CONTRACT

(Your name)

(Your address)

(Landlord's name)

(Landlord's address)

(Date)

Lettre recommandée avec Avis de Réception

Monsieur et/ou Madame

Dear Sir and/or Madam,

Je suis locataire d'un logement situé à (put address) *dont vous êtes le propriétaire et qui a fait l'objet d'un bail verbal.*

I am the tenant of… of which you are the landlord and which is subject to an oral tenancy.

L'article 3 de la loi du 6 juillet 1989 prévoit que j'ai le droit à un contrat écrit et je voudrais que vous me fournissiez d'un tel contrat écrit.

Article 3 of the law of 6 July 1989 provides that I have the right to a written contract and I would like you to provide me with such a written contract.

Je vous prie de croire Monsieur et/ou Madame en l'expression de mes sentiments distingués

Yours sincerely,

TENANTS' LETTER GIVING NOTICE OF TERMINATION
(*congé donné par les locataires*)

(Your name)

(Your address)

> (Name of proprietor)
>
> (Proprietor's address)
>
> (Date (eg *Vendredi 25 janvier 20…*))

Lettre Recommandée avec Avis de Réception

Monsieur et/ou Madame,

Dear Sir and/or Madam,

Nous sommes locataires de (put address) *dont vous êtes le propriétaire. Nous voulons résilier le bail à loyer que nous avons signé le 1er mai 1999 et nous vous donnons congé pour le 30 avril.*

We are tenants of… of which you are the proprietor. We wish to terminate the tenancy that we signed on 1 May 1999 and we give you notice of termination for 30 April.

Nous nous engageons donc à libérer les locaux le 30 avril en bon état de réparations locatives.

We undertake to vacate the premises on 30 April, leaving them in good condition and having completed the repairs required of a tenant.

Nous vous précisons qu'il conviendra de dresser un état des lieux lors de la restitution du logement.

We consider that an état des lieux should be drawn up once the premises are vacated.

Nous vous invitons à faire le nécessaire afin de nous restituer le montant du dépôt de guarantie que nous vous avons versé, soit… euros.

We invite you to make the necessary arrangements to return the deposit to us that we gave you, namely… euros.

Pour le bon régle nous vous serons reconnaissants de bien vouloir nous signifier votre accord.

We would be grateful if you would confirm your agreement.

Nous vous prions de croire, Monsieur et/ou Madame, à l'expression de nos sentiments distingués:

Yours sincerely,

PROCURATION
(letter of authorization required by the tenant's representative at a tribunal)

Je soussigné(e) (name of person to be represented)

demeurant (address of person to be represented)

donne pouvoir à mon (put relationship of person representing)
authorize my (eg *mon conjoint* (husband), *ma conjointe* (wife), *mon concubin/ma concubine* (partner), *mon père* (father), *mon beau-père* (father-in-law), *ma mère* (mother) *ma belle-mère* (mother-in-law), *mon beau-fils* (son-in-law), *ma belle-fille* (daughter-in-law))

demeurant à (put in their address) *pour me représenter à*
to represent me at
l'audience du (put in date of hearing) *et à toute autre audience ultérieure*
the hearing on and at any other hearing
devant le tribunal d'instance de (put in town in which tribunal is situated)
before the *tribunal d'instance* at
concernant un litige contre au sujet d'un logement de (put in the address of the property)
concerning a dispute relating to
a cet effet
with power to

faire toute déclaration, signer toute pièce et de faire tout ce qui sera nécessaire
to make any declaration, sign any document and do anything necessary

4

The purchase of your home

The first step: deciding on legal advice

Once you have decided to purchase a property in France you should seriously consider consulting a lawyer before you even start your search. Legal advice should cover the various ways in which you can own your French property, the options for mortgage finance and French inheritance and tax rules. This book is intended to highlight matters you should consider and is not an alternative to taking legal advice on your intended purchase or residency in France.

The French *notaire* and the solicitor

While the French *notaire* is in some ways similar to the English solicitor, he or she is, above all, a publicly appointed official. The *notaire*'s main function is to draft legal documents, ensure that all state taxes are paid on the purchase of a property and register the property transaction at the French land registry (*bureau des hypothèques*). The *notaire* also offers legal advice in relation to property purchases and such matters as the creation and merger of businesses, the financial arrangements on divorce, wills and inheritance. He can act for a client anywhere in the country.

In principle, *notaires* are required to be impartial. While it is difficult to see how a *notaire* can be entirely impartial in cases where he has known the vendor and his family for many years and the purchaser is a stranger to the area, the system appears to work.

It is the *notaire*'s job to check the preliminary contract (see below) and then verify that the vendor does have proper title and is able to sell the property. In addition to verifying the vendor's right to sell, the *notaire* is

responsible for checking planning regulations and charges against the property. His obligations in relation to planning regulations are limited. He should check on the present authorized use of the property and regulations that have a direct bearing on it, but the *notaire*'s brief does not extend, for example, to finding out if there are any plans to put a new railway line or motorway through or near the property. Where loans on the property exceed the monies available from the sale, the *notaire* is responsible for ensuring that creditors are paid from some other source.

While you have no choice but to involve a *notaire*, there is no reason why you cannot instruct a separate *notaire* to represent your interests. In theory, this should not increase the costs of the transaction as the two *notaires* are supposed to share the one fee. However, most foreigners buying in France are in a different position from that of the average French purchaser. It is likely to be important that the lawyer you instruct should have knowledge of both French *and* British taxation and inheritance law, as well as French property law. There are very few *notaires* in France who can both speak English very well and have a detailed knowledge of English, Scottish or Northern Irish law and procedures. Fortunately, there are some British lawyers who have chosen to specialize in this area and some of them have obtained qualifications in French law. They also have the advantage of being able to communicate with you in English. In addition, there are a few French lawyers who have moved to the UK, are dually qualified and represent clients purchasing property in France. Details of some solicitors are included in Appendix 1.

As a barrister, I have absolutely no personal interest in encouraging you to instruct your own *notaire* or a solicitor to represent your interests. My firm advice, however, is that you should obtain separate legal advice from a lawyer familiar with the laws and regulations of both systems. Whichever route you take, obtain a prior written estimate of their fees, setting out how their charges will be calculated (usually a percentage of the property price subject to a minimum charge, or an hourly rate). UK solicitors often charge 1 per cent of the purchase price (plus a further fee if they draft French wills).

Title insurance

There have been cases where the vendor's title to sell has been found to have been defective, or where unbeknown to the purchaser, the property is subject to rights of way. Insurance is available to cover such eventualities and you should discuss this with your lawyer.

Methods of owning property

This is one area where advice is most definitely appropriate and should be obtained fairly early on in the formulation of your plans. There are several options available, each with different financial consequences, including what happens with regard to the passing of the property on your death and inheritance tax liabilities. Unmarried couples and people in second marriages are particularly at risk of making the wrong choice and should proceed with special caution.

Joint ownership is frequently an option. There are two different means of jointly owning property. One is to purchase *en division*, which means that on your death your half of the property devolves in accordance with the French inheritance rules (subject to the limited provisions you can make in your will – see Chapter 13). The beneficiary is entitled to force a sale of the property, thereby compelling the surviving joint owner to leave.

On the other hand, if you purchase *en tontine*, your 50 per cent *automatically* passes to the surviving joint owner. For inheritance tax purposes, you may wish to include your children as joint owners or put the property in their sole names (reserving a right to live in the property for life). Further details relating to a purchase *en tontine* are set out in Chapter 13.

Purchasing via a limited company permits you to avoid French inheritance laws if you are not resident in France (French succession laws only apply to land held by foreigners, not shares in a company). Similarly, when you wish to sell the property, you can simply sell the shares in the company. The purchaser makes a substantial saving on the acquisition costs (there is no taxable transfer of the property, only a transfer of the shares). This enables you to negotiate a better price with the purchaser.

French law also allows the creation of a *Société Civile Immobilière*, which is a company that exists purely for the purpose of owning property. An SCI is frequently used by unmarried couples or when several people are jointly purchasing a property. The set-up cost ranges from £1000 to £1500 and there are running costs involved, too.

Other less frequently used options include purchasing via a trust, a French commercial company, or a UK or an offshore company.

Properties are often purchased via a company when the purchaser wants to let out the property. It may also be worthwhile considering this if you are purchasing a substantial property or one with a partial business use. Take professional advice.

Finding a property and negotiating with the vendor

There is a substantial amount of property available in France. This is partly owing to its low population density (France is four times the size of England, for example, but its population is only about a quarter greater). It is also because the last 20 years have seen substantial movements away from rural areas to the towns and main cities. Bordeaux, Lyon and Grenoble, for example, have dramatically increased in size.

Property is generally priced much lower than in the UK, with Paris and the Riviera being notable exceptions. In other areas, such as Normandy, the Dordogne and many coastal areas, the influx of foreign, particularly British, purchasers has caused prices to rise. Do be prepared to negotiate, however, as vendors in popular areas put an asking price on their property well above what any local purchaser might contemplate, in the hope of selling to a foreign buyer who doesn't know any better.

Always bear in mind that some day, perhaps rather sooner than you might like, you will want to sell this property. You are more likely to be able to dispose of it easily if it is the type of property that would appeal to potential French, as well as foreign, buyers. Property prices in France have tended to rise steadily, but on the whole by no more than the cost of living (though 2003 saw steep rises in some areas, including around 20 per cent in Paris and Marseille). Accordingly, with high acquisition costs, residential property for owner occupation is seldom a lucrative financial investment. Remember, too, that much of France can be as cold as or colder than England during the winter months and so the larger the house, the higher your heating bills. While derelict properties are inexpensive, renovation costs are high and it is important to work out a realistic estimate of the likely total cost of your purchase.

Recent years have seen the appearance of a number of specialist magazines aimed at prospective British housebuyers, including *Focus on France* and *French Property News* (see Appendix 1 for their respective Web sites). The articles in these publications are frequently helpful and informative. They also contain various advertisements by lawyers who are dually qualified and can provide legal advice in English, as well as estate agents who have set up agencies in France to assist English-speaking purchasers in their search for a dream home. They contain small ads from Britons, too, now wishing to sell their French home or the more adventurous French vendors.

You will also find a selection of such advertisements in the quality British newspapers, such publications as *The Lady* and even *Exchange & Mart*. Properties obtained via these sources are generally offered by vendors who have higher expectations than those selling through French estate agents, *notaires* and media. *French Property News* also holds exhibitions of French property in London, Birmingham, Harrogate and Taunton.

In your search for a property, three main possibilities present themselves. Firstly, there are the various advertisements in French and British publications and Internet sites with details placed by owners themselves. When you are in France, you could search through the small ads (including in the free newspaper normally known by its department number, such as *Le 06* – le zéro six – in Alpes Maritimes). It is also worthwhile consulting a specialist publication such as *de particulier à particulier*, designed to put vendors and purchasers in touch with each other (its Web site is www.pap.fr).

Once you have reached an oral agreement, you should not sign any documentation presented to you by the vendor as he may claim that what you have signed represents the whole agreement between you and seek to enforce the sale to you on that basis. It is essential that all the terms of your purchase are written down in a comprehensive contract drafted by a *notaire*. Avoid the standard printed contracts that you can find for sale in the high street.

Secondly, you could seek the services of an estate agent (*agent immobilier*). This is the most popular method among the British, although among the French only 50 per cent of property is sold this way. Estate agents vary in the quality of the service they provide, but many are extremely helpful and can provide much practical information relating both to the properties they offer and the local area. You should supply the agent with as much detail as possible as to your requirements. Agents are supposed to satisfy themselves that the properties they put forward are in a good state and will normally accompany you on a visit to the property. In most areas of France (though not in Paris or the Riviera), estate agents provide only very brief printed particulars, or none at all, and seldom include photographs. Do not be surprised if they ask you to sign a *bon de visite* – this is merely to safeguard their commission by confirming that it was they who introduced the property to you.

In France, estate agents have to be professionally qualified, licensed to practise and have appropriate insurance. You should avoid the many estate agents, including Britons, who work without satisfying these requirements. If you visit their premises, they should have certificates showing that they are licensed and insured. If you are dealing by telephone, fax or the Internet, ask agents to provide proof that they are licensed and insured (especially if you are proposing to hand any deposit over to them rather than a *notaire*).

If you decide to purchase a property, the agent should draw up a *promesse de vente* and forward this on to a *notaire*, who will complete the remaining paperwork to finalize your purchase of the property. The general rule is that the vendor pays the agent's fees. In the past, the agent's fees were paid by the purchaser – a practice that continues in some regions. Accordingly, you should check what the situation is with each agent prior to agreeing to buy a property. The fees of the *notaire*, on the other hand, are paid for by the purchaser.

Estate agents are free to set the level of their commission, although in most regions there is little price competition, with the usual rate being 5 per cent plus TVA (French VAT). Rates can be slightly lower or as high as 10 per cent. The commission is not payable until the sale has been finally completed by the *notaire*.

A large number of estate agents subscribe to the Internet site operated by the *Fédération Nationale des Agents Immobiliers* (FNAIM), the industry's trade association. The site is at www.fnaim.fr and provides a wide selection of properties. A list of estate agents is included in Appendix 1. Others can be accessed via the *Yellow Pages* Web site at www.pagesjaunes.fr.

There are also several UK-based estate agents, but often these are not licensed in France. Generally, the UK agents carry out searches of properties being offered by a large number of French agents over a wide area to identify properties that might be of particular interest to prospective British purchasers. They prepare particulars and photographs. In many cases they share the French agent's commission, there then being no extra cost to the vendor (or purchaser). On the other hand, extra (hidden) commission is often charged. The agent does this by advertising the property at a price above the vendor's asking price and taking the difference as commission. Ask for a breakdown of the sale price and the different agents' commissions. This may enable you to negotiate a lower price. If you feel that the agent is not being frank, ask for the contact details of the French agent and the vendor.

Do not assume that advice and information given to you by those with a financial interest in the sale of the property, whatever their nationality, is accurate or indeed truthful.

Thirdly, you can contact a *notaire* (see sample letter below). In addition to acting in their official capacity of drafting the documents of transfer, *notaires* sell nearly half the volume of property sold by estate agents. In rural areas, the percentage is generally much higher. A local *notaire* may be able to offer you a variety of properties for sale in the locality. While his commission of 2 per cent is paid by the buyer, a purchase via a *notaire* gives some room for negotiation with the vendor, who will then not have to pay the estate agent's much higher fee (normally 5 per cent, sometimes higher).

A substantial number of French *notaires* subscribe to immonot.com at www.immobilier-notaires.presse.fr. This site is particularly useful for finding properties in villages and the smaller towns. The site will also let you know when properties come on the market.

SAMPLE LETTER TO NOTAIRE ENLISTING HELP IN LOCATING A PROPERTY

Mr/Mrs/Ms Interested Purchaser
3 Acacia Drive
Somewhere
Hereshire
Royaume-Uni
Tel:
e-mail:

> *Somewhere, le 2 avil 2003*
> *Maître…*
> *3 rue des Vacanciers*
> *Parfait*
> *Code Postal*
> *France*

Maître,

Je souhaite acheter une propriété dans votre région, de préférence pas loin de Parfait.

I wish to buy a property in your region, preferably not far from Parfait.

Je cherche une maison ancienne de cinq ou six piéces qui a besoin d'être restaurée ou qui a assez de terrain pour agrandir, située à proximité d'un bourg ou d'un village.

I am looking for an old house with five or six rooms that needs renovating or that has enough ground to extend, situated near a small town or village.

Auriez-vous l'obligeance de me faire savoir si vous êtes au courant d'une propriété qui puisse me convenir, ainsi que les conditions de vente?

Would you be kind enough to let me know if you are aware of a property that might be suitable, and the conditions of sale?

Je vais rendre visite à Parfait en juillet, et je voudrais bien vous rencontrer si vous serez disponible.

I will be visiting Parfait in July and would like to meet up with you if you are available.

En vous remerciant à l'avance je vous prie de croire, Maître, à l'assurance de ma parfaite considération.

Thanking you in advance,

Yours faithfully,

In rural areas, properties are often not advertised at all but are sold by word of mouth. If you have set your heart on a particular rural area, you should also make enquiries in the local *boulangerie* or *tabac*.

Declaring at an undervalue

You may be asked to declare property at an undervalue and pay a proportion of the purchase price 'under the table' (*dessous-de-table*). This will reduce the tax you pay on your purchase and the vendor's liability to tax on his or her capital gain. This practice, though illegal, is widespread.

The drawbacks are that when you come to sell the property, unless you adopt the same procedure (by which time the authorities may well have clamped down on the practice), you will have a larger capital gain and a higher tax bill. Moreover, if the matter should come to the knowledge of the authorities, they can have the property valued. You will then be charged any additional tax plus interest and face a fine and possible prosecution. Furthermore, if the local authority decides to purchase your property as part of a local development plan, the price will be based on the price you paid (the declared price) plus a modest uplift. Lastly, if you decide to adopt the same practice on selling the property, do not assume that you will be paid the additional (under the table) sum by the purchaser.

Purchasing at auction

As in the UK, the best-value properties are often those sold at auction (*ventes aux enchères*) by banks that have repossessed, or where there is a dispute as to inheritance, or the owner has died without heirs and the property needs to be sold.

Auctions are advertised in the local press about six weeks before they are due to take place. For most auctions, it is only *avocats* and *notaires* who are permitted to bid and, accordingly, you will have to appoint one of these lawyers to represent you.

You will need to discuss with your lawyer the maximum price that you are prepared to pay and provide him with a refundable deposit charged by the auctioneer to entitle him to bid on your behalf. A deposit of 10 per cent is payable immediately a bid is successful. A purchase at auction involves higher fees, of between 15 and 20 per cent of the purchase price. These are payable within one month and the purchase price within two months. A purchase at auction is not conditional on you obtaining a mortgage and, accordingly, you must have the money already available.

It is essential to inspect the property prior to bidding or, alternatively, arrange for a local estate agent (for a modest fee) to visit the property and provide you with a description and some photographs. Purchasing at auction can become expensive if you have to make several bid attempts before you are successful, especially if you obtain a report from a surveyor or other expert on each occasion.

While your attendance at an auction is not necessary, in rural areas it is an experience that you may not wish to miss. Traditionally, once it appears that the last bid has been made, a candle is lit. Once the candle is extinguished (this takes about 20 seconds), a second candle is lit until it in turn goes out. If there are no further bids, a third candle is lit. On the extinction of the third candle, the bid is completed. This practice (*vente à la chandelle*) is gradually disappearing in favour of a system of lights.

After a successful bid, you will have to wait ten days before being certain that the property is yours. Anyone prepared to offer 10 per cent more than your bid during this period can force a fresh auction. Fortunately, this is a relatively rare occurrence.

Viewing the property

It is essential that you view the property several times, including in good and bad weather, and during the hours of darkness. Take care to listen to what noise is likely to affect you. Approach the property from different routes and consider how visitors might approach it. You might not appreciate them remembering that to reach you they have to turn left past the sewage works, continue on past the funeral directors or climb the hill past the refuse dump.

You should not be deterred from returning to the property before deciding whether or not to proceed. If possible, try to ascertain why the owners wish to sell and how long (and it may be a question of years, rather than months) the property has been on the market. It may help to remember that the estate agent will receive commission several times the percentage of a UK colleague, albeit generally on a lower-price ticket, and ought to be prepared to answer your questions and arrange your various visits to the property.

Consider the property's location in relation to access to public transport and proximity to shops – chemists and so on. Look carefully not only at the building, but also at the garden and the neighbouring properties. Are the boundaries clearly marked? Is there any reason to suspect that other people have a right of way over the property? What about that well-worn path running through part of the property? Is there a well? Having a well in your garden may appear like an attractive feature. Not so desirable if you are sunning yourself in a state of semi-undress when you look up to see your neighbours, or other inhabitants of the village, walking through your garden to exercise their right to draw water from your well! If there is a well, or some other feature of the property that concerns you, speak to the agent and vendor, then raise it with the *notaire*. Do not forget to note whether the house – in particular the garden, terrace, veranda or balcony – is south-facing. Check also that the light switches work, there is hot and cold running water and that the toilet bowls are not cracked.

Whether you are buying an established property, a new one from a developer, or purchasing a building plot, you should pay particular attention to the terrain. Attempt to ascertain whether the land is likely to flood or not. Some areas have suffered widespread flooding in recent years (see Chapter 1). While these areas are to be treated with particular caution, elsewhere you should still be alert to local flooding. A stream or river may be picturesque during the summer months, but overflow its banks during heavy rains, making your garden unusable even if your house remains untouched. Fortunately, some areas that are prone to dampness and flooding are easily identified by their names. For example, avoid locations such as *La Mare* or *L'Etang* (pond) and *Le Ru* (brook). In my youth, I spent one very wet summer working at a campsite named *La Grenouillère* (frogpond). The site remained damp for many weeks after the rain and tents were uninhabitable owing to the continuing humidity and the odours emanating from under the groundsheets. Always check in a dictionary in case the name of a road or the area in which you propose to buy in fact has a negative meaning.

Think twice, too, before buying a property at the foot of a hill. You may well wish to shelter your home from strong winds, particularly in Brittany, Normandy or the south (the mistral is renowned for the damage it does to properties on the Riviera, especially to windows). However, you also need to consider whether or not the property is likely to be the unhappy recipient of the rainwater that falls on the hillside above your home. The property may also be in danger from falling rocks or landslides.

Whether you are buying property or land, a surveyor can advise you if the land was or is suitable to build on, especially if he is familiar with the locality. In the eastern part of Normandy, for example, chalk mining has caused serious problems in this respect (see Chapter 2). Be alert also to the possibility that the land has been used as a dumping ground for refuse or chemical waste – this may be the explanation for the apparent bargain that you are being offered.

It is wise to visit the *section d'urbanisme* at your local *mairie* and ask to see the POS (*le plan d'occupation des sols*). This will indicate what improvements are planned in the locality, including any airports, motorways and TGV lines. Ask what planning permissions, if any, have been granted for neighbouring properties. Check whether or not the area is subject to flooding. It is also worthwhile visiting the *Direction Départementale de l'Equipement* (DDE) at your nearest *préfecture* to see what information they have about plans for your area.

A word of warning. In some areas – most notably Alpes Maritimes – many properties have been constructed or extended in blatant disregard of local planning restrictions. The cases fall into three categories. Firstly, there are the modest or small houses built by a small developer and sold on to an innocent purchaser.

Secondly, there are the many small restaurants, cafés and other small tourist businesses along more coastal areas where previous owners have encroached on public land or extended the property beyond the boundaries permitted by the planning permission. The businesses will often have changed hands several times, so the present occupier has been totally unaware of the breach until recently.

Thirdly, there are the huge mansions, often constructed on the coastline, by the most wealthy, often foreigners, again blatantly in breach of planning permission, sometimes building over twice the surface area permitted.

For many years, the local authorities sat back and did nothing. The climate has started to change, though, and, in some cases, the authorities

THE SURVEYOR'S VIEW

It's a curious fact that whilst prospective purchasers in the UK generally consider a survey in one form or another to be the prerequisite of buying a house, R-PS (Chartered Surveyors), who specialise in carrying out surveys throughout France, have found that once those same purchasers cross the channel, a surprising number adopt the French philosophy of simply assuming all will be well.

It is also acknowledged by most of the surveyors who act on behalf of UK purchasers in France that, whilst an ever increasing number of immobilier are coming to the realisation that a survey is likely to be required by their UK clients, many of the agents are still resistant to the idea although this usually proves to be a fear of the unknown and attitudes change once they have experienced the reality.

French vendors on the other hand are generally bemused when they witness a survey of their property although, interestingly, so far in 2004, R-PS have been instructed by three such French vendors who were so taken with the investigation of their homes that they decided to have a survey carried out on their purchases – a first time for everything!

Sadly, during 2003, over 10% of work carried out by R-PS on behalf of Clients involved advising on problems that had arisen as a direct result of not seeking professional advice prior to buying their homes in the sun, in some cases having relied on local builders. These problems ranged from relatively minor matters, where R-PS were able to put minds at rest, to more extreme cases such as structural defects and, worse still, hopelessly inadequate budgeting, all of which should have come to light in a traditional survey.

R-PS (Chartered Surveyors) stress that they do not see it as their role to frighten prospective purchasers with seemingly insurmountable problems, simply to ensure their Clients have balanced advice on the actual condition of their investment, enabling a realistic approach coupled with a sensible plan for the long range management of remedial work that might be required – as R-PS say "avoid your milestone becoming a millstone!"

have taken action. Already some properties have been demolished or are undergoing substantial alteration at the expense of their present proprietors, even though they were not responsible for the breach of the regulations. The only solution is to make as many enquiries as you can, specifically asking your *notaire* or solicitor to ensure that the vendor confirms that there have been no breaches. He should carry out thorough checks of the documentation. It would be sensible to insist on the vendor providing up-to-date plans of the property that you or your surveyor can confirm show the present position and then discuss with the *notaire* and your surveyor whether or not they correspond to the permissions granted.

Surveyor's report

In the UK, almost all lending institutions insist on a professional valuation by a building surveyor before agreeing to grant a mortgage. Any self-respecting solicitor will advise a client to have a survey carried out prior to committing themselves to a purchase. A building survey has two very important advantages. Firstly, it prevents you from purchasing a property that is structurally unsound, perhaps dangerous, will be expensive to restore and may be difficult to dispose of. It should identify any woodworm and any movement in the property (which may have caused extensive damage to underground drainage channels or undermined the stability of the property). Secondly, a good report, even a basic one, often identifies non-structural defects – often minor, sometimes more significant. These may not deter you from your intended purchase, but give you ammunition to negotiate on the purchase price.

In France, the practice is very different. French banks and, indeed, most British financial institutions in France, only require a valuation of the property, which is carried out by a valuer, not a surveyor. This is clearly a sensible way to proceed if you are purchasing a tumble-down cottage that requires extensive renovation and where you are essentially paying for the plot of land. Equally, if you are an experienced builder with a portfolio of properties that you are seeking to renovate and sell on, taking a risk in not obtaining a structural survey would be entirely rational. In my opinion, for the individual purchaser who is investing significant capital (including much higher acquisition costs than in the UK) or taking on the liability of a mortgage, a decision to proceed without a survey is sheer folly. Why do it in France, where building standards are, if anything, lower than in the UK, when you would not do it at home?

A full structural survey (*un bilan de santé*) from an *expert immobilier* can be expensive – about £200 to £500 for a basic survey and £500 to £1500 for a full survey. You will also need to have it translated. Translators should translate into their mother tongue, so you should instruct an English-speaker to do this. Remember, this expenditure may help you to negotiate a lower price and save you from taking on an expensive liability that will be difficult to offload. The estate agents, *notaire* and your lending institution should be able to advise you of the names of suitable experts. There are English-speaking surveyors (as well as architects and builders) who are now working in France and will provide you with a report in English. Some of the consulates keep lists of such professionals. One alternative is to have a professional valuer provide a valuation (see the *Yellow Pages* or www.pagesjaunes.fr under *Agents Immobiliers*) or have the property looked over by a master builder (*maître d'oeuvres*), who can also provide you with a written estimate for renovation works. The latter two options are particularly suitable where the property requires substantial renovation and the purchase price is only a modest proportion of your total outlay.

Whoever you instruct to inspect the property, ensure that a written report is provided and make it clear what is to be covered – that is, structural condition of roof, walls, foundations, all woodwork, drains connections with mains or the septic tank, plumbing, electrical and heating installations. Properties built within the previous ten years should benefit from a ten-year guarantee. You should ask for details of this and whether or not there have been any claims.

Occupants or owners of properties affected by termites or similar insects must declare the infestation to their local *mairie* and confirm that the appropriate treatment has been carried out. Check with the *mairie* if the area in which you are contemplating a purchase is a declared risk zone. In such areas, a survey must be carried out before any sale can take place and the vendor must provide the purchaser with a certificate (valid for three months only) confirming whether or not termites are present in the property.

Under recent regulations a vendor is also required to provide details of any asbestos components inside the property. Asbestos (*amiante*) was widely used in France during the 1960s and 1970s to insulate walls and ceilings. All buildings constructed prior to 1 July 1997 must be subject to tests (costing 180–1000 euros) covering all materials used in their construction. If the test is positive, remedial work must be carried out, and further tests made. Your lawyer should obtain documentation proving compliance by the vendor. Information is obtainable from the Ministry of Health and Housing (Web site www.sante.gouv.fr) and the *Association Française pour le Contrôle et la Maîtrise de l'Amiante*, tel: 01 44 30 49 36). As for asbestos, a vendor in certain regions (including departments in the Île de France, Bouche du Rhône, Saône-et-Loire, Hautes Alpes, Gironde, Haute-Loire and Vaucluse) must produce test results for the presence of lead (mainly in paintwork). No remedial works are required. Tests cost 400–700 euros.

Transfer of the property

You may be asked by an estate agent to sign an *offre d'achat* (an offer to buy). This states the purchase price that you are prepared to pay and the time in which you are willing to complete the transfer. On signing the offer you are asked to place a deposit of up to 5 per cent with the estate agent. If the offer is accepted, then a binding agreement is reached.

The principal drawback of this arrangement is the uncertainty faced by the buyer in the days or weeks waiting for the vendor's response. It is preferable to ascertain orally whether or not the vendor would be prepared to accept your price and for an *avant-contrat* to be drawn up. This should not be by simple exchange of letters, but by a *compromis de vente* or a *promesse unilatérale* signed by the vendor. The *avant-contrat* must indicate whether or not the price is to be paid by means of a loan. If the loan is refused and you are unable to obtain alternative mortgage finance, you can recover all the sums you have paid at the time the *avant-contrat* was signed. The contract is accordingly a conditional contract – conditional on a loan offer. It is possible to insert other conditions in the contract, such as the grant of planning permission, obtaining a satisfactory survey, sale of another property, provision of a certificate confirming the absence of termites or granting of rights, such as a right of way over an adjacent property.

The practice of signing an *avant-contrat* means that gazumping is almost unheard of in France. The *avant-contrat* should also set out all the extras that you are purchasing from the vendor, such as carpets and curtains. Remember, many items that would normally be included in a sale in England, such as fitted kitchens, are not included unless specifically mentioned.

The *promesse unilatérale de vente* and *compromis de vente*

In a *promesse unilatérale de vente* it is only the vendor who is committed. The purchaser is granted a period of reflection. The purchaser, in effect, has an option to purchase the property. This option has a cost – normally 5 to 10 per cent of the purchase price. Do not pay this direct to the vendor, but pass it to the *notaire* who is going to be responsible for completing the transaction together with the original of the *promesse*.

If the purchaser decides to proceed, then the deposit is deducted from the purchase price, but if he decides not to proceed, he loses this deposit. The *promesse* must be registered (by the *notaire*) with the local tax office within ten days of signature.

In a *compromis de vente* – the most widely used preliminary contract – both parties are committed. Once you have signed this, and once any conditions (*conditions suspensives*) have been satisfied, such as a mortgage offer, you are committed. Furthermore, even if the vendor and you were to agree that the sale should not proceed, this agreement would be considered by the tax authorities as a sale by the purchaser to the vendor.

Whichever agreement is used, it must indicate whether or not the purchase is going to be financed by a loan and set out any other conditions of the sale. It should also record any easements affecting the property, such as a right of way over it.

A 5 to 10 per cent deposit is usually payable (to the *agent* or *notaire*) and should preferably be by bank-to-bank transfer. If the purchaser fails to complete, the deposit is forfeited. If the vendor backs out, then not only is the deposit returned to the purchaser, but the vendor has to pay a similar sum to the purchaser as a penalty.

Always, always have the preliminary contract examined by a lawyer before signing it and always seek advice in relation to the rules concerning inheritance.

SIMONE PAISSONI

SOLICITOR

Member of the
Association for Franco British Lawyers

IN FRANCE – FOR FRANCE

Tri lingual English Solictor
based in Nice since 1995
provides advice and assistance
on all aspects of property
purchase and ownership in
France, with emphasis on
inheritance and taxation.

Tel: +334 93 62 94 95
Fax: +334 93 62 95 96
Email: spaissoni@wanadoo.fr
22, ave Notre Dame, Nice 06000.
France

A recent law now gives the purchaser the right to cancel the agreement within seven days of receiving the copy signed by the seller. If you do wish to cancel, do so by recorded delivery. Any deposit paid is refundable.

The *acte authentique de vente*

You will need to agree a fixed date for completion. This is often three to four months after signing the *avant-contrat* and is frequently subject to changes owing to administrative delays (such as the obtaining of the *certificat d'urbanisme*).

Immediately prior to the completion date, you should attend the property to inspect it. Ensure that its condition has not deteriorated or changed since the signing of the *avant-contrat* and check through the inventory annexed to the *avant-contrat* to satisfy yourself that the vendor has left behind the various items to be sold with the property. It is extraordinary what some vendors try to take with them!

If there has been damage to the property or items included in the sale are missing, you should contact the *notaire* and seek to agree a reduction in price or request that he or she withhold a proportion of the purchase price until matters are resolved.

If the area is in a zone affected by termite infestations, you should be provided with a certificate by the vendor confirming that the property is termite-free. Should the property be infested, you should discuss the options with your lawyer or *notaire* – avoiding the contract or agreeing a reduction in the purchase price to reflect the work you will have to have carried out, for example.

The *acte authentique* has to be signed by you in front of the *notaire*, who will read the document out loud. You may interrupt him if you require clarification, although you should have already been provided with a copy of a draft of it. The *notaire* will require proof of your date of birth, marital status and so on. Should you not wish, or be unable, to attend, you can sign a *mandat* (a limited power of attorney) appointing an *agent immobilier* or the *notaire* to sign for you.

The *acte* should include a clear identification of the land and buildings, a summary of the ownership of the land over the previous 30 years and set out relevant planning permissions, easements and guarantees. The purchaser becomes entitled to take possession of the property on the day of signature and payment of the full purchase price (by banker's draft or bank transfer to the *notaire*'s bank account). Using a banker's draft is to be recommended – you control the payment until the last minute, enabling you to withhold payment if there are any problems when you carry out your last-minute inspection of the property. The *notaire* will also ask for payment of his or her fees and the various disbursements. You will receive an *expédition* of your title to the property about two months after completion.

Fixtures and fittings

The parties can reach any agreement they wish as to what is to happen to fixtures, fittings and contents. However, if no express agreement is reached, the vendor is obliged to leave rather less than he or she would under English law. In brief, the vendor is required to leave everything that is indispensable to the property and everything that cannot be taken away without damaging the structure of the property. The sinks, toilets, and fixed fireplaces must be left. On the other hand, the vendor is entitled to take fitted kitchen units, heating apparatus, light fittings, mirrors attached to the walls and so on.

The costs of purchase

These include the taxes payable on the transaction, the disbursements by the *notaire* and the *notaire's* fees (*honoraires*). Taxes payable on the transfer (*départementale*, *communale* and *régionale*) and stamp duty amount to 7.2 per cent – very much higher than in the UK and, indeed, the rest of Europe. The land transfer fee is an additional 1 per cent.

The *notaire's* fees are calculated on a sliding scale. This is normally 5 per cent of the purchase price for the first 3000 euros, with a reducing rate to about 0.825 per cent for amounts above the first 16,750 euros. The *notaire's* fee for a property sold at 150,000 euros or above amount to about 1 per cent of the sale price. The fee is fixed by law and, hence, is not negotiable. If you have instructed a UK lawyer, his or her fee is likely to be in the region of 1 per cent, too.

The purchase of farms

Recent years have seen a number of UK farmers sell up and move across the Channel. There are various subsidies and grants available for the purchase of farmland. Advice can be obtained from the *Fédération Nationale des Sociétés d'Aménagement Foncier et d'Etablissement Rural* (FNSAFER), at 3 rue de Turin, 75008 Paris (tel: 01 44 69 86 00).

Local property taxes

There are two main annual local taxes:

▌ *taxe foncière*, which is payable by the owner – the *notaire* will normally make an adjustment between the vendor and purchaser to ensure that each pays the proportion of the year's tax according to their respective periods of ownership;

▌ *taxe d'habitation*, which is payable by the occupier – the person in occupation on 1 January in any year is liable to pay this tax in its entirety, irrespective of when he or she ceases to occupy the property, and usually no apportionment is calculated.

Insurance

The vendor's existing insurance policy will automatically continue unless you require him or her to cancel the policy. There are several UK-based insurance companies that will provide requisite alternative cover. The advantage of a UK company is that the policy will be in English and any claim can be made in English.

Whatever policy you take out, ensure that you have sufficient cover. If you under-insure you will not be able to claim your full loss. Public liability insurance is cheap and, accordingly, a high level of cover (consider 1,500,000 euros) is worthwhile.

When you need to claim, ensure that you do so within the strict time limits and by recorded delivery. If you intend to occupy the property for only short periods or to let it out, you should inform your insurers.

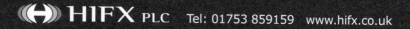

Why is currency such an important aspect of buying property in France?

Because when you agree to buy in France you will agree a price in euros. Until you buy those euros you don't actually know what they will cost you. Currency markets can sometimes move 5% in one month, so apply that to the price of your new dream home!

High street banks can convert your pounds into euros and send them to France but you are unlikely to receive the personal attention and advice that this transaction deserves. It is also a good plan to shop around and compare exchange rates. Specialist currency brokers can usually save you money and provide the service that you require; ask the agent or lawyer that you are using to recommend a broker.

So what is currency risk?

A French property priced at 100,000 euros would have cost £63,694 in December 2002 but increased in cost to £68,966 by March 2003 (an extra £5,272 or 8% in just 3 months).

To try and predict currency movements is a foolish pastime. If you are buying a property in France the most sensible course of action is to fix the costs straight away; in the example above you could have fixed your costs in December by either buying and paying for the euros or reserving them on a "forward contract" using a slightly adjusted exchange rate and a 10% part payment as a security deposit. This then removes all the currency risk. Now, you might say that is just hindsight trading, which of course it is but it is the prudent course of action regardless of whether the rate subsequently moves up or down. You would never agree to buy a property in the UK if the costs were not fixed so do not be tempted to "play around" with the currency markets.

Let us assume that you don't subscribe to the 'prudent plan' above; you are convinced that the exchange rate will improve and you are willing to risk it? The word risk is exactly what you are taking, so ask yourself what price you place on peace of mind? If you do decide to wait for a better exchange rate then be sure to work out the lowest acceptable rate that you would accept (the rate below which you go over budget) and be sure to buy the currency at that level if things go wrong. Equally, if the rate improves, do not be too greedy. Be sure to buy significant amounts of currency "on the way up" so that your average rate keeps improving. To wait too long and find yourself back or below where you started would be very depressing.

Remember: if you buy the euros now and the exchange rate subsequently improves you would be mildly annoyed. If you do nothing in anticipation of a better exchange rate that fails to materialise you would be very annoyed! Saving money is nice but unnecessary price increases are very unwelcome!

Written by HIFXplc 01753 859159 info@hifx.co.uk www.hifx.co.uk/france

5 Mortgages and financial assistance for the housebuyer

Taking out a mortgage is a serious and long-term commitment. For this reason many foreign residents prefer to deal with institutions where the documentation and discussions are in English. There are several banking institutions that provide these. The most popular are Abbey National, Barclays, the Banque Woolwich and Banque Populaire, with Web sites in English advising on the services they offer in France.

All mortgage lenders go through a very similar procedure to that applicable in other countries. The bank will need to check your financial standing and requires details of residence status, employment position, income and tax status. If you are self-employed, you will be asked for your accounts and tax liabilities for the preceding three years. Generally, you may not commit more than 30 per cent of your gross monthly income to mortgages, liability for rent and payments on loans outside France. The arrangement fee is generally about 1 per cent of the amount of the loan.

Local French institutions favour shorter loan terms, with 10 to 15 years being the most common, whereas British lending institutions are more prepared to grant longer repayment terms. The French tend to favour fixed interest rate loans, but variable interest rate loans are available, as are loans that include a combination of fixed and variable elements.

Generally, it is more difficult to obtain a 100 per cent mortgage from the main institutions, although this is available from Abbey National. Banque Populaire has a limit of 90 per cent of the purchase price, Barclays and Banque Woolwich 80 per cent. The mortgage will not cover the substantial acquisition costs of a property in France. The banks will levy an adminis-

WITH OUR INTERNATIONAL TRANSFER SERVICE YOUR MONEY WILL FLY AROUND THE WORLD

Whether you're sending cash to relatives overseas or buying a home in the sun, we can get your money to wherever it has to go, quickly and reliably. What's more, the funds can be sent in a wide range of local currencies, as well as in sterling. So, if you're after a full range of international payment services that are quick and easy to use, we'd suggest you fly along to your nearest branch of Halifax.

08456 077 767 (Lines open 24 hours a day, 7 days a week). Please quote ref: PB0013

HALIFAX Always giving you extra

tration charge (*frais de dossier*) on completion of the loan. Life insurance is mandatory.

Before deciding on a mortgage lender, you should shop around the main institutions to consider the variations and any special promotions that they may be running. Ensure that you fully understand the policies on offer. Taking independent advice may well save you substantial financial loss, not to mention anxiety and heartache.

In France, mortgage lenders do not require a survey, although some ask for a property valuation. The latter is merely designed to estimate the market value.

Once the lender has approved your application, you will be sent a mortgage offer. There is then an 11-day 'cooling-off' period, during which you can change your mind. Most major institutions are willing to process applications prior to you locating a property to indicate how much they would be prepared to lend to you and on what terms.

The other main characteristics of French mortgages to note are:

- only repayment mortgages are available, with interest and capital being repaid in equal instalments throughout the course of the loan; variable interest rate loans are available;
- every contract for the purchase of property must state whether or not it is subject to a mortgage. If the proposed loan is refused, the purchaser must try to obtain an alternative loan. If he is unsuccessful the purchaser is entitled to avoid the contract and have the deposit refunded (this is known as *la loi scrivener*);
- mortgage offers must be in writing and have a time limit of 30 days for acceptance;
- the purchase must be completed within four months of the acceptance of the loan offer.

One option is to raise the finance in the UK by using any UK property as security. The cheapest option may be to ask your existing mortgage lender if it would increase the mortgage facility, thereby avoiding legal fees, land registry fees and even an arrangement fee. You could also take the opportunity of considering remortgaging your UK property – you may succeed in reducing your existing repayments to partly offset the costs of financing your French property.

The main drawback of borrowing in the UK is that interest rates have tended to be higher than in France. On the other hand, if you are paying your repayments from funds in the UK, your repayments will not increase if the value of sterling falls.

Raising your funds in the UK allows you to avoid having to take out further life insurance (frequently a requirement in France). Note, however, that if you are intending to let your French property, you will almost certainly not be able to set off the mortgage interest on a UK loan against the rent received for French income tax purposes.

Loans and financial packages for the house purchaser in France

For those resident in France, there are a number of schemes to assist purchasers, including the following.

Le prêt à taux 0%

This interest-free loan of up to 27,000 euros is available from certain financial institutions to those with a net income below about 23,000 euros a year for single person and below about 38,000 euros for family unit of five or more.

It is restricted to the purchase of new property or old property where the costs of renovation works are at least 35 per cent of the total cost.

An advantage of this loan is that it counts as part of a person's personal capital outlay when applying for a main mortgage, thereby reducing the proportion of the cost of the property that you are required to provide yourself.

Le prêt à 1%

Loans at 1 per cent are available up to a maximum of about 18,000 euros to the employees of some companies.

Again, this is counted as part of your personal outlay when you apply for a mortgage to fund the balance of your purchase.

Le prêt fonctionnaire

These loans at favourable rates are available only to French civil servants, although this term covers a large number of employees in France, including teachers and postal workers.

Compte Epargne Logement (CEL) and Plan d'Epargne Logement (PEL)

The CEL allows you to save up to 15,000 euros for your intended house purchase over a period of 18 months at a favourable interest rate. When you come to purchase your home, you are entitled to a guaranteed loan up to about 23,000 euros at a favourable interest rate (about 3.5 per cent). The state will also give you a grant equal to half the interest accrued up to a maximum of 1100 euros.

The PEL is a similar scheme over 4 years with a limit on savings of 60,000 euros and a maximum loan of about 90,000 euros. Banks look favourably on applications for mortgages from holders of a PEL or CEL.

Le prêt conventioné (PC)

This is a loan granted pursuant to schemes agreed between the government and financial institutions that involve the grant of financial assistance (*Aide Personalisée au Logement*).

A PC can finance up to 90 per cent of the purchase and can be added to the other loans mentioned above. It can last for 5 to 25 years. This type of loan is available to all, but those of modest means are also entitled to a loan guaranteed by the state (*le* PAS – *le Prêt Accession Sociale*).

Buying a future retirement property to let

There are other schemes providing assistance for those purchasing property for letting. These are worth considering if you intend to retire to France at least nine years after your purchase and are prepared to let the property in the meantime. This is considered further in Chapter 10.

Other financial assistance

There are numerous tax deductions and grants available:

▌ tax relief on interest payments on your principal residence;

▌ tax relief on the costs of substantial works of renovation, repair and improvement to your principal residence;

▌ tax relief in relation to installing systems using renewable energy sources or the installation of heat or sound insulation;

▌ improvement grants from *L'Agence Nationale pour l'Amélioration de l'Habitat*;

▌ improvement grants from your local council (available via the *mairie*);

▌ improvement grants from the *Direction Départementale de l'Equipement* (DDE);

▌ grants in relation to installing systems using renewable energy sources (see Chapter 8).

Grants are often limited to those of 'modest' means, though not grants relating to renewable energy resources.

6 Buying a new property and having a property built

If you are buying a new property, you will almost certainly have to buy it unseen and wait at least a year for it to be constructed. Buying a plot of land and having a house built for you is invariably much cheaper than buying a house built by a developer, with a saving of 25 per cent or more. Whether you are buying from a developer or purchasing a building plot, you should pay particular attention to the terrain and the matters set out in Chapter 4 under the heading Viewing the property.

Building plots

The vendor of land that is sold as *terrain à construire* or *terrain à bâtir* is obliged to ensure that everything is in order as far as the *certificat d'urbanisme* is concerned (see below). He is supposed to tell you of any known problems. If you purchase from a professional, then he or she has to guarantee that there is nothing about the land that will prevent construction, whether he or she knew, or could have known, about it or not.

The nature of the underlying surface could have a major impact on the costs of construction. Granite, for example, is not susceptible to being broken up or hewn out, even with pneumatic tools – expensive explosives will be required. The key is to ask as many questions as you can, not merely from the vendor, but also of neighbours and at the local *mairie*. Above all, have an expert examine the land.

If you are being pressed to commit yourself and feel that you really cannot risk this plot slipping through your fingers, insist on having a condition in the contract that enables you to avoid the contract if an expert advises that the land will be expensive, difficult or impossible to construct on.

Ideally, you should be able to buy or build a property that is south-facing, with the minimum exposure of doors and windows to the prevailing winds.

You can obtain advice from the local branch of *Conseil d'Architecture, d'Urbanisme et de L'Environnement* (CAUE), including via the *mairie*. This association provides free advice to those embarking on the construction of new homes, in relation to both design and building work and the various formalities, such as planning permission.

If the plot is not *viabilisé* – that is, connected to the various services – you should check if there are any problems with connecting the property to the mains water and mains sewerage (*le tout-à l'égout*), gas, electricity and telephone networks. Even if these services extend to neighbouring properties, you will almost certainly bear the costs of connecting to the networks. Check on access to the property, including for works vehicles that will need to deliver supplies or carry out works at the property during construction. Also, if the boundaries are not already fenced, the contract of sale is likely to require you to erect fencing at your expense.

Besides the option of instructing an architect to design a property, there are various companies that offer a range of standard properties that they will construct for you and to which they will make internal modifications to suit your requirements. If this option appeals, ask to see examples of properties already constructed by the company. You need to be absolutely certain what is included in the price, in particular in relation to fittings in the kitchen and bathroom, as well as the garage and garden. This is obviously a cheaper option than the individually architect-designed route and, as the companies have constructed their *modèles* with the approach of the local planning authorities in mind, you should be less likely to encounter problems from that quarter.

If you intend to join those who have constructed their own homes themselves, advice can be obtained from the *Confédération Nationale d'Autoconstruction Castors* (*castors* means 'beavers'), 69 rue des Près aux Bois 78000, Versailles (tel: 01 30 24 15 98).

Employing an architect will obviously increase the costs of construction. Depending on the degree of his involvement, the fees will range from 3 to 12 per cent of the total price of the house.

Planning and building regulations

Land in France is zoned into three different types of areas – *résidentiel, artisanal* and *industriel*, the construction of homes being restricted to the first of these. You will need to have an understanding of the terms *certificat d'urbanisme, permis de construire, déclaration d'ouverture de chantier* and *certificat de conformité*.

The development of an area and planning and building regulations are handled at your local *mairie* and by the *Direction Départementale de l'Equipement* (DDE). There you will able to inspect the *Plan Local d'Urbanisme* (PLU), sometimes referred to by its previous name of *Plan d'Occupation des Sols* (POS). This is often a very detailed assessment of the area, its resources, facilities, roads and public buildings and what changes are underway or planned. It sets out restrictions on the height of buildings, building materials and even colours that can be used. Changes are frequently made to the PLU, so ensure that your information is up to date. Some areas are not covered by a PLU and are subject to the more general *Réglement National d'Urbanisme* (RNU).

The first step is to ascertain whether or not a *certificat d'urbanisme* has been obtained for the property. This indicates merely whether or not building is permitted – it does not constitute planning permission. If there is no *certificat* (or the 12-month validity period has expired), you will need to submit an application. You should also ascertain the *coefficient d'occupation des sols* (COS) – this is the percentage of the land on which you can build. It can vary between 100 per cent in a very built-up area to 10 per cent in more rural areas.

There are two categories of *certificat d'urbanisme* – *le certificat simple* and *le certificat détaillé*. The latter provides more details of the type of building project that is permittted, such as the type of architecture. Application forms are available from your local *mairie*. Take the four copies along with a plan drawn by a *géometrie* to the *mairie* and obtain a receipt. Alternatively, send these by *lettre recommandée avec avis de réception*. It will take about two months to obtain the *certificat*.

Neither certificate constitutes planning permission for a specific building, for which a more detailed application is necessary. Furthermore, a *certificat* is valid for one year only and, accordingly, an application for planning permission (*permis de construire*) should be submitted fairly promptly, particularly if you are applying for any state grants as this will

inevitably take some time. You will almost certainly need the assistance of an architect or a builder. Indeed, an architect is obligatory for any property with a surface area (including all floor surfaces, not just the ground floor) exceeding 700 square metres.

Once you have your *permis de construire*, you will need to apply to the *mairie* for a *déclaration d'ouverture de chantier* (an authorization to start work), which you must do within two years of obtaining the *permis*. Take the forms to the *mairie* or send them by registered post (see above).

After completion of the works you will need to obtain a *certificat de conformité* to establish that the building complies with the permission that was granted. This is an essential document that is necessary for the payment to you of any state grants and to obtain exemption from property tax for the first two years after completion. Take the *certificat d'achèvement* (certificate of completion of works) to the *mairie* or send it by registered post as indicated above. The *certificat de conformité* should be sent to you within three months.

Should one or more of your applications be refused or only granted on conditions that seem unnecessary or unreasonable, you can make an amended application for planning permission or take your case to an administrative tribunal within two months of the refusal of your application. If you are successful before the tribunal and the refusal of your application is quashed, you must then make a renewed application that cannot be refused on the same grounds as before. The best way to avoid problems is to discuss matters with the officials at the *mairie* on an informal basis from the outset.

Note that planning permission is granted *sous réserve du droit des tiers*. A disgruntled neighbour who considers that the building work is contrary to regulations or is concerned that he or she will lose a view or exposure to sunlight still has the right to object. If there is an objection, then this will clearly delay the work and perhaps result in amendments having to be made to the plans.

The building contract

Whether you buy a property from a developer, purchase the land yourself and purchase a standard building package, or instruct an architect and builder to design and build a house for you, the building contract should contain the following standard terms:

- a detailed description of the property to be built;
- the quality of the materials to be used;
- a schedule of construction and ancillary work;
- penalty clauses for late completion of the work (and late payment by yourself);
- insurance cover during the period of construction;
- stage payments.

You must take a careful look at the contract to ensure that every detail is covered, from doors and windows, to kitchen, bathroom and toilet fittings, to wall and floor finishes. If the construction is being handled by a single enterprise, the contract should be what is termed a *contrat de construction de maison individuelle* (CCMI).

Under a CCMI, the price should be fixed from the outset, with any unexpected increases in costs to be met by the construction company. Ask for advice, including on terms of the contract, from the local branch of the *Association Nationale pour l'Information sur le Logement* (called *Association Départementale d'Information sur Le Logement* – ADIL), and preferably a *notaire* also. The ANIL Web site is at www.anil.org.

If you have doubts after signing the contract, remember that the law has recently introduced a seven-day cooling off period, during which you can withdraw from the contract. If you wish to withdraw, do so by registered post.

The amount of the stage payments varies according to whether the promoter is offering his own guarantee or the guarantee is provided by another party, such as a bank. Where the promoter provides his own guarantee, the schedule would be along the following lines:

5 per cent	on signature of the contract (satisfy yourself that planning permission has been granted before signing);
15 per cent	on completion of the foundations;
35 per cent	following completion of walls and roof;
40 per cent	on completion of the building;
5 per cent	on final completion at the time of the *réception* (see later in this chapter, under heading The four guarantees).

Where the guarantee is provided by a third party, the above schedule is amended so that 30 per cent is payable on completion of the foundations and 25 per cent on completion of the building.

Do not be surprised if the work takes longer than envisaged. The developer is bound to hit some problem or other and is allowed some leeway to complete the task. Do visit the construction site from time to time to satisfy yourself that matters are proceeding properly and raise any concerns that you have. An error in the construction can be much more easily and speedily corrected if identified at an early stage.

Buying from a developer

The majority of new properties are sold by developers (*promoteurs*) prior to construction, although you may be able to inspect a showhouse (*maison-témoin*). A reputable developer may well have sold the entire stock before work has even commenced. Purchasers buy on the basis of plans (*sur plan* or *en état futur achèvement*). Indeed, you should be suspicious if a development is nearly completed and a number of properties remain unsold – it may be an indication that the developer is overcharging or that something else is wrong with the development or that the developer is putting others off.

Other writers on the French property market present a healthy picture of the French construction industry, with its various guarantees (see below) and stage payments. However, a number of French television documentaries over the past two years or so have highlighted cases of construction companies going out of business, leaving purchasers with half-finished badly constructed properties that they are unable to inhabit and do not have the means to complete. These are apparently not isolated examples, but part of a major problem.

You or your lawyer should check on the financial health of the developer and on the guarantees (insist on a bank guarantee, not the builder's own guarantee) and insurance cover.

If you are intending to buy from one of the British companies operating in France, you should proceed with the same caution. The builder has probably set up a French company and will probably seek to avoid using the financial strength of the UK business to bail out the French subsidiary should it run into difficulties.

There is also a quality mark that promoters can apply for and you should ask if one has been obtained for the development they are proposing. The programme is examined by an organization called Qualitel (136 boulevard Saint Germain, 75006 Paris; tel: 01 42 34 53 29; Web site www.qualitel.org). To obtain the mark, the programme has to obtain a score of three out of five in seven different categories. Besides being a quality benchmark, properties bearing the label Qualitel also have advantages in relation to obtaining a loan.

Initially, you will be asked to sign a *contrat de réservation* and pay a deposit of 2 to 5 per cent. This is not paid to the developer, but is put into a separate account with a bank or *notaire*. The promoter does not receive this deposit until the sale goes through. You are not obliged to proceed with the purchase, although you will lose your deposit if you do not. Equally, the promoter is not obliged to proceed with the development, in which case the deposit is returned to you. Once the *contrat de réservation* is signed, the next stage is to proceed to the *contrat de vente définitif*. If you have not already involved a lawyer (and my firm advice to you is that you should have done so before signing anything), you must do so now.

There are various advantages in purchasing a new property – a bright new and clean property of which you are the first occupier, the likelihood of double glazing, up-to-date insulation, central heating, good ventilation and good security (bars on the windows in some areas, such as the Riviera). If you are one of the early purchasers on the development, you will have considerable freedom in choosing the precise location of your house or apartment. On the financial front, there is a lower deposit (normally 2.5 or 5 rather than 10 per cent), lower property taxes, reduced conveyancing fees, and a ten-year warranty. In addition, you avoid the expense and inconvenience of renovation works, yet have the freedom to choose your own colour schemes and materials, as well as the ability to agree some variations.

In the case of purchases from a developer, the total price is fixed at the outset. Many developments consist of a complex with various sports and other facilities, including a swimming pool. A major disadvantage is that you are paying for the property for perhaps a considerable period of time while still having to finance your existing accommodation.

The four guarantees

After completion of the work, you and a representative of the developer have to meet together for *la réception*. I strongly recommend that you instruct a surveyor or architect to inspect the property on your behalf at this point. It is the occasion when a record is made as to whether or not you accept the work and, if you accept it, whether this is with or without any reservations. If you accept without reservation, then the balance of the purchase price is payable.

If the property does not correspond to your expectations as set out in the contract, then a list is recorded (a *procès verbale*, or snag list) of what is missing or faulty.

The third option is the *refus de construction*. This is where the outstanding or faulty works are more substantial than a few little niggles and the parties agree a new date for completion of the work. If you cannot reach agreement, the matter will have to be referred for arbitration by a judge, who can require the developer to pay a daily penalty for late completion.

By law, developers are obliged to provide three guarantees:

- *la garantie de parfait achèvement*, which is valid for 12 months following completion and covers all the items recorded in the *procès verbale* and, in some limited circumstances, other faults;
- *la garantie de bon fonctionnement*, which is valid for two years and covers various non-structural items, such as plumbing, radiators, doors and windows;
- *la garantie décennale*, which is valid for ten years and covers structural defects, such as a faulty roof, cracked walls, subsidence and so on.

In addition, you are obliged to take out (and pay for) *l'assurance dommage construction*. This is a back-up to the ten-year guarantee and covers all building defects. The advantage is that if a problem arises during the ten years, you do not have to prove which of the contractors involved was at fault, and, accordingly, your complaint should be remedied in a matter of weeks or months rather than years.

These policies are expensive (often in excess of 1500 euros) and, despite being obligatory, are not always taken out by a purchaser. If you are purchasing a property under ten years old, check that there is a valid policy in force. If you are buying a new property, you should shop around for policies, as some are better value than others, but have a notary check the policy over before you sign.

To claim under a policy, you should notify the insurer within five days of noting the defect. Notification should be by registered letter with *accusé de réception*. The insurer should notify you within 60 days whether or not it will take responsibility for the necessary works. It then has another 45 days to let you have a provisional payment.

7 The purchase of an apartment or private property on a housing development

Nearly half the population of France lives in apartments. Furthermore, a substantial number of houses form part of a private estate or development, of which there are many along the coast and in the more popular areas. The latter include many detached houses and townhouses. All these properties are owned *en copropriété*. This means that each proprietor owns the private parts of an apartment or house, but also owns a proportion of the parts that are shared. The common parts include lifts, hallways and stairs, the entranceway to the building, the approach road, gardens, pathways and so on.

Such properties are often more affordable and have a number of advantages over other types of housing, including a higher level of security, easy maintenance and less responsibility than owning a separate dwelling. Property taxes are generally lower, too, and developments frequently have facilities such as pools and gardens that you can enjoy without the inconvenience and burden of the extra maintenance required.

On the other hand, you have less privacy, are more at risk from disturbance by your neighbours and can be subject to large service charges/community fees over which you have little control. In some instances, factions can develop among the *copropriétaires*, with deep animosity between them and arguments erupting about every conceivable detail of how the development should be run.

In holiday resorts, you may find that the communal swimming pool or sports facilities are so overloaded as to be of no benefit. Accordingly, you would do well to have your initial visit during the peak season and ask what restrictions are placed on the use of such facilities.

Before agreeing to buy such an apartment or home, it is imperative that you ask to see the rules of the *copropriété*, the charges that you will have to pay and how these charges can be increased. The *règlement de copropriété* sets out the rights and obligations of proprietors and the rules for the smooth functioning of the development. They will govern what you can and cannot do. They may prohibit you from exercising any business or profession or impose restrictions on renting. The keeping of pets is normally permitted, although you should ask for confirmation. These rules also set out what is covered by the service charges and how the cost of these is to be divided.

In most cases, the everyday management of the development is carried out by a *syndicat* (or *synd*), subject to overall control by an *assemblée générale* of all the property owners (*les copropriétaires*). A general assembly convenes once a year and on other occasions if necessary. You are entitled to attend and vote by proxy.

The *charges de copropriété* include the costs of maintaining, repairing, cleaning, lighting, heating and insuring the common parts and the administration involved for the development. All proprietors have to pay a share of these costs in accordance with the proportionate value of their property (*la quote-part* or *les tantièmes*). The costs of a lift, and of any communal heating system are borne by all the proprietors irrespective of whether or not they make use of them. There is no rebate if your property is unoccupied for prolonged periods of time, so take care if you are looking for a holiday apartment.

In addition to the rules of the development, you should also ask for copies of the service charges for the last few years and minutes of the last two or three annual general assemblies. These may well highlight problems with the development.

You would be especially well advised when considering the purchase of such a property to introduce yourself to neighbours, if the opportunity arises or can be created. A very short conversation may immediately warn you off, and a longer conversation may reveal problems with the management of the development that at least require questions to be asked by you or the *notaire* of the vendor and/or the agents. Ask them bluntly 'Would you buy again?'!

Look carefully at the condition of the development. Are any major expenses likely to be required in the near future? Owners should reveal details of impending expenditure to a potential purchaser prior to the signing of a contract.

Note that garage and parking facilities often have to be purchased separately.

You are free to sell or rent out your house or apartment and any rule that requires the consent of other proprietors is illegal. The only restriction is where a proprietor owes arrears of service charges – that will prevent a sale unless provision is made for the arrears to be cleared.

If another proprietor is rowdy or endangers the health and safety of the block or development or other proprietors, he cannot be expelled, but proceedings can be brought against that person to compel him to comply with proprietors' obligations and for compensation for the breaches that have already been committed. Alternatively, it is possible to invoke the criminal law by calling the police and/or notifying the *mairie*.

If you suffer from the actions of a neighbour, it is for you to take what action you consider appropriate and not the responsibility of the *syndicat*. However, if the offender is causing a general nuisance to other occupiers, then the *syndicat* can and may be prepared to take action.

8 Heating your home and optimizing your utility bills

Choosing how to heat your home

Heating requirements vary greatly according to the location of your home, its type, size and insulation, whether you live at the property throughout the year and whether it is occupied throughout the day. In deciding how to heat your home you also have to consider the present heating system in the property, the costs of installing a new system, the life expectancy of a new system and your estimated consumption.

It is worth noting that both *Agence de l'Environnment et de la Maîtrise de l'Energie* (ADEME, tel: 01 47 65 20 00; Web site www.ademe.fr) and EDF-GDF provide advice on energy use. ADEME will provide you with a report from one of their inspectors at a cost of about 300 euros, setting out your heating needs and the various options (including costings), and advise you on insulaton. The EDF-GDF assessment is free of charge and advises you of your energy needs in relation to all electrical appliances, on how to minimize your electricity bills and on the operation of the various tariffs.

Electricity

Electricity is a popular form of heating, especially for smaller flats and properties in the south. It has the great advantage of being easy and inexpensive to install, so it is often the choice of landlords.

The disadvantage of electricity, however, is that the running costs are high. This can be mitigated to a certain extent by carefully considering the various choices provided by EDF-GDF – in particular the tempo option (see below) – and by making use of modern systems that can automatically activate electrical appliances during off-peak periods only. Nevertheless, electricity is unlikely to be the most appropriate means of heating a large house inhabited most of the year.

Oil (*mazout or fioul*)

Traditionally, oil-fired central heating has been expensive, produced pollution and had an odour. More recently, improvements in the quality of fuel have reduced these drawbacks.

Gas

While natural gas is now available to 80 per cent of the French population, there are still many rural areas that are not yet connected to the system. However, the network is being extended constantly, so it is worth enquiring at the local *mairie* and of EDF-GDF if there are plans to lay pipelines in the near future.

You may wish to opt for a short-term solution until your property is served by natural gas. One possibility is to use propane. The same boiler can be used for natural gas and the rented gas tank can be returned to its owner.

The advantages of gas are that it is clean and relatively economical. On the other hand, the initial outlay is fairly high and it can be dangerous if it is not functioning properly.

Wood

For those living in the countryside, wood is an option well worth considering – especially if you live in or near a wooded region. France has numerous huge forests, covering over a quarter of its national territory and with well-managed replanting programmes. Over 6 million French homes have some form of wood-burning heating appliance.

The efficiency of wood-fuelled heating depends on the quality of the appliance, type of wood used and humidity of the wood. Do not use driftwood or discarded wood from old furniture and so on as it may well have been treated and contain harmful toxins.

You will need a place to store your supply of wood. It should be left to dry out under a shelter or tarpaulin, with the sides of the pile left open to aid the drying out process. Ideally, wood should be left to dry out for up to two years. The best woods for heating are the harder woods, such as oak, acacia, maple and ash. Less efficient, but still effective, are beech and silver birch.

Wood is sold in *stères* (cubic metres) or in *brassess* (= 4 *stères*) and an average-sized property will need 20 to 30 *stères* per year, at a cost of about £600 to £900 according to my French source. I have been informed by one British-run supplier operating in France that UK stoves are more efficient than this, and that annual consumption should cost about £400. Prices are lower if you live near the woodcutter's business, if you can collect or if you cut the wood into logs yourself.

Most of the heat from a log fire literally goes up the chimney. Enclosing the hearth with a glass door in a stove immediately reduces much of this heat loss.

The costs of installing a wood-fuelled boiler system range from 2000 euros to 11,000 euros. A wood-burning stove will cost between 500 euros and 3000 euros. The latter, however, is only effective in heating a single room or adjacent rooms.

The main drawback of this form of heating is the work involved in the collecting, cutting and storing of the wood, and cleaning the grate and lighting the fire.

An advantage is that if you purchase an appliance using renewable energy, such as wood or solar energy, you are entitled to a tax credit of 15 per cent of the total cost of the equipment. Furthermore, if you install such a system in a house that is more than two years old and your prinicipal residence, the TVA (VAT) due on your purchase is reduced to 5.5 per cent.

Solar energy

Solar energy is renewable, clean, silent and free. Moreover, a system that uses solar energy requires very little maintenance and should last 20 or 30 years.

Solar energy is particularly popular for heating water in Austria and Germany. The southern half of France has rather more hours of sunshine and so solar energy is capable of meeting the majority of your needs for heating both your rooms and your water.

A major disadvantage is the relatively high installation cost. However, as part of its campaign to encourage the use of renewable energy sources, the government, through its agency *Agence de l'Environnement et de la Maîtrise de l'Energie* (ADEME, tel: 01 47 65 20 00; Web site www.ademe.fr), provides substantial grants towards these costs. A second drawback is that you will need a back-up system (though portable electric radiators may suffice).

The total installation costs for a water-heating system range from about 3500 to 5000 euros. Against that you can set off a grant from ADEME of between 700 and 1200 euros. In addition, you may be entitled to a further regional subsidy of up to 1400 euros, giving a total financial assistance package of up to 2600 euros. Costs of a comprehensive system for heating rooms as well as water are considerably higher, with a range of about 13,000–22,000 euros. A higher level of grant is payable from about 2600 euros up to about 4000 euros, to which you can add any regional subsidy.

Entitlement to these grants requires that you use a certified installer (*agréé qualisol*). The installer will be able to guide you as to the current level of national and any regional grants available and assist you in submitting your claim to ADEME.

In addition to the above state subsidies, you can also take advantage of hire-purchase schemes (usually over ten years). Remember, when buying appliances using renewable sources of energy, you are entitled to a tax credit and, in some circumstances, to a lower rate of TVA (VAT) on your purchase (see under the heading Wood above).

Carbon monoxide poisoning

A word of caution: each year 400 people in France die of carbon monoxide poisoning and a further 8000 are known to suffer from the effects of intoxication. It is likely that the problem is, in fact, more widespread, with many people being unaware of their exposure and the cause of symptoms they are suffering. Symptoms resemble those associated with flu – headache, fatigue, nausea and problems with vision and hearing.

A colourless, odourless gas, it is associated with gas, oil, wood- and coal-burning appliances. Almost invariably, the problem arises from a faulty or incorrectly used appliance. Appliances should be regularly serviced and replaced when appropriate. A faulty appliance is not only dangerous, but is inefficient and accordingly more expensive to run.

Electricity bills

Electricité de France and Gaz de France combined to become one large energy supplier known as EDF-GDF.

Utilities bill every two months in France, rather than quarterly. Your bill will consist of a subscription for the service, which varies according to the level of the power supply you choose, plus an amount depending on the quantity of electricity consumed. You must decide first the level of kilowatt-hours (kWh) of your electricity supply. This can range from as little as 3kWh if your needs are limited to lighting and running such electrical appliances as a television, refrigerator and vacuum cleaner. If you wish to be able to run a washing machine, dishwasher and electric cooker, you will probably need a supply of between 9 and 18 kWh – the latter being probably the most popular choice for a family. For homes with numerous electrical appliances likely to be switched on at the same time or with an electric system for heating rooms or water, you should discuss your needs with a representative of EDF, with a view to having a higher level of power, up to 36 kWh.

The appliances that place the greatest demands in kilowatts on your system are (figures indicate the maximum the appliances would use):

- water heater 4500
- electric plates 4000
- dishwasher 3000
- washing machine 3000
- tumble-dryer 3000
- electric kettle 1800
- oven 1200
- iron 1100
- hairdryer 1100.

Accordingly, a family household in which a water heater, kettle, washing machine, oven and hairdryer could well be operated simultaneously would require up to 11.6 kW without taking into account the less hungry items, such as lighting, televisions, computers, fridge, freezer and so on.

There are three pricing structures:

▌ *l'option base*;
▌ *l'option heures creuses*;
▌ *l'option tempo*.

With *option base*, the charge you pay per kWh remains constant. With *option creuses* you pay a higher subscription charge, but have the benefit of two different rates. Most of the day, during *les heures pleines*, you pay the same rate per kWh as with the *option base*, but you benefit from a lower rate applicable during eight hours during each day (*les heures creuses*).

If your consumption during the off-peak period is likely to be high, then you will almost certainly benefit from the option *heures creuses*. You may be able to choose hours for your off-peak period, but this is often not possible. In these cases the off-peak period is frequently 1.00 a.m. to 7.30 a.m. and 12.30 p.m. to 2.00 p.m. You will need to discuss the options with EDF-GDF.

There is no charge for moving to the option *heures creuses*. In late 2002, EDF-GDF introduced changes to their options, enabling consumers to extend their off-peak periods to cover the whole weekend (in addition to the eight hours for each weekday). This option is not presently available, but may be extended again in the future.

The third option, *l'option tempo*, is particularly suitable for summer holiday homes. For 300 days of the year, you pay a much lower rate per kWh (*jours bleus* – blue days). The rest of the year includes 43 *jours blancs*, on which you pay a higher rate per kWh not very different from that applicable to the *option base*. The drawback relates to the 22 *jours rouges* (all between 1 November and 31 March) on which you pay a very high rate (between four to eight times the normal off-peak rate). The 22 days are selected in advance by EDF-GDF and coincide with the days of greatest demand on the system. You are provided with a device to indicate the colour of the day and the colour of the following day. The standing charge for *tempo* is lower than for *l'option heures creuses*. There is no charge for changing to *tempo*. You can have a light or buzzer installed to provide a half an hour's warning of the start of a higher rate and arrange for the appliances that have the heaviest consumption to switch off automatically during the high-rate period and switch on again afterwards. Your system can be set so that certain appliances only operate during off-peak periods.

You can obtain advice from your local EDF-GDF branch, which will, at no charge, arrange for someone to meet with you to discuss your needs and advise how best to reduce the level of your consumption. EDF-GDF also publishes a leaflet in French and in English setting out its services and charges.

When purchasing electrical appliances, ensure that they are marked with the label PROMETELEC, indicating that they have satisfied French safety requirements. Electrical materials should be marked NF (*normes Françaises*). The power supply is at 220–240V and, accordingly, you will need a converter or step-down transformer for some electrical equipment, such as items from the USA, which are rated at 110V. This does not work for all items – notably those with motors designed to run in the USA at a frequency of 60Hz, such as automatic washing machines, cookers, electric clocks and tape recorders. These items cannot be used in France if they have not been designed to operate at a frequency of 50Hz.

Gas bills

Four rates are available, depending on your consumption. There is a rate for those who use gas only for cooking and a rate for homes using gas for cooking and heating water. The other rates are for those with gas central heating.

Water bills

In France you pay according to the quantity of water used. It is common practice to have a contract for the supply of a given amount, with a higher charge levied for usage in excess of that amount. A leaking tap can prove to be very expensive.

An average family uses about 500 litres of water per day. About 60 per cent of consumption relates to the taking of baths and showers and the flushing of the toilet. Accordingly, substantial reductions in consumption can be made by taking showers instead of baths and choosing the toilet cistern carefully – more modern cisterns use a third or less of the amount used by older toilets. Always check where the main stop valve or stopcock is located in case you need to turn off the water supply in an emergency.

The telephone

To subscribe or cancel your telephone line, telephone 1014. To subscribe, you will need to provide your exact postal address and proof of residence (*justificatif de domicile*), such as a tax demand, an electricity or gas bill, and a copy of your *carte d'identité*. If you wish your number to be ex-directory (*Liste Rouge*), a monthly fee of about 3 euros is payable.

Standing orders

The French are much hotter on prompt payment of utility bills than the UK. If you do not pay a bill within the time shown on the bill, interest is added. They are also quicker to cut off electricity and gas supplies or telephone lines than in the UK. There is, accordingly, much to be said for paying by direct debit, particularly if you are away from home for extended periods.

The *prélèvement automatique* consists of a fixed sum per month being deducted from your bank account. At the end of each year, a bill is sent out showing the amount outstanding or to be repaid.

EDF-GDF attempt to read your meter every four months. If they are unable to gain access to it, an estimate is entered on your statements. Meters have to be read at least once a year.

Moving house

When you come to move, telephone EDF-GDF several days before your move to cancel your contract and arrange for the meter to be read, thereby avoiding being billed for the new occupant's consumption. There is no charge for this. The bill will be sent to your new address.

As to your new home, contact EDF-GDF about two days before the move. If your requirements match those of the previous occupier, there should be no interruption in the gas and electricity supplies and a bill will be sent to you through the post consisting of a fee for the changeover to your name and the first period's subscription charges.

You may want to make changes to the electricity system (such as increasing the level of the power supply to avoid a power cut if you have many electrical appliances that may be running at the same time). If so, you will need to make an appointment to meet up with a representative of EDF-GDF. Arranging this over the telephone appears not to be an option. You will have to pay the costs of the attendance and of the change to your system.

9 Settling in

Your right to stay in France

Citizens of the European Union are entitled to live and work in any of the member states. No special documentation is required for your first three months. However, before the expiry of that period you should apply for a *carte de séjour* (residence permit). People with second homes in France who stay in the country for more than three months each year seldom apply for the *carte de séjour*, and appear in practice not to need it. Those who are living and working in France on a permanent basis should apply.

In the near future EU citizens will no longer have to apply for a *carte de séjour* in order to stay in France. In reality, however, you may still wish to obtain one if you do not want constantly to carry your bulkier passport, or present your 'foreign' ID document every time you pay by cheque. Applications for a *carte de séjour* are made to your local *mairie* in rural areas and elsewhere to the *Service des Etrangers* at the *Préfecture* of the department in which you live. You can make your application by post, but it is probably preferable, and certainly quicker, to attend in person.

You need to produce a valid passport, three passport photographs and proof of residence (a utility bill, for example). If you are not working, you will need proof that you can support yourself (your last six bank statements will probably be sufficient). If you are of working age, you will need to produce your contract of employment or proof that you are registered with a *chambre de métiers* or *chambre de commerce* applicable to your occupation. Some *chambres* may insist on a *carte de séjour* before registering you, in which case, ask for temporary membership pending obtaining your *carte de séjour*.

Citizens of Australia, Canada, New Zealand, Norway, Switzerland, the United States and a small number of other countries do not need a visa to go to France. However, obtaining employment in these circumstances is not straightforward and you should contact your local French consulate prior to leaving your home country. No residence permit is required in order to buy property in France.

It is advisable to carry your *carte de séjour* with you at all times as it (or your passport) can be requested at any time by a police officer. It is also required if you wish to pay by cheque.

Retiring to France

France is a popular location for people who are retired or planning their retirement. It is hardly a surprising choice, given the mild weather in many regions, lower housing costs, the efficient French health service, cheaper motoring costs and modest local taxes. In most cases, the sale of your British home will enable you to buy a very comfortable home in France and still have a substantial surplus.

It is important, however, to be realistic, for it is retired expatriates who are the most likely to return home. Consider what you are likely to miss in the UK, and whether you are likely to feel at home in France. How will you manage with the French language? How will you cope with illness, advancing age and the loss of a partner?

If you do decide to make the move, there are several areas, in particular in the Dordogne and the Riviera, where much of what you may miss about life in Britain is duplicated, including cricket, the great British pub, British food and Anglican church services. Details of what is available in each region are set out in Chapter 2. These areas tend to be more expensive than elsewhere in France, but you may find them more conducive to making a home and developing a feeling of belonging.

There is no problem with receiving UK state and private pensions in France, and, if you are a retired person, you are entitled to use the French health system on the same basis as a French citizen. The two matters that you do need to consider are exchange rate fluctuations and inheritance. As to the former, the problem will disappear when the UK eventually adopts the euro. In the meantime, you could move some of your investments to France. Alternatively, you could just accept that there is a risk that sterling may suffer modest falls in value and discuss with your financial adviser how quickly you could move your investments if it was felt that sterling was likely to become particularly weak. Issues relating to inheritance are covered in Chapter 13.

Payment of other UK benefits while living in France

The principle of free movement of labour within the European Union requires that citizens of member states should not be impeded from living and working in other member states. Accordingly, citizens of EU countries should not lose any of their rights to welfare benefits by moving to France. Those currently in receipt of an old age pension, invalidity and disability benefits, widows' benefits or benefits received as a result of an accident at work or an occupational disease are entitled to have their benefits paid to them irrespective of where they choose to live. They should be paid gross and the payment should include any increases. Incapacity benefit will only be paid to those who have paid Class 1 or Class 2 and Class 4 National Insurance contributions.

If you have not yet retired, your existing entitlement to a UK pension will be frozen and you will receive a reduced pension from the UK authorities when you reach retirement age. For those approaching retirement, it may be worthwhile making voluntary payments to bring your National Insurance contributions up to the level entitling you to a full pension. You should contact The Pension Service's International Pension Centre (part of the Department for Work and Pensions, a renamed part of the DSS that was, on tel: 0191 218 7777) and the Inland Revenue's Centre for Non-Residents (tel: 0845 070 0040, to ask for up-to-date information and advice, including whether you should pay Class 2 or Class 3 contributions. The former is the more expensive option but entitles you to incapacity benefit.

As to unemployment benefit, those out of work are entitled to have the Jobseeker's Allowance paid to them in France for up to 13 weeks. You must have been registered as a job seeker for at least four weeks before you left the UK and have been available for work up until your departure. You must be leaving the UK in search of work and register as seeking work with the French authorities within seven days of your last claim for Jobseeker's Allowance in the UK. You must contact your Jobcentre Plus office or Jobcentre before leaving and complete the appropriate forms if you have not done so already to claim benefit. If you cannot find employment during that 13-week period, then you will have to return to the UK if you wish to continue to receive benefit. You are only entitled to claim Jobseeker's Allowance abroad for one 13-week period in between periods of employment.

Attendance Allowance and Disability Living Allowance are not normally payable once you move abroad permanently.

If you are living in France but remain liable to UK income tax and National Insurance, you or your spouse are entitled to claim Child Benefit from the UK authorities. This is not means tested, whereas French child benefit is only payable to those whose earnings are below a certain threshold.

Entitlement to French state benefits

For those not in receipt of benefits when they move to France, but who subsequently become entitled, the rules are different. Generally, you are insured by the country in which you work and pay tax and social contributions. Those who work in more than one EU country are governed by the rules of the country in which they live. The French system makes a marked distinction between those who are employed and those who are self-employed. The rules governing the former provide for entitlement to the whole range of different French state benefits, whereas the self-employed are entitled to only maternity and sickness benefits and have to look to various other arrangements via professional bodies for entitlement to other benefits.

If you lose your job in France, you are entitled to claim unemployment benefit from the French authorities. They take into account the National Insurance contributions you have paid in the UK or other EU country. You should ask your Jobcentre Plus office or Jobcentre for the forms you would need to enable you to make any claim in France.

Importing your belongings

There are no restrictions on EU citizens bringing personal belongings into the country, although you are required to have an inventory that can be produced to customs officials. Non-EU nationals are required to pay VAT on any possessions that they bring into the country that they have owned for less than 6 months and on all belongings brought into the country 12 months after their residence began (there are some exceptions). To import personal belongings, non-EU nationals are required to make an application to the *Direction Régionale des Douanes* in the area in which they will be living. Reputable international removal companies are familiar with the various procedures and should advise you of the necessary details. France has similar restrictions to the UK in relation to importing such items as drugs and firearms. There are also regulations relating to the importing of animals, animal products, plants and items with a possible military use. If in doubt, you should ask for advice from French Customs.

Pets

To take a pet to France, no permit is required from the French authorities, but you will need an export certificate. The form for this is obtainable from the Department for Environment Food and Rural Affairs (DEFRA – the MAFF has been renamed) on tel: 08459 335577. You will also be sent a summary of the regulations governing the importing of your animal into France. There is also a Web site explaining the procedures, www.defra.gov.uk. You must travel with your pet or meet it at the port of entry. Dogs and cats must be at least three months old and you may only import a maximum of three cats or dogs at one time.

While there is generally no difficulty regarding taking your pet to France, complications arise if you wish to bring it back into the UK. Advice and assistance is available from the Pets helpline run by DEFRA (contact details as above).

In brief, you will need to have your pet fitted with a microchip and then vaccinated against rabies. You will then have to arrange to have a blood test to check that the vaccine has been effective. The whole procedure takes about eight months, so you will need to plan ahead. Check with the centre that is to test your animal's blood how long they are currently taking to return results (there is a wide variation – I have been told that Institut für Virologie, Frankfurter Strasse 107, D-35392 Giessen in Germany, tel: 00 49 641 99 38350, returns results reasonably quickly). Just before leaving, you will need to have your pet treated for ticks and tapeworm. There are relatively few companies that have made arrangements permitting them to bring pets into the UK (a list is contained in Appendix 5). More routes are anticipated in the coming years and you should contact DEFRA (see above) for information.

Once in France, your pet is allowed much more freedom than in the UK and can be taken to most shopping centres, cafés and restaurants. Small dogs are often seen being carried in supermarkets.

You are required to give your dog an annual rabies injection, tattoo it (*le tatouage*) or have a microchip inserted, and register it with the *Société Centrale Canine* (see below). Tattooing consists of recording a number tattooed on the animal's skin, usually in its ear. This will help trace your dog if it is lost. Should you lose your dog, notify the *Société Centrale Canine*, 155 avenue Jean-Jaurès, 93535 Aubervilliers (tel: 01 49 37 54 54), which keeps a central list of tattoo numbers. Also consider contacting your local branch of the SPA (*Société Protectrice des Animaux*) under SPA in the *White Pages*.

Your car

You will not have to pay VAT if you bring your car into France, provided that you have owned it for at least six months.

You are supposed to register your vehicle within three months of arriving, although some people wait until after they have obtained their *carte de séjour*. You will need to obtain a *certificat* from your local *inspecteur de mines* (the contact details are available from your local *préfecture*), confirming that the vehicle corresponds to French safety specifications. Owners of right-hand-drive vehicles should normally be required to change the headlights. You will then need to take this *certificat*, your passport or *carte de séjour*, car registration document, insurance certificate and MOT certificate to the branch of your *préfecture* that handles car registrations. You will be issued with a new number and registration document (*la carte grise*). You should then arrange for your new plates to be fitted.

There is no need for EU nationals over 18 and with a valid driving licence to obtain a French driving licence (EU Directive R123-E/97).

Car insurance is more expensive than in the UK, but it is worth shopping around. You should carry a *constat amiable* (available in many petrol stations) with you at all times, in case of an accident. This document is in duplicate and should be completed and signed by both parties. Copies are available in English. You should ensure that the answers, in particular the various boxes, are completed correctly as it will prove very difficult, if not impossible, to correct these details at a later stage. You should forward your copy to your insurers.

Your vehicle will be examined by an *expert* – often at the garage where you wish the repairs to be carried out. The *expert* will determine what damage requires rectifying and how much this is going to cost. Your insurers should then provide the garage with an authority to proceed with the work and settle the bill directly. It is possible to arrange for the work to be carried out immediately after the *expert* has visited, thereby avoiding having to part with your vehicle on two occasions. A courtesy car (*véhicule de prêt*) may be available.

If you wish to purchase a car in France, you will find that the prices (certainly in 2004) are considerably cheaper than in the UK. Interest rates for finance, too, are lower.

All cars over four years old have to undergo a *contrôle technique*, which is similar to the annual MOT in the UK. The first test must take place during the six months prior to your car having been on the road for four years. Thereafter, the 133-point test must be carried out every couple of years and be completed at a certified centre at a cost of about 40–60 euros. These centres are listed in the *Yellow Pages* under the heading *Contrôle Technique*, where you should also find a brief summary of the requirements associated with *le check-up*.

If your car fails the test, you have two months to carry out the necessary work, failing which the vehicle will have to be completely retested.

Adolescents are entitled to ride a moped from the age of 14, but must first take the level one test of the ASSR (Attestation Scolaire de Securité Sociale). A further obligatory test takes place at age 16.

Taking and transferring money to France

There are no restrictions on transferring money to France. Once you have a French bank account, it is easy to make transfers by telephone from your UK account into your French account. UK banks normally tell you that it will take up to five working days, but in practice a transfer in euros may be credited to your French account the next working day. Initially, my UK bank charged £20 per transfer, irrespective of the amount, and my French bank charged another £7 or so for receiving it. Changing to a French bank that was part of the same group as my UK bank reduced this to a total of £10 per transfer. EU regulations now prohibit a receiving bank from making a charge.

Taking money out of France is not so straightforward – there is a limit of 8000 euros at any one time. This rule, however, is relaxed for foreigners wishing to take out the net proceeds from the sale of their property.

A French bank account

You will need a French bank account. In addition to a cheque book (with your name and address printed on each cheque) you should be given a *carte bleue*. This is not a cheque guarantee card and you will need to present your passport and, subsequently, your *carte de séjour* as proof of identification when paying by cheque. The *carte bleue* is a payment card and is widely used in France even in fast food outlets. You type your code into the shop's machine. No signature is required.

You should check with your bank how much you are permitted to take out of your account each month by cheque and by using your *carte bleue*. If you do not comply with these limits, you could face the embarrassment of having authorization to use the card refused in the supermarket queue, even if you have ample funds in your account. If you have no cheque book with you, the cashier may be indulgent enough to wait while you make a cash withdrawal from the nearest cashpoint (*distributeur de billets*).

Failure to have sufficient funds in your account when a cheque is presented is taken extremely seriously in France. Any oversight or the late presentation of a cheque that you have issued can cause you considerable expense. You need to contact your bank and put matters right as a matter of urgency. A second such oversight in a 12-month period will lead to loss of your cheque book. Repeated such oversights can result in a prohibition on the use of that account or any other bank account in France for two years. Bouncing a cheque can also result in steep fines.

Your account is likely to be managed by a particular individual and it pays to be on friendly terms with him or her. If you suspect that you may exceed the limit on your overdraft (*découvert*), telephone the person handling your account to let him know and ask for assistance. The rigid rules are imposed by the Banque de France and your bank may be willing to help, in so far as it is able. The rules apply equally to British banks operating in France.

You can use your UK cheque cards to make withdrawals from cashpoints in France.

As with UK banks, notify your French bank immediately of any loss or suspected theft of your cheque book or card – you are responsible for any loss until you do. Your account will then be frozen and you should request alternative arrangements to cover you for the immediate future.

Many foreigners have a *compte étranger* – either a current account or deposit account. Overdrafts are not permitted on *compte étrangers*. Interest is paid gross on deposit accounts and must be declared.

To open a resident's account, you will need your *carte de séjour* and proof of address (a utility bill will suffice). In the unlikely event that two banks refuse to open an account for you, the third bank to which you apply is obliged to accept you.

British banks are quite well represented in France, especially in Paris and on the Riviera. Barclays and Abbey National have fairly extensive branch networks in France.

Your *régime matrimoniale*

On marriage, French couples have to indicate which *régime matrimoniale* should apply to their financial affairs. If they opt for common ownership of assets (*communauté de biens*), then all the assets acquired by either of them after their marriage (including assets in the name of just one spouse) belong to them both. Under the *régime* of *séparation de biens*, each spouse owns his or her assets separately. The latter regime is more akin to the position in the UK.

The choice of matrimonial regime is important for tax and inheritance purposes and you should take advice from your financial adviser or lawyer. Most British couples retain a system of separate ownership (save, of course, for property that is specifically held jointly, such as their home, and a joint bank account). When purchasing property, a *notaire* can simply describe your civil status by stating that you did not enter into a marriage contract, but that you were married under a British regime equivalent to a *séparation de biens*.

Pacte Civil de Solidarité

The PACS is a contract that permits two adults to organize and formalize their life together without being obliged to marry. Two adults of the same sex may also enter into a PACS. Partners to a PACS gain certain rights (and obligations) relating to inheritance, tax relief, social security and housing rights. Partners are also liable for each other's debts. Not all the rights are immediate, and partners have to wait for two or three years before some rights can be acquired. A PACS is registered by a joint declaration at a local court.

Your children

A family with three or more children is termed a *famille nombreuse* and is entitled to various discounts, including on public transport and entrance to museums. You are liable for any damage caused by your children and should insure against this (see below under household insurance).

Fitting your children with shoes is not as straightforward as in the UK. British children tend to have broader feet than their French friends and there is no equivalent to Clarks or Start-rite.

For children's clothes there are plenty of expensive boutiques and also large shops selling very cheap children's clothes that are often of poor quality. One chain of smaller shops selling clothes for children from 12 months to 14 years that is worth visiting is Du Pareil au Même. It has branches throughout France (see their Web site, www.dpam.com).

For healthcare and education, see Chapter 11.

Pool safety

In the summer of 2003 no less than 28 children aged one to five died in France after drowning in a swimming pool, and a further 77 were hospitalized. It is hardly surprising that legislation has been introduced imposing safety standards (indeed, it was passed in December 2002 in response to high numbers of incidents in previous years). As from 1 January 2004 *all* newly constructed pools must be fitted with a standardized safety device. Owners of pools built before this date have until 1 January 2006 to comply, though landlords of seasonal lettings have only until 1 May 2004.

There are a number of standardised devices, as follows:

1. safety barriers and gates (NF P90–306). The barrier, which can incorporate walls and sides of buildings, must be at least 1.10 metres high and non-climbable. There is a recommendation that the barrier be no less than 1 metre from the pool;
2. a perimeter or immersion alarm system (NF P90–307). This must be audible in all the properties using the pool;
3. a safety cover (NF P90–308) or pool shelter (NF P90–309) to prevent a child falling in. It must support a body weight of 100 kilograms.

There are a number of Web sites with information on pool safety, such as www.protectachild.com, www.richardewingnet/poolsafety (operated by Robert Ewing, a French qualified lifeguard) and the French government Web site www.fncesel.fr. The French body responsible for the regulations is AFNOR (Association Francaise de Normalisation). Details of some suppliers and installers of equipment are included in Appendix 1.

Household insurance

In France, you are required by law to be insured against causing damage to third parties. This cover – including insurance against damage by your children to other children at school – will normally be part of your household insurance. A policy must be in force before you complete your house purchase. Indeed, the vendor's insurance cover automatically transfers to the purchaser unless it is specifically cancelled. You may wish to make alternative insurance arrangements, especially if the existing policy is expensive.

As in the UK, you should insure your property for its full worth, taking into account the value of the land, but also the cost of demolition and rebuilding. Similarly, with contents, you should insure their full value if you are to be certain of having a claim met in full.

Your insurers need to know if the property is vacant for much of the year and if you are letting the property. The premiums will be higher, but failure to notify your insurer will result in the disallowance of relevant claims.

Insurance contracts are automatically renewable, and if you wish to change insurance companies, you generally have to give notice to your present insurer well before the anniversary of your insurance contract.

In an apartment, building (but not contents) insurance should be included as part of the service charge.

Claims normally have to be submitted within a very short time of an incident (5 days is common or 24 hours in the case of theft), so you should check the terms of the policy. Thefts and break-ins also have to be reported to the police as a condition of the policy, usually within 24 hours.

Communications: the telephone and postal system, fax, Minitel and the Internet

The French postal service is usually extremely efficient, with next-day delivery common within France. Letters and parcels to the UK generally take two to five days. You have a choice between *prioritaire* and *économique*.

A convenient way to send parcels of up to 500 grams or 2 kilograms is to purchase pre-paid envelopes (*les prêts à poster*). The envelopes, for which there is no extra charge, are extremely strong and have an inner bubble-wrap bag. These parcels are treated as priority mail and are generally delivered to the UK address within two to three days. Furthermore, you generally do not have to queue to post the envelope, but can just pass it through the screen at the counter.

If you are sending important documents and require proof of posting, you should ask for the letter or parcel to be sent *recommandée avec avis de réception*. This is a recorded delivery service where confirmation of receipt is posted back to you by the post office after delivery.

Other facilities available at *La Poste* include bank and savings accounts, public telephones, a fax service and Minitel (see below). As in the UK, you can have mail redirected to a new address (*ordre de réexpédition*) for a modest fee. Post offices are also invariably equipped with automatic machines that weigh your letter or parcel, tell you the cost of postage and print out a franked label. These are very easy to operate and save substantial time.

Main post offices are generally open from 8.00 am to 7.00 pm from Monday to Friday and on Saturday mornings. Most post offices in the provinces close for a long lunch break, although the larger branches do not. Remember that stamps (and telephone cards) are also available wherever you seen the sign *tabac*.

France boasts a sophisticated telephone system. Prices of calls have fallen in recent years following deregulation of the system and there are various providers, including IC Telecom. For land lines, you still require a contract with France Telecom. Teleconnect advertises a rate of 0.04 euros per minute for calls to the UK and US during a 'happy hour' of your choosing.

Public telephones are no longer coin-operated and you will need to use a phone card or a *carte bleue*. In France, each department has its own *White Pages* and *Yellow Pages*. To use the *White Pages*, you need to know the *ville* in which a person lives, as the numbers for each main town are listed separately. For directory enquiries, telephone 12. For international enquiries dial 3212.

France Telecom has a very similar range of services to those offered by British Telecom. If you wish to be ex-directory, you are required to pay a modest monthly fee to be on the *liste rouge*. To avoid your name and address being used on mailing lists, you should ask France Telecom to put you on their *liste orange* (there is no fee). At the back of the *Yellow Pages* is a practical section containing information on the local area, and details of how to obtain assistance and information on various matters, such as housing, employment, legal disputes and so on.

There are several providers of mobile telephones, with packages that vary by the day. Special offers are often advertised in television magazines, such as *TELE Magazine* (available at most supermarket checkouts). If you wish to take your British mobile phone to France, contact your service provider. It can be quite expensive. You may be able to install a French SIM card in your mobile phone.

Minitel first appeared in France in the mid-1980s. While it is being abandoned in favour of the Internet, you will still find Minitel posts in French post offices and many French people have one in their home. It is a telephone line-based videotext and teletext information system that enables you to obtain information on a large number of business and government services.

France has lagged behind the UK in the spread and popularity of the Internet. That said, it has grown rapidly in recent years and most large businesses, government departments and local councils have Web sites providing a vast quantity of information. Providers (*fournisseurs d'accés*) include wanadoo (France Telecom) and AOL. Some basic Internet vocabulary is included in Appendix 3.

Television and satellite

There are five main television channels – TF 1, France 2, France 3, Arte (a Franco-German channel) and M6. Canal + and France 5 are also available through a rooftop aerial.

You are required to pay an annual television licence fee of about £80. When you purchase a television, the retailer is obliged to inform the *Centre Régional de la Redevance de l'Audiovisuel*, which will then send you a demand for payment. You need one licence only per address.

There are several ways in which to obtain British TV and radio programmes via satellite.You could subscribe to the French Canal Satellite, which has BBC World and Sky News and broadcasts many films in their orignal version. British TV and radio (including BBC Prime) is also available using a TPS system, and BBC Prime is available as a stand alone channel with a Via Access receiver and viewing card. Several channels can be received free of charge using a receiver that you can purchase from a dealer or electrical retailer. Many Britons in France receive BBC 1, BBC 2, ITV, Channel 4, Channel 5 and Sky by using a receiver available from specialists and a card from the UK for which they have to give a UK address. This is contrary to UK licensing and copyright laws that restrict the use of the card to the UK but as far as I am aware no steps have been taken to enforce these. A list of suppliers and installers of satellite equipment is included in Appendix 1.

Welcome to France

There are some French associations for welcoming newcomers to an area, in particular the *Accueil des Villes Françaises* (AVF). A modest joining fee is payable. There is a branch of AVF in nearly every large and medium-sized town, where you will find a whole range of organized social and sport activities, as well as classes in French and foreign languages.

Adapt in France, based on the Côte d'Azur, is run by a Breton lady who felt that there was insufficient help for foreigners in the area. The association, sponsored by local councils, has a resource centre in Valbonne, provides support sessions, runs workshops (on, for example, education, taxation, finance, healthcare, setting up a business) and has a Web site. Most of the information is in English (with some in Spanish, German and Danish) and the majority of those joining her association are British. Annual membership fees range from 50 to 150 euros. The Web site is www.adaptinfrance.org and the telephone number 04 93 65 33 79.

If you wish to integrate fully into French life, and especially if you live in a more rural area, you must make contacts among the local French community. Even if you are the only British family, you are probably not the only newcomers in the area – many Parisians leave the capital in favour of a home in the countryside.

There are steps you can take to ease the transition to your new home and environment. Prior to purchasing, or indeed renting, you would do well to introduce yourselves to your immediate neighbours in order to ask them about the property and the neighbourhood. Once you have moved in, renew the acquaintance. You have the perfect pretext in that you are new to the area and can ask them for information or advice about the area or alterations and improvements that they have made to their property.

There will be local sports and cultural associations in which you can participate. If you have children at the local school, you will find that they soon make friendships. This will bring you into contact with other parents in the area, some of them keen for their children to establish links with English-speaking people in the hope that this will help them in acquiring what remains by far the most important world language.

Most villages have regular festivals (*fêtes, kermesses, festivals*). Each local school will have its annual *kermesse*. Integration inevitably requires participation. If you are in a village, do carry out some of your shopping locally. Do buy and look at the local newspaper. It is not only about becoming part of the community, it may be the first notification you have that a new motorway is planned that will directly affect your daily life and/or the value of your property. On this note, some expatriates have taken an active part in campaigning on local issues. In Lot, in south-western France, the British residents who had helped revive the area led the opposition to EDF's (*Electricité de France*) plans to erect 100 pylons over a 40-km stretch of scenic countryside. British residents have had the vote in municipal elections since 1999, and in some areas form a potentially significant group of the electorate.

There are many English-speaking associations throughout France, but particularly concentrated in Paris, Lyon, Marseilles, Lille and Bordeaux, the Côte d'Azur, Normandy and the Dordogne. They are mainly British, but include American, Irish, South African, Canadian and Australian and some that are specifically Scottish or Welsh. They range from churches and religious groups to cricket clubs, women's groups, activities groups for children and retired servicemen's associations. There are also various British and Franco-British cultural centres and groups – most notably the British Council. Friendships are often quick to form among the expatriate community. Whatever your age and circumstances, you may find their help and advice indispensable, including in relation to finding employment.

You may be reluctant to immerse yourself completely among expatriates. One possibility is to participate in the joint Franco-British or Franco-American groups, such as the *Association France–Grande-Bretagne*. Details of its local branches can be obtained from its central office in Paris at 183 avenue Daumesnil, 75012 Paris (tel: 01 55 78 71 71).

A list of organizations is included in Appendix 1 under the heading Support services. Substantial local information is contained in Chapter 2.

Speaking and learning the language

In Paris, the Dordogne or the Riviera, it is very easy to live in an almost totally English-speaking environment in which you rarely have to speak a word of French. However, if you are to truly settle, you really do need to have some understanding of the language. Indeed, it is essential if you wish to obtain employment with a French employer. It is important, too, if you are to confidently handle emergency situations and for your dealings with the various administrative bodies.

There is no doubt that French is a difficult language – more so than Italian, for example. Its genders, complicated grammar that the French themselves have difficulty mastering and its rules of pronunciation can make the task of learning the language seem formidable. However, there is no better place to learn it than in France itself.

There are many different courses. A detailed list can be found on The French Directory: Learn in France Web site, www.europa-pages.co.uk/france. Many courses will be in 'target' language only (ie French), with no English spoken. The most well-known organization is the *Alliance Française* (the central Paris number of which is 01 45 44 38 28) that runs courses in all the main cities. One option for complete beginners is a course at your local branch of the *Accueil des Villes Françaises* (AVF, see above), for which only a nominal charge is made for members. If you are officially unemployed, have a residence permit and a basic knowledge of the language, you can obtain free lessons to improve your French via your local *Agence Nationale Pour l'Emploi* (ANPE). There are (expensive) total immersion options available in which you spend a period of time in a French family, attending courses during the day.

For the serious student, there are many qualifications that can be gained. Study for O and A level French is possible via correspondence courses with the National Extension College, as is the External Degree in French at London University. The Open University has courses for complete beginners up to a Diploma in French, in which the level of language is equivalent to university level.

There are various examination centres in France, although you should check with the individual examining body. French qualifications include examinations from the *Chambre de Commerce de Paris* and the *Diplôme d'Etude de la Langue Française* (DELF), and the more advanced DALF that may be required prior to entry to any French university.

The best way to advance your French is obviously to use it. Making French friends will prove invaluable. So, too, is the French media. Watching and listening to television is a must, but ensure that your viewing is *selective*. Avoid the most difficult programmes to follow, such as chat shows (everybody always talks at the same time!) and French TV series.

Translations of English-language films or television series are invariably in standard French and you seldom have to cope with the difficulties of regional accents. You will also be more familiar with what is being shown pictorially (such as courtroom scenes, police investigations, lifestyles and so on). The programmes will accordingly be easier to follow (and enjoy) as well as to learn from. If you record the programme, you can replay it to hear something that you have missed. News bulletins are also worth watching – newsreaders tend to speak clearly and are accordingly easier to understand. News is repeated throughout the day, so if you did not pick something up the first time round, you will have another opportunity to do so.

Radio is inevitably more difficult to follow. However, time in your car could be usefully spent learning the language and, if you are not listening to French language tapes, consider a news channel, such as France Info, especially on long journeys. Consider listening to the BBC News or, preferably, a local English radio station (such as Radio Riviera in the southeast of France) that has local and national news. This will give you an idea of the main news items and help you to follow them on French radio.

You will find that many people try to speak to you in English. You should politely persist in speaking French. They may well be simply trying to impress a third party and their knowledge of English is probably limited to only a few words. It will not compare to your own level of French after you have been in the country a short time.

If you wish to study the language in the UK prior to moving to France, consider the courses run by the *Alliance Française* in London, Oxford, Cambridge, Bristol, Bath, Belfast, Exeter, Milton Keynes, Manchester, York, Jersey and Glasgow. The Web site is www.alliancefr.org. Some of these courses are run at cultural centres where you can also learn more about France and French culture, see French films and meet French people living in the UK.

Formalities

In many ways the French remain far more formal than the British or other Anglo-Saxons. This is most apparent in business and other correspondence. Where an English-speaker would write 'Yours sincerely' or 'Yours faithfully' to end a formal letter, the French would write something along the lines of: *'Veuillez agréer, Monsieur, l'assurance de mes sentiments distingués.'* Books on how to address, write and terminate correspondence are sold in far greater numbers than in the UK and are available in the larger supermarkets.

The French frequently address each other as *monsieur* or *madame*, even after knowing each other for years. The use of the more personal *tu* or *toi* to address each other remains restricted among adults. I once met a couple who still used *vous* to each other after years of marriage!

Friends and acquaintances shake hands, although the French frequently *bise* each other – the *bise* consists of a cheek-to-cheek embrace on each side, generally repeated once or twice. Children are expected to undergo this ordeal from almost every adult they meet, including the parents of their school friends and, on occasions, their teachers. Some Britons explain that they are British and shake the child's hand with a warm smile. Incidentally *la bise* also means the North Wind!

Be wary about calling univited on your French neighbour. You should telephone first and give plenty of advance warning.

The black market

Anyone thinking of having work done to or at their property, even gardening, would do well to decline the lower rates offered by those working in the black economy. Ask for a copy of their *carte d'identification* issued by the *Chambre des Métiers*.

Should you take on someone who has an accident in your home and who is not properly registered, you may find that the courts deem him to be your employee. You could find yourself in the situation experienced by one British couple – liable for the medical bills that the injured person is required to pay because of lack of insurance, but cannot meet because of lack of resources. Also check that they have professional insurance, to ensure that you receive compensation for any damage they may cause to your property or its occupants while working for you.

Your neighbours and you

If a recent French documentary is to be believed, neighbour disputes are a serious and growing problem in France. The key to minimizing problems is always to attempt to establish a good relationship with your neighbours from the outset, even if you are going to keep them at arm's length. At some point, you may well need each other – especially if you live some distance from shops and other facilities. If a dispute does arise, do your utmost to settle disagreements without recourse to the courts, perhaps asking a third party to act as an arbiter (such as a *notaire*). Litigation may only fuel animosities and leave both sides with substantial legal bills.

The following is a brief guide to the rights and obligations between neighbours:

▌ your neighbour is obliged to cut the branches of trees that have grown on to your land; you are entitled to cut roots and brambles extending on to your property, but note that if the tree has extended into your property for over 30 years or is only near the boundary because a piece of land has been divided, the overhanging branches are permitted to remain overhanging;

▌ you have no right to go on to your neighbour's property to collect fruit from your trees without your neighbour's consent, nor is your neighbour allowed to pick the fruit, though he may pick up fruit that has fallen;

▌ trees and hedges should be planted at least 50 cm from the boundary and, if they are higher than 2 metres, they should be planted at least 2 metres from the boundary;

▌ a wall is normally a party wall (ie it belongs to *both* neighbouring properties) if it separates two buildings, two yards, two gardens or a yard and a garden. Similarly, a fence between two fields will usually, though not always, be a party fence. These assumptions do not apply if there is evidence to the contrary in the title deeds, or there are strong signs to the contrary or where the wall has been treated by a proprietor as his or her sole property for 30 years or more;

▌ in the case of a party wall, the costs of maintenance are to be shared equally. Where there is no fence, you can require your neighbour to share the cost of constructing one, though, if the construction is clearly solely for your benefit, then you should bear the entire cost;

▌ one party is entitled to increase the height of a party wall at his or her own expense without the consent of the other, but can face a claim for compensation for any easement lost, such as the loss of light;

▌ neighbours can settle disputes about the location of the boundary between themselves or call in a surveyor to assist – in either case, you should have the agreement recorded officially by a *notaire*;

▌ each proprietor has a right of access over his or her neighbour's property to carry out *essential* repairs that cannot otherwise be carried out, although the arrangements should be agreed prior to work commencing and any interference to the *neighbouring* property should not be disproportionate;

■ the construction of a new property on neighbouring land that complies with planning and building regulations but deprives you of a right of light will not normally entitle you to any remedy;

■ if a neighbour, or indeed any other party, parks a vehicle across the entrance to your property, you are entitled to call on the police to take action and serve the offender with a *procès verbale*.

■ if your neighbour decides to keep pigs or poultry and the smell or noise significantly interferes with your enjoyment of your property, you can oblige the neighbour to move his livestock away from the boundary between the two properties. However, if this nuisance was already in existence at the time you purchased or rented your home, the law is not on your side.

Noisy and nuisance neighbours

You have no right to complain about a nuisance that is no more than a norm for the neighbourhood (such as church bells that have been rung for centuries, but which might lead to mental instability if you were unwise enough to purchase the house next door). This is merely a characteristic of the neighbourhood that you are obliged to accept. For abnormal nuisances, however, there are rules and regulations governing such matters as noise and pollution.

If a noisy or nuisance neighbour has ignored your polite and reasonable requests, you should write to him by recorded delivery (*lettre recommandée avec avis de réception*). If this does not have the desired effect, you will have to contact your local police force and/or raise the matter at the *mairie*, which has powers to take action against disturbances of the peace. Before doing so, or if the disturbance persists in spite of a police warning, you should seek the assistance of other neighbours prepared to give statements.

You may obtain assistance from the ADVTV (*Association de Défense des Victimes de Troubles du Voisinage*), 11 rue de 8 mai 1945, 60800 Crépy en Valoy (tel: 03 44 87 57 17).

Taking French nationality

Once you have lived in France continuously for 5 years, are over 18, can prove your ability to speak and write French to a reasonable standard, are of good character and can prove yourself loyal to France, you are entitled to apply for French citizenship. 'Good character' means that you have not been convicted of a criminal offence punishable with a sentence of imprisonment of six months or more. You must also derive your earnings from within France.

Applications are made to your local *préfecture*. An investigation is then carried out to assess your assimilation into French society. The procedure takes about 12 months. The five-year residence requirement is reduced to two years if you have successfully completed at least two years of further education in France, or if you are able to be of particular service to the French state. You do not have to give up your British citizenship – neither the British or French governments have any objections to dual nationality.

The conditions for citizenship entitlement are less demanding for your children if they are born in France or for you if you marry a French citizen. Remember that citizenship carries with it responsibilities and obligations – a citizen, even one living outside of France with dual nationality, may be called on to do military service in the event of a war. National service has been abolished in France.

10 Letting and selling your French home

If you do not intend to occupy your French home full time, you may wish to cover part of your costs by renting it out. There are various options.

Holiday lettings

If you only intend to spend short periods in the property, you could consider trying to let it out to other holiday visitors during the holiday seasons. France remains the top destination for tourists and, in some areas, the summer holiday letting season can start as early as May and extend for five months until the end of September. In addition, there are the other school holiday periods, during which you may be able to let the property. In the most popular resorts, most notably on the Riviera, there is substantial unmet demand for both holiday and longer-term lettings. The location of the property is obviously important for its letting potential. It should also have the basic facilities, such as those required by Gîtes de France (see below).

Even if you intend to live in the property more or less continuously, you may still wish to consider letting for short periods. On the Côte d'Azur, for example, many permanent residents let their homes out for the whole of the summer or during August and go to live elsewhere or take an extended holiday. The rental income during this busy season is several times their monthly mortgage instalments.

Many French property owners manage lettings themselves, placing advertisements on a number of Internet sites (see Appendix 1) or in newspapers and magazines in the UK (such as *Chez Nous*) or, indeed, in France (such as *de particulier à particulier*). If you work in a large organization, such as a local authority, hospital or private company, or have a good friend who does, you may be able to circulate details among the employees. Your own small Internet site (at a modest cost of about £400) is also worth considering. If you are not going to be there, remember that you will need someone who can arrange to have the property cleaned for you and deal with handovers and any emergencies that may arise. Ideally, you should also have that person place some basic supplies, such as fresh bread, butter, milk and mineral water in the property in preparation for the arrival of your guests.

Alternatively, you can instruct one of a number of French or English-speaking (primarily British) management agents. Management agents charge a hefty commission – generally 20 per cent of the rental income plus VAT – and vary tremendously in the quality of the service they provide. You will need to keep a close eye on them to ensure that they are keeping the property as fully let as possible and are providing a good service to your clients (especially with regard to keeping the property clean). Insist on being provided with a week-by-week schedule of rental income with contact details of tenants – some agencies have been known to keep part of the rental income for themselves during peak periods or to fail to inform proprietors of a letting during the low season. If you know someone who lives nearby who can make spot checks, so much the better. A list of estate agents who can arrange management of a property is given in Appendix 1.

The return that you can expect from renting out your French property will depend on a number of factors, not least the effort that you put into finding clients, the location of the property, accessibility from UK ports and airports, and the attractiveness of the property. With reasonable effort and availability throughout the summer, you should be able to make a return of between 4 and 7 per cent. Returns in the more popular areas (notably in Paris and the coastal resorts) will be towards the top of that range, while those for inland areas will be towards the lower end.

You should prepare a brief information pack. Of crucial importance are good directions to the property – if these are complicated, then potential tenants may be put off. In your description of the area, you should include references to the main tourist attractions, particularly those in close proximity to the property, as well as local restaurants, supermarkets, banks, markets, pharmacies, doctors and hospitals. A good map showing the

The French Government have published the final standards for pool safety equipment and these are now law.

This law has added to and amended the "Code de la construction et de l'habitation", the building regulations in French law.

From 2004 onwards, all new pools and pools and rental properties in France must have a standardised security system installed. Failure to comply has a penalty of a 45,000 euro fine.

The four official AFNOR standards were announced in the Journal Officiel on 20th December 2003.

- Safety Barriers NF P90-306
- Pool Alarms NF P90-307
- Safety Covers NF P90-308
- Pool Shelters/Abris NF P90-309

It is therefore important to choose a safety device that conforms to the law. We recommend you speak to a specialist Pool safety company to ensure you comply. Safer Pools have 30 offices in France. All the products they supply and install conform to the stringent safety standards published by AFNOR and their english speaking agents are on hand to provide you with quotations and allocate installation dates for suitable safety devices for your pool. See our advert.

property, main landmarks and attractions is essential. The best bookings are from clients who wish to return.

If you are prepared to make your property available for letting for at least three months a year, including throughout the summer and during the longer school holiday breaks, one possibility worth considering is Gîtes de France. This organization oversees about 50,000 houses in France that are available to let to tourists. The properties on its list must come up to certain minimum standards – they must have hot water, electricity and cooking facilities, a bathroom, an indoor toilet, beds and standard kitchen equipment plus washing machine. The properties have to be available for the exclusive use of the client and have an independent entrance. Properties are categorized into four different standards (being given one to four *épis*, ears of corn) depending on the property and its location. Obviously a tourist location, a garden and a swimming pool all help to increase the number of *épis* a property is given. Commission is payable by the holiday resident. Your liability, termed *la contribution représentative du droit du bail,* amounts to 2.5 per cent of the rent.

Note that landlords of seasonal lettings had until 1 May 2004 to comply with the new swimming pool safety standards (see the section on 'Pool safety' in Chapter 9).

Longer-term lettings, unfurnished

Before letting out your property on a longer-term letting, I recommend that you read Chapter 3, Renting a home in France, which details many of the procedures relating to the letting of unfurnished property.

The first point for a prospective landlord to remember is that the rental of *unfurnished* properties is subject to extensive regulation under French law. These provisions override the terms of any written or oral rental contract. Tenants have rather more rights than in the UK, at least when it comes to security of tenure. In ordinary circumstances, a tenant is normally entitled to stay in the property for three years and has a right to a further three-year extension, making a total of six years. During this time, it is impossible to obtain possession of the property if the tenant wishes to remain, save on fairly narrow grounds, such as substantial rent arrears or damage to the property. Even in these cases, obtaining possession can be a lengthy process and the courts may refuse to grant you possession, giving the tenant one or more opportunities to remedy the default. No eviction is permissible anyway between 1 November and 15 March.

There are circumstances in which a proprietor can, for family or professional reasons, let a home for less than three years. These include if the owner is working abroad, or within France but a great distance away, and wishes to return to live in the property at a later date (for further details see Chapter 3).

When you let out a property on a longer-term letting, you are entitled to demand a *caution* (deposit). This is limited to two months' rental and is payable on the commencement of the tenancy. It should be repaid within two months of the tenancy coming to an end, less any sums owed by the tenant.

Before a tenant moves in, you should arrange for an *état des lieux* to be drawn up, setting out the condition of the property. This is often carried out by a *huissier* at a cost of around 230 euros, split equally between landlord and tenant, but can be carried out by the landlord and tenant together (an example is included at the end of Chapter 3).

As a landlord, you are responsible for maintaining the structure of the building, including the roof and boundaries, stairs, shutters and windows, boiler and chimney. The tenant is responsible for running repairs, such as minor works of maintenance to prevent the building falling into disrepair – painting, replacing windowpanes, cleaning and minor repairs to pipework, taps and radiators, replacing the odd broken floor tile, that sort of thing.

Longer-term lettings, furnished

When letting a property on a longer-term basis, you should very seriously consider letting the property furnished. The furnished sector is not regulated. You can therefore rent out for periods of 6, 12 or 24 months and be entitled to regain possession at the end of the rental period.

To qualify as a furnished letting, the property must contain all the basic requirements to enable the tenant to live in the property as a home. These include curtains, beds, wardrobes, table and chairs, refrigerator and cooker, sofa and so on. If you do not adequately equip the property, you risk the courts declaring that it in fact falls into the unfurnished category.

The result will be that your tenant will become a protected tenant and entitled to continue in the property after expiry of the tenancy agreement.

You should ensure that a tenant signs an inventory listing the contents.

You are entitled to take a deposit as for unfurnished properties. Of course, you are responsible for maintaining the structure of the property. You would also be well advised to have an *état des lieux* carried out (see above).

The nightmare tenant

Whether you are letting your property for short-term holiday lets or for longer periods, there is always the risk of encountering a tenant who will not leave or only does so after causing extensive damage to your property. You can take out insurance against such eventualities. There are various policies available with different levels of cover.

You are not permitted to require payment of rent by a direct debit or direct from a tenant's salary.

Insurance

You should make your insurers aware that you are letting the property and the type of lettings involved. Failure to do so may result in a claim being disallowed.

Income tax

Income from French property is subject to income tax. There is a significant distinction between unfurnished and furnished rentals.

For unfurnished letting, you can set off the owner's property tax (*taxe foncière*) and a fixed 14 per cent of the gross income to cover your various expenses (receipts should nevertheless be kept).

Furnished lettings are taxed differently and for the most part according to the Micro BIC scheme, under which you can opt to be taxed

on only 30 per cent of gross income, with 70 per cent being allowed to cover expenses. You have the option of calculating your expenses in case they should exceed 70 per cent of gross income.

Financial incentives for prospective landlords

Do obtain expert advice as to the various financial incentives and tax consequences if you are contemplating purchasing for rental. Incentives are available to encourage the building and acquisition of properties for renting, including *la loi Besson*. This provides certain tax advantages where a property is to be let for at least nine years (a possible option for a couple purchasing a home for their future retirement).

'Leaseback' is where you purchase a new or renovated property, usually an apartment, in part of an approved scheme. A purchaser grants a lease of the apartment for at least nine years to the company managing the development at a fixed rent with annual increases. That company

185

then seeks to rent the property to tourists. The company takes on the entire responsibility for managing the property. The agreement normally provides for the purchaser to use the property at no charge for two or three weeks per year.

These leaseback developments are concentrated in tourist areas where the government has been concerned about the shortage of holiday accommodation. Properties purchased as part of an approved scheme are exempt from VAT (19.6 per cent), resulting in a major saving for the purchaser. It is generally possible to obtain mortgage finance on these properties for more than the usual 80 per cent of the purchase price. At the end of the nine-year period, the purchaser can sell, continue to rent or live in the property.

Selling your property

Selling property in France generally takes rather longer than in the UK. You can seek assistance and obtain a valuation from a *notaire* or an estate agent (*agent immobilier*).

An agreement with an estate agent – *un mandat* – must be in writing, for a fixed duration and specify the commission. There are two different types of agreement. The *mandat simple* gives you the option of instructing several estate agents, providing you do not instruct any one of them on an exclusive basis. Such agreements normally reserve the right for you to sell the property yourself without an agent. Alternatively, you can enter into a *mandat exclusif*, an exclusive agency, under which all or part of the commission will be payable, even if you were to locate a purchaser yourself. A sole agency agreement can be irrevocable for up to three months only. Thereafter, you can revoke the agreement at any time by giving 15 days' notice to the agent by registered letter. If the agent finds a purchaser willing and able to go ahead, but you change your mind, you will probably find yourself liable for damages and have to pay the agent a sum equal to the value of the commission.

Estate agents' commission is generally between 5 and 10 per cent, plus VAT. It can be payable by the vendor or purchaser, but is usually included in the advertised purchase price.

Capital gains tax is likely to be payable on a second home (see Chapter 13 in which I set out the basic position). The tax is collected by the *notaire* handling the sale. You should attempt to agree with the *notaire* how much he is going to deduct from the proceeds of the sale and seek guidance as to what steps, if any, you should take.

Some of the expenses that you may have incurred in relation to the property may be deductible from your gain, including the various purchase and sale costs and some of the costs of your mortgage or any loan to cover building and other work to the property. Also deductible are the costs of modernization and renovation (but not decoration and painting). If you have carried out such work yourself, the costs of the materials are deductible and the total is multiplied by a factor of three to take account of your labour. It is obviously important to keep a file of receipts and bills as they can reduce your apparent gain considerably and may well even extinguish any liability.

11 Education and health

Pre-school care

The facilities available include:

- *crèches*, which are day nurseries, generally municipal, for children from two months to three years, open from 7.00 am to 7.00 pm, the cost being determined, in part, by the income of the parents;
- *halte-garderies*, which are for children from three months to six years;
- *assistantes maternelles*, who are similar to childminders in the UK and are authorized to look after one child or more over three months old in their own homes;
- *gardes d'enfants à domicile*, who are employed by parents to look after a child at home – parents may obtain financial assistance to do this from the *Caisse Allocation Familiale* and a proportion of the cost is deductible against tax.

Nursery school education

Education does not become compulsory in France until children are six years old. However, most children (well over 90 per cent) attend an *école maternelle* from the age of three.

Many parents of British and foreign children choose to send their children to an *école maternelle* even though they may have already decided to opt for some form of English-speaking, bilingual or international school for the primary and secondary years. Firstly, the *écoles maternelles* are free of charge. Secondly, attendance at an *école maternelle* enables children to learn to speak French during the years that they are most receptive to acquiring a second language.

To enrol your child in a village school, you can simply attend and speak to the headteacher, preferably in or before March in the year in which you wish your child to start school. If you live in a town, you will need to consult your local *mairie* to register and find out which school catchment you fall into. In either case, you will need your child's *carnet de santé*, so that you can show that he or she has received the requisite vaccinations, and proof of residence such as a utility bill.

Nursery school is divided into three year groups, namely *petite section, moyenne section* and *grande section*.

Choices for primary and secondary education

Your choices will depend very much on where you live. International, bilingual and British educational options are greater in and around Paris, Marseille, Lyon, Lille, Bordeaux, Toulouse and on the Riviera. The possibilities are as follows:

▌ **International private schools** These are primarily day schools. They are expensive, especially if you have more than one child, as fees range from £5000 up to £10,000 per annum for day schools. Discounts for second and third children are, at best, modest. Some of these schools are essentially British, others are more American and others more internationally focused. The British-orientated schools tend to follow the UK curriculum (SATS, GCSEs and AS/A levels). The others prepare their students for the International Baccalaureate (in English). These schools generally start from nursery and go all the way through to 18. A list of international private schools can be found at http:/ydelta.free.fr/school.htm.

▌ **International assisted/public schools** These are often French state schools with an anglophone section. Parents have to pay a contribution to cover the costs of the anglophone staff (£1000–£1250 would be typical). A list of these can also be found at http:/ydelta.free.fr/school.htm.

▌ **Assisted private schools** These schools are self-governing (referred to as *sous contrat*) but the salaries of teaching staff are paid for by the state. They are primarily Church (Catholic) schools that are attended by substantial numbers of French children. These schools are listed in the *Yellow Pages* under *Enseignement primaire: écoles privées* and *Enseignement secondaire: collèges privés*.

▌ **Non-assisted private schools** These include some boarding schools, and some schools that claim to be bilingual, but are primarily French. They are listed in the *Yellow Pages* under *Enseignement primaire: écoles privées* and *Enseignement secondaire: collèges privés*. There are few Protestant schools (about 8). Only 2 per cent of the population is Protestant. These schools are French. They are mostly for younger children, although two or three take children up to 18. Details can be obtained from www.huguenots.net (Rubrique 94 – jeunes – éstablissements scolaires).

▌ **State schools** As with all types of schools, standards vary considerably. On the whole, the French state schools are considered superior to British state schools. Certainly, the average French school leaver speaks a higher level of French than his or her British counterpart speaks English. These schools are free, but parents are expected to pay for exercise books, pens, pencils, crayons and so on.

General guidance can be obtained from the ELSA-France (English Language Schools Association), tel: 01 45 34 04 11, e-mail elsa.france@ wanadoo.fr. See also under Schools in Appendix 1 and Chapter 2 for regional information.

The French system – state and private

A major difference between French schools and their British or American counterparts is the relatively low emphasis on art, drama, music and sport. These activities tend to take place away from school. Nearly all schools are mixed. French schools, public, international public and private are divided into *écoles* (primary), *collèges* (for ages 11 to 16) and *lycées* (for 16- to 18-year-olds).

The start of the school day varies but is usually about 8.15 am. There is a two-hour lunchbreak, from 11.30 to 1.30, during which there is often little organized activity. School generally finishes at 4.00 or 4.30 pm, but can be earlier. In some secondary schools, start and finish times are staggered to avoid the traffic chaos caused by parents all arriving to drop off or collect their children at the same time. Children attend school for longer hours than in the UK (if you include their two-hour lunchbreak), but for fewer days in the year. For many primary school children, there is now no school on a Wednesday (in which case the school terms have been extended to make up for the half days lost). A good number of schools, however, have retained the Wednesday half day and some have kept Saturday morning school.

There are rather more bank holidays in France than in the UK, to which you also have to add *jours pédagogiques* – teacher training half days when primary school children do not attend school.

School trips, educational (*classes de découvertes*) and otherwise, take place during school terms, not during the school holidays. School holidays in the spring and winter are staggered depending on your area, in an attempt to persuade parents not all to take holidays at the same time, and so reduce road congestion.

The school year starts in early September (*la rentrée*). *La rentrée* is not made easy for parents of children in French schools, especially if they have more than one child. While there is no school uniform to find, each pupil will have received a long list of different and very specific types of exercise books (each of which also has to have a cover in a specified colour), together with what needs to be in their pencil cases. Many teachers insist on a particular make of pen, rubber, correction fluid and so on.

The *rentrée* has become extremely commercialized. Finance companies offer loans for parents having difficulties meeting the demands placed on them. Supermarkets rearrange their shelves to prepare for the mad rush of parents jostling with each other, clutching lists of demands set down by teaching staff. All this appears on the television news, with parents who have several children being interviewed to explain how they approach this ordeal. You will be lucky to complete the task without several visits to your local supermarkets. You may be better advised to present your list to your local stationery shop (*papeterie*), where staff will do the job for you and probably give a modest discount on the (higher) prices. The *papeterie* may not be able to provide everything on your list, however, so you may still have to join the majority jostling in the supermarket aisles, but at least your list will be shorter.

Once a child has started school, he or she will not be permitted to move up into the next year without attaining a certain level of education. If a child does not, he or she is '*redoublé*' – that is, has to repeat the year (while classmates and friends move up). This can happen up to twice during the course of a child's school life.

Ecole primaire (from ages 6 to 11)

Primary school (*école primaire*) is divided into *cours préparatoires* (CP – the first year), *cours élémentaires* (CE1 and CE2 – the second and third years) and *cours moyens* (CM1 and CM2 – the fourth and fifth years).

In primary school a child refers to his teacher as *le maître* or *la maîtresse*. The headmistress is *la directrice*.

Children receive annual health checks.

The five years in primary school are sometimes referred to as 11*ème* to 5*ème* (the former being the first year in primary school). The first year in secondary school is termed 6*ème*. The terms *instituteur* and *institutrice* usually refer to a teacher (male and female respectively) in an *école primaire*, whereas a *professeur* is the term used for a teacher in a *collège* or *lycée*.

In the primary years, your child will learn to read and write and understand some of the complex rules of French grammar. Standards are high, with much effort being put into learning the French language. There is far more emphasis on learning rules of speech and grammar than in English-speaking countries, where we tend to learn 'by doing' on a rather more piecemeal basis.

Considerable effort is put into learning and reciting poetry. English is meant to be compulsory from CM1, but implementation of the new regulations is not universal.

In the colder months, schools often organize *ateliers* (workshops) for part of the lunchbreak on some days. These range from judo to chess, creative arts and dance.

Physical education is included in the curriculum. Swimming instruction is provided, but you may find that your child will only attend lessons for a few terms during the five years spent in primary school.

Wednesdays

Children up to the age of 11 do not generally attend school on Wednesdays or, if they do, will finish at about 11.15 am. The reasoning is that children up to that age cannot cope with five consecutive days of schooling and need a break in the middle of the week.

Various activities are organized by the local *mairies*, such as artwork, music, dance and sports. Some of these activities are based in school buildings, especially in rural areas. Further information can be obtained from your local *mairie*.

Collège (from ages 11 to 16)

As with primary schools, you will need to enrol for a state *collège* via your local *mairie*. If you do not like your nearest school, then application can be made to enter another school and sometimes even a school in a different *commune*.

The emphasis is still on mathematics and French. History and geography are taught as one subject. English is taught from the first year, with a second foreign language being added two years later (the start of 4*ème*). At the end of the fourth year in *collège* (3*ème*), students sit an examination – *le brevet*.

In 3*ème*, major decisions will be taken that will affect your child's future career path. The results of the *brevet* and your child's annual report will determine the path of his or her remaining school years and, in particular, the type of *lycée* that he or she can attend: a *lycée générale et technologique* or a *lycée professionelle*.

Lycée (for ages 16 to 18)

After sitting *le brevet* at the end of 3*ème*, and provided he or she has reached a sufficient level of study, your child will move up to the *lycée*, which may be within the same school campus as the *collège* or may be at a totally different location.

Here, from the 2*ème*, your child will study for the *bac* (or *baccalauréat*). There are different *bacs* available, including a general *bac*, depending on your child's ability and career plans. Written and oral examinations are taken at the end of the *première* (*le bac de Français*) and the marks from these count towards the ultimate *bac* result. The final examinations are taken at the end of the *terminale*. Resits are possible.

Bilingual children

I have seen claims that children under the age of eight can acquire a competence in the language within three months and near fluency after six months, while at age eleven fluency can take *up to* a year. This is contrary to the views of many experts in this field. The Doman Institute in the United States, for example, claims that a child's capacity to acquire a second language is at its highest between the ages of three and five and drops dramatically from the age of six. In my experience, the reality is somewhere in the middle, with complete fluency in two languages requiring considerable effort on the part of the child and its parents. If you do want your children to speak fluent French, it would be advisable to seek out French company as much as possible and, ideally, place them in a French school rather than an international school.

Equivalent stages of education for France, the UK and the US

AGE	FRANCE	UK	US
2–5	*MATERNELLE* *petite section* *moyenne section*	NURSERY	NURSERY
5–6	*grande section*	Yr 1 (infants)	KINDERGARTEN
ECOLE PRIMARE			
	PRIMAIRE	PRIMARY	ELEMENTARY
6–7	CP (11*ème*)	Yr 2 (infants)	1st grade
7–8	CE1 (10*ème*)	Yr 3 (junior)	2nd grade
8–9	CE2 (9*ème*)	Yr 4 (junior)	3rd grade
9–10	CM1 (8*ème*)	Yr 5 (junior)	4th grade
10–11	CM2 (7*ème*)	Yr 6 (junior)	5th grade
COLLEGE			
11–12	6*ème*	1st form	6th grade JUNIOR HIGH
12–13	5*ème*	2nd form	7th grade
13–14	4*ème*	3rd form	8th grade HIGH SCHOOL
14–15	3*ème*	4th form	9th grade
LYCEE			
15–16	*seconde*	5th form	10th grade
16–17	*première*	Lower 6th	11th grade
17–18	*terminale*	Upper 6th	12th grade
	UNIVERSITE DEUG	UNIVERSITY	UNIVERSITY
	Licence	BA/BSc	
	Maîtrise	MA	

We have three children who were aged seven, six and four when we arrived in France four years ago. They now all speak fluent French. Fluency is not automatic and considerable effort was required by my wife and myself, who are both fluent French speakers. We speak English in the home, but our approach when working with the children has been very much bilingual. We consider that this has been helpful both for their acquisition of French and the continued growth in their knowledge of English.

Transferring from one language to another is a skill in itself that needs to be nurtured. Effort is also required to maintain your child's fluency in English – a language that many foreigners spend a great deal of time and money trying to acquire and which your child should not lose.

University education

Tuition at public universities is free. In order to save costs, students tend to favour their local universities so that they can live at home. The entrance requirement is generally a pass at the *bac* or the equivalent, such as A levels.

Students who have successfully completed the first two years are awarded a DEUG (*Diplôme d'Etudes Universitaires Générales*). Completion of the third year leads to a *Licence* (on a par with a BA or BSc) and the fourth year to a *maîtrise* (MA), followed by studies for a doctorate.

University in France is far more focused on academic study than is the case in the UK or US. Extra-curricula sport, drama and arts are virtually non-existent.

Registrations are made in January for courses starting the following September. If you are accepted, this will be conditional on your satisfying a French language test.

Les grandes écoles

These are higher education establishments for students of commerce, industry, politics and public service. Most of France's political and industrial leaders have passed through their doors.

Entry is very competitive and candidates prepare for the entrance examinations over one or two years after obtaining a good result in their *bac*.

Distance learning – *l'enseignement à distance*

The state organization *Centre Nationale de l'Enseignement à Distance* (CNED) offers a range of different courses at relatively low cost. Consult the Web site, www.cned.fr, or tel: 05 49 49 94 94.

There are several private institutions, including *Educatel*, that provide vocational correspondence courses in such areas as childcare, nursing, secretarial, hairdressing, tourism and commerce (tel: 02 35 58 12 00).

Obtaining information

Information generally can be obtained from Onisep (your local branch should be given in the *White Pages* under Onisep). See also its Web site, www.onisep.fr. Information can also be obtained from your local *Centre d'Information et de Documentation Jeunesse* (CIDJ) and its Web site, www.cidj.com.

Other useful Web sites include:

■ www.education.gouv.fr
■ www.francealacarte.org.uk/education
■ www.edufrance.fr
■ www.expat-moms.com

Access to the 'Guide de l'Etudiant Etranger', which gives information to students about higher education, is via the Web site www.egide.assoc.fr.

The Open University

The OU's distance learning programme is available in France. The cost is substantially higher than in the UK. However, if you or your spouse pay UK income tax, you should be able to avoid paying the supplement.

Summer schools for the OU's French classes are held in Caen, Normandy.

Information can be obtained from the OU in the UK or Rosemary Pearson in Paris, tel: 01 47 58 53 73 or e-mail r.pearson@open.ac.uk. For the Open University Business School, contact Barbara Wilson, tel: 04 93 77 06 28 or e-mail b.a.wilson@open.ac.uk. The respective Web sites are www.open.ac.uk and www.oubs.open.ac.uk.

Healthcare and the French health system

The French are preoccupied with the state of their health. France spends more of its national income on health than any other nation save the United States. The French do not feel that they have received adequate care from their doctor unless they leave an appointment with a *list* of prescriptions. Indeed, the government presently has a television campaign explaining to viewers that antibiotics are ineffective against viruses and is attempting to persuade doctors to reduce prescriptions of antibiotics. The presumption has to be that doctors were knowingly prescribing useless drugs to satisfy patient-led demand.

The general consensus in the English-speaking press in France, however, is that the French system is far superior to that in the UK and that if you were to develop cancer or heart problems you could expect to be treated more quickly and more effectively than in Britain. Indeed, in a recent survey of the quality of healthcare by the World Health Organization, France came out top. The average life expectancy for women in France – 83 – is the highest in Europe, and for a man it is 75.

There are more doctors in France than in any other country in the EU – nearly twice as many per head of population than in the UK. There are nearly twice as many pharmacists, as well as nearly twice as many hospital beds.

Doctors command more respect in France than in the UK, but the average doctor earns nothing like the remuneration received by his British counterpart. Many are dissatisfied at the poor returns after the long periods of study and training required. Indeed, in 2002, some of them took to the streets and could be seen struggling with riot police. Unfortunately, arrogance among many doctors is just as marked on the French side of the Channel as it is on the British side.

Under the French system:

▪ you have complete freedom over your choice of doctor and, accordingly, it is very easy to change doctors or seek a second opinion;
▪ you do not need to obtain a GP referral before consulting a specialist, thereby avoiding an unnecessary visit to a GP (*le médecin généraliste*)

and a day off work, when you already know what type of specialist to consult;

I while you pay for a medical appointment, the cost is modest (at least if the doctor is one of the 80 per cent of doctors who are *conventionné*) – the standard fee for a consultation was raised in 2002 to 23 euros (less than £16 and a fraction of the cost of a private appointment in the UK), although some doctors charge up to 36 euros (about £24);

I if you are covered by the state health system, about 70 per cent of the standard rate is recoverable and you have the option of taking out an additional insurance policy (a *mutuelle*) in order to claim the balance. You may consider that the benefits of such insurance cover are not worth the premiums as hospital treatment (the most expensive aspect of healthcare provision) is generally refundable in full under the state system, including important surgery, treatment for serious illnesses, antenatal care and delivery of a baby;

I waiting lists to see a consultant or to attend hospital for a consultation or surgery are very short;

I in relation to hospital treatment, you have the option of insisting on a consultation with a particular person, such as the head of the department. You may have to consult him or her on a private basis, but you only have to pay a top-up fee, with the state being responsible for about 70 per cent of the balance;

I if you are covered under the French social security system, 100 per cent of hospital bills are covered and you do not have to pay these and then seek reimbursement. You do have to pay *le forfait journalier* – a modest daily sum to cover the cost of meals. A parent of a child in hospital can usually stay overnight in the same room with a bed provided (rather discriminatingly called *une chambre mère-enfant*), the daily cost of which is about 45 euros, including meals;

I in most non-rural areas, doctors, including specialists, are very available and you will not have to travel far for an appointment – they are listed in the *Yellow Pages* under *Médecins*, the entries being separately set out according to specialty;

I there are many women specialists (far, far more than in the UK, where, outside the field of general practice, there are very few female doctors);

I for the most part, doctors are more user-friendly than in the UK, with patients being able to telephone a consultant to ask a question that they forgot to ask at an appointment, without a further fee. In the case of hospital-based doctors who will probably be in theatre on a regular basis, it is advisable to ask at the appointment if this is acceptable and check what day and time is most convenient for them to take a call;

▪ as far as children are concerned, save in rural areas, it is frequently a paediatrician who is the first port of call and, on the whole, because they are dealing entirely with children, they have a greater range of experience than the UK GP, particularly in relation to the less common ailments;

▪ a child is provided with a *carnet de santé* in which is recorded the major incidents of his or her medical history, including vaccinations, growth charts and so on. This is obtained from your local *Caisse Primaire d'Assurance Maladie* (see *Yellow Pages* under *Sécurité sociale*) – it is kept by his parents and facilitates the transfer of healthcare from one doctor to another. When a woman knows that she is expecting, she should contact the local *Caisse d'Allocations Familiales* and she will be given a *carnet de maternité* that sets out the basic information that she and her partner require;

▪ alternative medicine is readily available, and where prescribed by a doctor, the costs are frequently recoverable under the social security system.

One should avoid the temptation succumbed to by many Britons in France to view the French health system with rose-tinted spectacles. France has had its own health scandals, such as that involving the contamination of blood supplies, and the patients poisoned at Nice's new hospital L'Archet 2. In the latter, repeated tests carried out with help from the US eventually excluded sabotage in favour of a chemical component of an insecticide used in the hospital to keep down house dust mites!

As a barrister having practised in the field of medical negligence, I can vouch for the difficulties claimants face in the UK regarding getting doctors and hospitals to admit and rectify their mistakes. In France, if things do go wrong, you may find it even more difficult to take on the opposition and hostility from the medical profession when you come to complain. Notwithstanding the difficulties, the number of malpractice suits is increasing and there have been growing calls for doctors to be required to undergo continuous professional education to keep them up to date with the pace of change in medical knowledge.

It is also worth remembering that to gain entry to a UK university to study medicine, applicants generally need to obtain high grades in specialist science A levels, with two As and a B having been a common requirement. In France, the emphasis is firstly on first a more general education for sixth-form students, and secondly greater access to university studies. Even sixth formers taking a science baccalaureate (*bac*) continue with studies in French, geography, history and a foreign language. Furthermore, the *bac* is not graded in the same way as GCE A levels; rather the emphasis is on 'pass' or 'fail', with few distinctions being awarded. The pass rate is very high, with most students obtaining the right to go on to university studies, including medicine.

France has twice as many doctors as the UK, and on average they almost certainly have had a wider general education than their British counterparts. Though the French system gives greater choice to the patient than in the UK it does not follow, however, that the average French doctor or surgeon is any better trained than his or her UK colleagues.

Your rights to medical care in France

If you are going to France for a short stay only or as a student, obtain and complete a copy of Form E111 from your local post office (it is attached to a guidance booklet). This will cover you for emergency treatment while in France for up to 90 days (pensioners are entitled to both emergency and routine treatment). You will be required to pay a modest contribution, as you would if you were living and working in France. From June 2004 the E111 is to be gradually replaced with a pan-European medical insurance card.

If you take a regular prescription and will need to obtain further supplies while in France, be sure to obtain a Form E112 and the generic name of the medication from your doctor. This will enable the French pharmacist to identify the version of the drug available in France. Help and advice is available from the Overseas Section of the Department of Health (tel: 020 7210 4850).

If you are intending to reside in France, you should contact The Pension Service's International Pension Centre, which is part of the Department for Work and Pensions, tel: 0191 218 7777 or write to The International Pension

Centre, Newcastle upon Tyne NE98 1BA. In Northern Ireland, you should contact the Northern Ireland Social Security Agency, International Services, tel: (028) 9054 3245 or write to them at 24–42 Corporation Street, Belfast BT1 3DR. In either case, ask for copies of the various leaflets applicable.

Those living and working in France are generally required to join the French social security system governing pensions, sickness, unemployment and healthcare. If you are employed, both you and your employer are obliged to make contributions. The self-employed are also required to make contributions, but the system is not identical to that applicable to salaried employees and you will need to check the up-to-date position. Medical and health care for your spouse and children are covered by your social security contributions.

If you are a UK national and have been sent to work in France by your employer, you should be entitled to cover under the French health system while still paying your contributions to the UK system.

If you are in receipt of a UK state pension, you are entitled to treatment under the French health system without contribution. You will need to obtain Form 121 to establish your entitlement.

The system of reimbursement

This has been dramatically overhauled, making reimbursement simpler and quicker. If you are over 16 and entitled to cover under the French system, you should eventually be issued with a *carte vitale*. This is an electronic card resembling a credit card that contains information relevant to your entitlement to cover. You present this to your doctor, pharmacist or other medical professional along with your payment. Your card is then inserted into a machine that electrically notifies your claim for reimbursement to your local *Caisse d'Assurance Maladie*. There are no forms to fill in and you should be reimbursed within five days directly into your bank account.

There may be some delay in obtaining your *carte vitale*, in which case you will be given a *feuille des soins* by your doctor (and a similar form by the pharmacist). You should complete this and send it to your local *Caisse d'Assurance Maladie*.

Language difficulties

Many French doctors claim to speak English, but relatively few speak it to a high standard. Assistance is available from:

- the consulates of the various English-speaking nations, which keep lists of English-speaking doctors;
- private health insurance and traveller's associations – these often provide details of English-speaking doctors to their clients;
- British and American hospitals, including in Paris;
- the English-speaking press (see Appendix 1), which may be able to provide you with details, despite the fact that doctors are not permitted to advertise in their pages;
- you can consult the English *Yellow Pages*. Doctors are not permitted to advertise here either, but, if you telephone the publication's hotline (tel: 08 92 68 83 97, 0.34 euro per minute), they will supply you with a name and contact details of an English-speaking doctor;
- in the Côte d'Azur, one doctor has recently set up *Riviera Medical Services*, an English version of the French emergency medical service. If you phone 04 93 26 12 70, you will be put through to a doctor, dentist or nurse who speaks English (as at 2003, the service covered the area from Menton to Grasse, but there are plans to extend this further afield).

The names and contact details of doctors on night or out-of-hours duties are posted on the door of the local *pharmacie*. However, if you telephone most doctors out of hours, you should be put through to a switchboard that can put you in touch with the doctor on duty.

Emergency treatment

For medical emergencies, you should phone 15 to contact *Service d'Aide Médicale Urgente* (SAMU). For the police, call 17, and, for the fire brigade, 18. In addition, in the larger towns and cities, there is an SOS medical service available 24 hours a day.

Vaccinations

These are obligatory for diptheria, tetanus, poliomyelitis and tuberculosis. Vaccination is compulsory for entry into a nursery or school. The French words for the diseases commonly vaccinated against are:

- chickenpox – la varicelle
- diphtheria – la diphtérie
- measles – la rougeole
- mumps – les oreillons
- poliomyelitis – la poliomyélite
- rubella – la rubéole
- tetanus – le tétanos
- tuberculosis – la tuberculose
- whooping cough – la coqueluche.

Reform of the health system

The French health system is proving increasingly expensive. There was a deficit of 10 billion euros in the health budget in 2003 and that is set to increase to 66 billion euros by 2020 if expenditure is not brought under control. Major targets include expenditure on medication (which currently accounts for a staggering 20 per cent of the budget, with GP prescriptions costing several times as much as in the UK) and thalassotherapy (which is currently reimbursed).

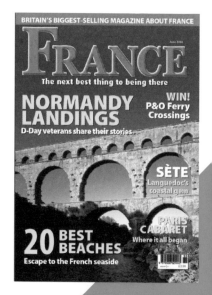

12 Working and setting up a business in France

Employment

Citizens of EU countries are entitled to live and work anywhere within the European Union, although you should ensure that you obtain your *carte de séjour* (see Chapter 9). There are English-speakers who are employed within the English community, particularly on the Côte d'Azur, and speak hardly any French, even after years of living in the country. However, while your chances of obtaining work will be increased by networking among other expatriates, if you are to obtain employment with a French employer, a reasonable knowledge of French and a willingness to improve it are essential.

Job seekers should register in person with their local office of the *Agence Nationale Pour l'Emploi* (ANPE). The larger offices have a member of staff specializing in advising migrant workers seeking work within the EU. Make contact with recruitment agencies by sending them a CV and covering letter requesting an appointment. Purchase a copy of *Le Figaro* each Monday, as it contains the most comprehensive selection of job advertisements. Other newspapers advertising appointments include *Carrières et Emplois* each Wednesday. *Le Monde* has a good selection of higher-paid jobs on Mondays and Tuesdays. Job advertisements often refer to *Bac, or Bac +3 or Bac +4*. *Bac* is short for *baccalauréat*, the French equivalent to GCE A level. *Bac +3* means that the post is restricted to those with three years of higher education. The two free English-speaking publications in Paris, *France-USA Contacts* and *The Free Voice*, have job sections with appointments of particular interest to native English-speakers. It may be worthwhile placing a paid advertisement in the monthly review issued by the Franco-British Chamber of Commerce (tel: 01 53 30 81 30, Web site www.francobritishchamber.com). On the Riviera, Radio Riviera has a jobs spot, though it is, for the most part, limited to the yachting industry, security services, childcare and appointments of domestic staff. Finally, it can be worth sending unsolicited well-written letters and CVs to companies you are interested in.

A covering letter must always be hand-written and in perfect French. The CV should be very brief and to the point (one page only) and in the French style. There is no need to include referees at this stage. The paper should be of good quality and the envelope should be white. I include a sample CV below, but, ideally, you should look at one of the specialist books on the bookshelves of most large supermarkets on how to present different types of CVs and how to address and set out your correspondence. Never begin a letter with *Cher*, but rather with *Monsieur* or *Madame*. If you know the person's title, use this, preceded by *Monsieur* or *Madame*.

Contracts of employment are either fixed-term ones of up to nine months (*contrats à durée déterminée*) or indefinite contracts (*contrats à durée indéterminée*). The latter are the most common. While the contract of employment does not have to be in writing, most large companies will provide you with a written document. This should normally include a job description, name the place of work and the remuneration.

France operates a minimum wage, which is about 1200 euros per month. A higher minimum wage of up to 50 per cent more applies to semi-skilled and skilled workers. Salaries are generally paid about five days before the end of the month. Most French employers pay an annual bonus equivalent to one month's salary – the thirteenth month. Many companies have profit-related bonus schemes.

The restrictions imposed by the 35-hour week have now been relaxed to permit employees to work additional hours. Five weeks' paid leave per year is the standard holiday entitlement, with most employees taking much or most of this during August. In addition, French employees benefit from a total of 11 bank holidays.

Grounds for dismissal are very similar to those in the UK. A complaint of unfair dismissal is brought before the *Conseil des Prud'hommes*, the equivalent of an industrial tribunal.

Example of a CV

(Name)

(Address)

(Tel)

(E-mail)

Né en Angleterre, le 20 mai 1970
Marié, trois enfants

ETUDES SECONDAIRES
XXXXXX High School

CSE/O levels (notés A – E)   *Note reçue* (put grade in list below)
    Mathématiques
    Anglais langue
    Anglais littérature
    Français
    Histoire
    Chimie
    Physique
    Géographie

A levels (notés A–E) – équivalent bac
    Mathématiques
    Economie
    Français

ETUDES SUPERIEURES

UNIVERSITE DE .... ANGLETERRE 19XX–XX

       ....Bachelor/Master of Arts/Science
(or other qualification)

QUALIFICATIONS PROFESSIONNELLES

(List.)

EXPERIENCE PROFESSIONNELLE

(List job experience to date, starting with the most recent.)

LANGUES ETRANGERES

Français lu, écrit, parlé

Income tax

Anyone resident in France, or who spends at least 183 days working or living in France, is liable for income tax. There is no system equivalent to PAYE and, accordingly, tax is not deducted by employers. Instead, you are obliged to submit a *déclaration des revenus* to your local *hôtel des impôts* each year setting out your income for the year to 31 December of the previous year. The deadline changes each year but is normally between 1 and 15 March.

You should complete the declaration even if your income is below the tax threshold, as you may be entitled to receive a *prime*, or benefit. You can obtain your first form from your local *hôtel des impôts*. Thereafter, you will be sent a form each year with much of the standard sections covering many of your personal details already completed for you. You should receive your tax assessment several months after lodging your declaration.

Tax is payable in three instalments, with the first being on 15 September. Thereafter, you will make payments on 15 February, 15 May and 15 September each year. The first two instalments will be based on your previous year's tax liability, with a balancing amount being paid on 15 September of each year. Alternatively, you can pay by ten direct monthly debits from January to October of each year based on your previous year's tax liablity, with any balance being paid in November and December.

The system for calculating income tax is extremely complicated. The following is only a brief outline of the most salient points. The incomes of husband and wife are considered as one for tax purposes. The amount of tax payable will depend partly on the number of dependants, with couples with larger families having significantly smaller tax bills than couples without children. Interest on a number of savings schemes and a certain level of income from letting out your home are not taxable. In addition, there are various deductions (all set out on the income tax forms), including maintenance payments, payments to a parent or disabled adult child and pension contributions. Finally, there are some tax credits covering, in particular, charitable donations, renovation costs of your main home, some childminding expenses, a certain amount payable for domestic help and allowances for children in school. Those living in retirement homes benefit from a reduction in income tax. Elderly and handicapped people living at home can offset the cost of installing necessary equipment against income tax.

In addition to income tax, there is a hefty bill to pay for social contributions (up to 13.6 per cent of gross salary), although the contributions are deductible when calculating income tax.

The present income tax rates are set out in the table below.

The rates of income tax (2004)

Band of taxable income (euros)	Rate (%)
Up to 4,262	0
4,263–8,382	6.83
8,383–14,753	19.14
14,754–23,888	28.26
23,889–38,868	37.38
38,869–47,932	42.62
Above 47,933	48.09

Starting and running a business in France

Setting up a new business in your home country is fraught with difficulties. Most new businesses fail in the first 12 months as a result of a variety of problems associated with inexperience, lack of planning, changing market conditions and plain bad luck. A major problem is lack of liquidity or cash flow, caused by overly optimistic sales forecasts and underestimating start-up costs.

Those seeking to set up business in France face other hurdles:

▌ You will be operating in a foreign land in which, to begin with at least, there will be more unknowns as a result of not being in your native surroundings. Furthermore, you are unlikely to prosper unless your business has a broad enough appeal to attract the local French population. Unfortunately the French do tend to prefer their own and the British are not their favourite foreigners.

▌ To a greater or lesser extent, you will be operating in a foreign language. Even if your clientele is mainly English-speaking, your suppliers may not be and your dealings with public officials and bodies will be in French.

▌ The taxation and social security burden on businesses is higher than in the UK. In France, taxation and social charges represent over 46 per cent of the GDP – it is under 37 per cent in the UK.

▌ Bureaucracy is acknowledged by the French themselves to be very burdensome for businesses. Indeed, a *Commission Pour Les Simplifications Administratives* (renamed the *Conseil d'Orientation des Simplifications Administratives* in 2004) was created in 1998, and as a result there have been some improvements.

The last two factors, according to a recent documentary on French television, have caused some French businesses to relocate in the UK – a factor that has only served to increase the calls for steps to be taken to reduce the bureaucratic formalities facing businesses.

There are a substantial number of businesses that rely on the expatriate British and other English-speaking communities, including bars, English bookshops, newspapers, financial advisers, estate agents, suppliers of British and American food and other produce, security and services relating to the yachting industry. Nevertheless, as a foreigner, you, or your business partner, will need to speak French to a reasonable level or at least have a business adviser who is fluent in both languages. He must be familiar with matters of finance and have (not merely claim to have) substantial experience of advising businesses in France.

There are various agencies that provide help and assistance in establishing a business. Prior to leaving the UK, you could contact the French Chamber of Commerce at 21 Dartmouth Street, Westminster, London SW1H 9BP (tel: 020 7304 4040, Web site www.ccfgb.co.uk).

Ask for the guide, in English, entitled 'Setting up a Business in France for non-French Nationals', which costs 7 euros. Other guides include 'Business and Economic Regulations', 'Finance', 'Taxes', 'Welfare Questions' and 'Daily Company Life'. Ask what other help and assistance is available. In some areas, chambers of commerce run courses in English on how to set up a business.

Once in France, you should contact the local *chambre de commerce et d'industrie*. Advice and information is also available from the *Délégation à l'Aménagement du Territoire et à l'Action Régionale* (DATAR). This body provides grants and investment incentives and has offices abroad under the name Invest in France.

You can also get some advice from branches of the British Chamber of Commerce in France.

While any citizen of an EU country is entitled to live and work in France, a *carte de séjour* is not sufficient to enable you to start a business. If you form a limited company, you should be given a *K-Bis*, which is a business registration certificate. If you are a sole trader, you should have a *carte d'identification* from the *chambre des métiers*.

Registration of any business is essential before starting to trade even if you are working out of your home. There are substantial fines for trading prior to completion of the necessary formalities, not to mention the possibility of having equipment confiscated, being deported or, in a worst-case scenario, receiving a sentence of imprisonment. The costs of completing the registration formalities (including obtaining some expert advice) are unlikely to be less than 1500 euros, but could be substantially more.

You should find a competent chartered accountant (*expert-comptable*) or commercial lawyer to advise on what form your business should take and assist with the necessary formalities. It is vital that you choose someone with experience of doing business in France.

If you are a sole trader, you should consult your local *centre des formalités des entreprises*. These centres are there to handle your dealings with various official bodies and help smooth your path. They can save you substantial time and effort. They enable the sole trader to complete in one place and on one form the various legal, fiscal, social and administrative formalities required for setting up the business.

A number of occupations – from doctors to hairdressers – are subject to specific restrictions and regulations, so you will need to make enquiries of the relevant professional body. A French doctor who recently set up a medical service in London has expressed his amazement at the ease with which he was permitted to set up practice. An English doctor making the journey in the opposite direction is unlikely to find the administrative practicalities so easy to handle.

The following vehicles are available for the running of a business:

▮ *Entreprise individuelle* – sole trader. Suitable, in particular, for tradesmen and shopkeepers. The start-up costs are relatively modest and taxes and social charges are less than for a limited company (see below). As in the UK, a sole trader is personally liable for the business's debts and losses. This is probably the most common choice of those working alone from home.

▮ *Profession liberale* Similar to the *entreprise individuelle* and the vehicle used by doctors, lawyers, architects and those in related professions.

▮ *Société à Responsabilité Limitée* (SARL). This is a limited liability company with several shareholders (at least a couple and no more than 50), each person having a number of shares in the business. The minimum share capital is 8000 euros, but shareholders' liabilities are limited to the value of their shares should the business fail. This is a vehicle often chosen by a married couple working from home. A managing director must be appointed to run the company. He could face personal liabilty if he mismanages the company. Successful companies can change to *Société Anonyme* (SA), the equivalent of a PLC in the UK.

■ *Entreprise Unipersonelle à Responsabilité Limitée* (EURL) A limited company formed by a single shareholder. Again, share capital of at least 8000 euros is required.

■ **SNC (an unlimited partnership)** This is less costly than a SARL, but partners remain personally liable.

There are other less commonly used alternatives. These include the *société en commandité*, a kind of mix between a limited company and a partnership, in which the liability of sleeping partners is limited, and the *société civile*, most frequently used where the ownership of property is an important feature of the business. A *société civile immobilière* (SCI) is a property holding company, often formed by landlords wishing to purchase and rent out property. Two other options are establishing a branch office or a subsidiary of a UK registered company.

In addition to the initial formalities, French businesses have to lodge annual audited statements with the local commercial court. These consist of balance sheets detailing fixed and current assets and liabilities, a profit and loss account and confirmation by an approved auditor that the statements provide a true picture of the state of the business.

Taxation of businesses

Social charges

This makes up the largest slice of the tax burden and pays for healthcare, maternity, disability, state pensions and family allowances.

The minimum for a sole trader is 2400 euros a year, even if the business is running at a loss. You may well not receive notification for payment until your business has been running for 18 months or more. These charges are paid retrospectively and, accordingly, you should ensure that you have funds set aside to meet this bill. An employer's social charges can amount to 27.8 per cent of an employee's gross salary. An employee has to pay up to 13.6 per cent of gross salary.

Social charges are higher for limited companies. The real cost to the business of an employee will approach about twice his or her take-home pay when all the various charges relating to his employment are taken into account.

One way to reduce your business' liability for social charges – whether you operate as a sole trader or as a limited company – is to use independent contractors who are liable for their own social charges. They will normally expect to be paid more than an employee. You need to ensure that they are properly registered and declaring their income or the tax authorities could look to you for payments.

Business taxes

Le taxe professionelle is a tax on businesses. It is a local tax and the amount levied depends on the value of the business premises and salaries paid and on the area where you set up your business. It can be substantial. *Impôt sur les sociétés* (IS) is paid by limited companies and is the equivalent of the UK corporation tax. The rate is from 25 per cent up to just over 38,000 euros and 33 per cent thereafter. New businesses are exempt for three years.

For the sole trader, his profit is taxed as personal income. Taxable income is calculated after making various reductions, including the social charges that have been paid.

When deciding on investing in the business by purchasing substantial assets, such as a computer system, you should note that not all the costs will be deductible against tax in the year in which they are purchased. The cost of such assets will be spread over a number of years and only a fraction will be deductible against tax in the year of purchase. You may wish to consider leasing equipment so that tax deductions are more in line with your expenditure.

You must charge VAT – TVA in France – on your supplies once your turnover exceeds 26,675 euros, or 76,225 euros in the case of a retail business. Accordingly, if your business is going to succeed, you will only be exempt from TVA in the very early stages. You have to account to the

TVA authorities every month or quarter and pay over the TVA you have charged less the TVA you have paid on your inputs. The rate is 5.5 per cent for food, pharmaceuticals and water, 22 per cent for cars, perfumes and some other luxury items and 19.6 per cent for other products and services. Medical and educational services are exempt from TVA. TVA paid on company cars (*voitures de société*) is not recuperable and your business will have to pay a company car tax of between 1000 and 2000 euros, depending on the horsepower of the vehicle. TVA can be recuperated on commercial vehicles such as lorries, vans and trucks. Road tax (the *vignette*) remains payable on company cars and commercial vehicles.

There are other charges that have to be met by any business. Once you take on an employee, you will be liable to pay the *taxe d'apprentisage* used to finance training courses. You have a choice as to whom to pay this tax. However, if you pay this to the organization responsible for training entrants to your own field of business activity, you are more likely to be asked to take on a trainee at little or no cost to your business.

The purchase of a business

The sale and purchase of a business or business property are handled by the *notaire*, who acts on behalf of both parties to the contract. His fees amount to about 17 per cent of the purchase price. If you are instructing an estate agent, he can handle all steps, save for completing the *acte de vente*. His fees are unlikely to exceed 10 per cent, but you will have to add in a further amount to cover the *notaire*'s completion of the formalities. Transfer duties (*droits d'enregistrement*) are payable on the transfer of a business – 7 per cent on the value from 15,250 to 45,750 euros, and 14.2 per cent on the value above 45,750 euros.

The safest course of action when contemplating the purchase or creation of a business, however, is to obtain the services of an *avocat* or *conseil juridique* specializing in this field. Their charges are based on an hourly fee, rather than a percentage, and may not cost you any more than instructing an estate agent or *notaire* and may even cost somewhat less. An expert lawyer specializing in commercial matters should have a thorough understanding of the relevant legislation, business practices and the type of advice required by a business. The *avocat* or *conseil juridique* is not permitted to complete the *acte de vente*, which is the sole province of the *notaire*.

Business premises

The conveyancing procedure is very similar to purchasing a house. About half of business property in France is leased. Like the residential tenant, the business tenant benefits from considerable protection under the law, including a right to the renewal of his or her business lease. This right is subject to exceptions and the completion of the necessary formalities, including applying for an extension in writing six months prior to the termination of the tenancy. As in the UK, if the landlord is entitled to refuse a renewal, then, provided the tenant has complied with his obligations under the lease, that person is entitled to compensation for being compelled to leave. The landlord will be seeking to find some default on the part of the tenant to avoid having to pay this.

The responsibilities of tenant and landlord are similar to those applicable to residential lettings, with obvious variations. The landlord will take a deposit of three to six months' rent. He may restrict the kind of business activity that may be operated from the premises.

Bank finance

Having a business plan, in French, is essential if you are to obtain a bank loan to finance your business. You will need to provide an assessment of the demand for your product or service, likely revenue, assets being introduced into the business, your fixed and variable costs and some cash-flow forecasts. Loans are sometimes available from trade or professional organizations, but only for amounts totalling under half the value of the business.

State aid

There are various subsidized loans, grants and subsidies available from the EU, central, regional and local government, particularly in the less prosperous regions. In addition, there are several tax incentives and allowances in the early years of a business. Up to a quarter of the set-up costs (subject to a ceiling of 1500 euros) can be set against personal income tax.

Jeune Enterprise Innovant (JEI)

From 1st January 2004, certain new businesses will benefit from tax relief for a period of up to 8 years. This also applies to businesses created prior to the 1st January 2004. For further information see: www.impots.gov.fr (recherche JEI).

Insurance

It is mandatory for businesses to have insurance cover for their vehicles, health insurance for their employees and property insurance. In France, insurance policies are automatically renewed unless you give at least two months' written notice before the renewal date that you do not want to renew. The notification period for claims is very short – 5 working days, reducing to 24 hours for theft.

13 French inheritance laws and the taxation of capital

Rules of succession

While the 1989 Hague Convention provides that citizens of Europe can choose that the national laws of their home country should apply to their estate, France has not ratified the convention (any more than has the UK). Accordingly, the position is as follows:

■ **Land and property in France (immovable property)** French inheritance rules apply irrespective of your country of domicile. If you own property through a company, however, the shares do not constitute immovable property. The shares held by non-residents are not subject to French inheritance rules.

■ **Movable property in France and abroad** This devolves according to the rules of your country of domicile. The French tax authorities consider you to be domiciled in France if your main home is in France or, in some cases, if you spend more than 183 days in France in any tax year (even if your main home is not in France). You are also deemed to be domiciled if your business is based in France and, in most cases, if you work in France. If you have a *carte de séjour*, you are assumed to be domiciled in France, unless you can prove to the contrary.

■ **Land and property outside of France** The rules applicable are those of the country in which the property is situated.

French succession law is very restrictive, despite several amendments in recent years. The basic principle is that automatic precedence is given to blood relatives to whom you must leave a certain proportion of your estate. The original code of 1804 gave no succession rights at all to a surviving spouse.

Until 2002, if a deceased person had not made a will (as is very frequently the case in France), his estate would be divided between the children in equal shares. The surviving spouse received only a life interest in one-quarter of the deceased's estate. From the beginning of 2002, however, a spouse must now receive one-quarter of the deceased's estate outright. Furthermore, a spouse now has an automatic right to remain in the couple's principal residence and retain the furniture for life. The surviving spouse has to pay the other beneficiaries a 'rental', but not for the first 12 months.

Even if you make a will, part of your estate – *la réserve héréditaire* – is reserved for your children, including illegitimate and adopted children, who must inherit as follows:

- one child – at least one-half;
- two children – at least two-thirds, shared equally;
- three or more children – at least three-quarters, shared equally.

If a child dies before you, his or her children will inherit that child's share. If there are no surviving children (or grandchildren) on your death, your parents must inherit at least one-half of your estate and take precedence over the surviving spouse. You cannot deprive them of this right. Until recently, grandparents, brothers and sisters also took precedence over the surviving spouse.

These rules apply regardless of the state of a person's relationship with his children or parents or their conduct. The only exclusions are where a child has been convicted of killing, or attempting to kill, his parent or is accused of attempted murder by the parent or is deliberately refusing to reveal the perpetrators if the parent has been murdered.

The law does provide that if the deceased has children, he may leave a life interest (*un usufruit*) in the entire estate – that is, the income from the estate – to the surviving spouse. A further permitted alternative is to leave one-quarter of the estate to the surviving spouse absolutely, with a life interest in the remaining three-quarters. However, where there is a life interest, those who would not otherwise inherit until the death of the surviving spouse have the right to receive an amount in cash representing the value of their interest. If you wish to exclude this right, ask your lawyer about the possibility of including a clause in your will.

It is not easy either to gift one's estate to a spouse during one's lifetime (or indeed to anyone else) – any of the 'compulsory' beneficiaries can apply to have the gift set aside.

Avoiding the restrictions: the *tontine* clause (resident and non-resident)

The principal method employed by the French to side-step these restrictions and provide the surviving spouse with greater protection is to include what is termed a *tontine* clause when purchasing your home. The effect of such a clause is that on the death of the first spouse, the surviving spouse automatically becomes the absolute owner of the property. This avoids the property becoming part of the estate for inheritance purposes.

A *tontine* clause does not, of course, prevent other assets falling into the estate and being subject to the rights of the children if, for example, you are domiciled in France. One advantage of a *tontine* clause is that it can reduce the total inheritance tax liability.

A *tontine* clause is only available on the purchase of a property. If you have already purchased in joint names, then the best obtainable outcome for the surviving spouse is that he or she receives one-quarter of the spouse's share in the property absolutely and a life interest in the remainder of his share. Added to the half share in the property that was already his, that gives him five-eighths of the property absolutely and a life interest in the remaining three-eighths.

The historical rules relating to the *tontine* mean that you can only safely enter into a *tontine* with others who have a similar life expectancy. If there is a significant discrepancy between the ages of the owners, as there might be, for example, in a second marriage, the validity of the *tontine* can be challenged. The children of the first marriage could do so on the grounds that the *tontine* was in reality a disguised gift, to deprive them of their inheritance rights.

A second disadvantage of a *tontine* is that the property cannot be sold unless *both* partners agree – a major problem if two partners fall out.

Avoiding the restrictions: purchasing via a company (non-residents)

If you are a non-resident, you should consider purchasing your property via a company. The shares of the company do not constitute immovable property and, hence, are not automatically subject to French inheritance rules – succession to the shares will be determined by your country of domicile.

Some residents have attempted to avoid French succession laws by creating trusts, but in many cases these have not been recognized by the courts. You should take (early) expert advice if your estate is likely to be significant.

Making a will

You would be well advised to make a French will dealing with land and property that you own in France if you are not resident there or dealing with your entire estate if you are a French resident. Reliance solely on your existing English will can have disastrous consequences, in terms of both inheritance rules and taxation. Your English will should be amended to exclude your French property.

You should keep copies of your wills and leave copies with your lawyer or executor. You may register your French will with a central body at a cost of about 70 euros. The most recent will takes complete precedence over previous wills, provided that it indicates clearly that all previous wills are revoked.

There are three types of French wills, namely *authentique, olographe* and *mystique*. A will can be changed or revoked at any time. It is a document whereby you set out what is to happen to that part of your estate you are free to dispose of – *la quotité disponible*.

■ *Le testament olographe* This must be hand-written, signed and dated. A typed will is invalid. On the other hand, the will can be written on any material – a will written in blood on a washing machine by a person committing suicide has been upheld.

■ *Le testament authentique* This is prepared by a *notaire*. The testator is supposed to dictate it to the *notaire* who writes it down and then reads it back to him. Fees vary, but about 200 euros would be fairly standard, and this includes the cost of registering it with the central body. The will is signed by the testator and witnessed by either two *notaires* or one *notaire* and two other adult witnesses who all sign the will. A spouse may not witness the will, nor should any of the beneficiaries or their relatives.

▌ *Le testament mystique* (secret will) This hand-written or typed document is signed by the testator in the presence of two witnesses and sealed in an envelope. The envelope is then given by the witnesses to a *notaire*, who signs the sealed envelope and also records on it the date and identities of the two witnesses.

Procedure on death

There is no French equivalent of the British system of the appointment of personal representatives or obtaining a grant of probate. Estates are frequently administered by a *notaire,* but can be administered by an *executeur testamentaire* appointed in the will. He should not be a major beneficiary under the will. If the estate is small, with no property or shares and a value of under about 5000 euros, the beneficiaries can handle the estate themselves. This is done by obtaining a *certificat de hérédité* from the deceased's local *mairie* or *tribunal d'instance*. Otherwise, recourse must be had to a *notaire*.

An heir may find himself liable for the debts of the deceased, even where they exceed the value of the inheritance! The answer is to either officially renounce the inheritance completely or opt for a provisional acceptance of the inheritance in order to take stock. The latter course enables you to accept the inheritance *sous bénéfice d'inventaire* – subject to debts up to, but not beyond, the value of the assets you inherit. Anyone who is concerned that acceptance of an inheritance might involve liability for substantial debts should take legal advice as soon as possible.

If you wish to take advantage of accepting *sous bénéfice d'inventaire*, it is extremely important that you do not deal with the deceased's property or belongings in any way – by taking away a piece of furniture that the deceased had promised to leave to you, for example. If your action is discovered, you are likely to find yourself held responsible for the deceased's debts, however great they may be.

There are specific provisions governing what is to happen to business assets in certain cases in which spouses have been in business together. You should consult a *notaire* regarding these.

Inheritance tax

A declaration must be submitted by the beneficiaries of the estate to the tax authorities – *la recette des impôts* – within six months of the date of death. This should be completed by the *notaire*, if one has already been instructed.

The form requires a number of details concerning the deceased and the beneficiaries, including details of gifts made by the deceased in his lifetime. If the deceased was domiciled in France, then all his assets must be declared, including assets held abroad. By virtue of a number of double taxation agreements, inheritance tax paid to tax authorities abroad is deducted from the amount of French inheritance tax.

Inheritance tax (*droits de succession*) is paid by the beneficiary according to how much he inherits and his relationship to the deceased. It applies to all assets and, if you are domiciled in France, this includes property abroad. If you are not domiciled in France, then only your immovable French assets are caught by the *droits de succession*. Tax can be paid in instalments over up to five years (interest is payable).

The current rates of inheritance tax for the surviving spouse are as set out in the table below.

The rates of inheritance tax (2004)

	%	TOTAL SPOUSE INHERITANCE (including lifetime transfers in previous ten years)	TAX PAYABLE BY SPOUSE
Up to 76,000 euros	0%	76,000	Nil
Next 7600	5%	83,600	380
Next 7400	10%	91,000	1,130
Next 15,000	15%	106,000	3,380
Next 490,000	20%	596,000	101,380
Next 330,000	30%	926,000	200,380
Next 850,000	35%	1,776,000	497,880
Above 1,776,000	40%		

A spouse who inherits 180,000 euros pays approximately 17,430 euros. In the UK, transfers between spouses, whether during the deceased's lifetime or on death, are exempt.

For (non-married) partners to a *Pacte Civil de Solidarité* (PACS) the first 57,000 euros is exempt, providing the PACS was concluded at least two years prior to death. The next 15,000 euros is taxed at 40 per cent, and the remainder at 50 per cent.

The following table sets out the inheritance tax payable by each child or grandchild beneficiary.

Tax payable by children who are beneficiaries of a will

	%	CHILD'S INHERITANCE (including lifetime transfers in previous ten years)	TAX PAYABLE BY CHILD
Up to 46,000 euros	0%	46,000	Nil
Next 7600	5%	53,600	380
Next 3800	10%	57,400	760
Next 3600	15%	61,000	1300
Next 505,000	20%	566,000	102,300
Next 330,000	30%	896,000	201,300
Next 850,000	35%	1,746,000	498,800
Above 1,746,000	40%		

It is important to remember that the total inheritance includes not merely sums received on death of the deceased, but also gifts received in the ten years prior to death. In the case of beneficiaries who are disabled, the tax-free allowances are increased by about 46,000 euros.

Gifts during your lifetime and reducing your liability to inheritance tax

Lifetime gifts are subject to rules that are similar to those for the passing of property on death.

The tax authorities take no account of gifts made more than ten years before death. These must have been declared to the authorities and must not have exceeded 76,000 euros in the case of a spouse and 46,000 euros in the case of children. In other words, you can give away up to 76,000 euros to your spouse every 10 years and 46,000 euros to each of your children every 10 years without them incurring any liability for inheritance or gift tax. Note that the tax on lifetime gifts payable where the donor is under 65 is reduced by 50 per cent and by 30 per cent for those between 65 and 74. The government has recently introduced a temporary measure to encourage lifetime gifts – all lifetime gifts made between 25 September 2003 and 30 June 2005 will benefit from a 50 per cent reduction, irrespective of the age of the donor.

The rules in relation to *droits de succession* (inheritance tax) and *droits de donations* (gift tax) are complex and subject to change. Accordingly, you should take advice from a *notaire* or financial adviser in relation to any substantial transfers, whether during your lifetime or on death.

Wealth tax

L'impôt de solidarité sur la fortune (ISF) applies to those who have net taxable assets exceeding 720,000 euros.

For those domiciled in France, their assets worldwide are taken into account, and for those domiciled abroad, only their French assets are included in the assessment.

Married couples submit a joint declaration, as do unmarried couples, unless they are married to someone else, in which case the joint declaration is with their spouse.

For the purposes of the assessment, assets of children under the age of 18 are attributed to their parents.

The ISF applies to all assets save for business assets, antiques, works of art and intellectual property, such as literary and artistic rights. The tax therefore applies not only to land and buildings, but also to bank accounts, stocks and shares, boats and yachts, horses, jewellery, gold, precious metals and even furniture and contracts of life insurance.

All assets are assessed at their current market value – something that is often difficult to determine. Various items are deductible, including tax liabilities, mortgages and bank overdrafts. The date for the valuation of assets and liabilities is 1 January of each year.

The rates on assets held on 1 January 2004 were:

- 720,000–1,160,000 – 0.55 per cent;
- 1,160,000–2,300,000 – 0.75 per cent;
- 2,300,000–3,600,000 – 1.00 per cent;
- 3,600,000–6,900,000 – 1.30 per cent;
- 6,900,000–15,000,000 – 1.65 per cent;
- 15,000,000 plus – 1.80 per cent.

These bands and rates have not changed for several years.

Example calculations

An individual or couple with net assets amounting to 750,000 euros would pay 0.55 per cent of 30,000 euros, amounting to 165 euros.

A couple with assets of 1,200,000 euros would pay 2,720 euros, calculated as follows:

720,000 – 1,160,000 × 0.55 per cent = 440,000 × 0.55 per cent = 2,420

1,160,000 – 1,200,000 × 0.75 per cent = 40,000 × 0.75 per cent = 300

Total ISF = 2,720

A couple with assets of 1,500,000 euros would pay 4,979 euros, calculated as follows:

720,000 – 1,160,000 × 0.55 per cent = 440,000 × 0.55 per cent = 2,420

1,160,000 – 1,500,000 × 0.75 per cent = 340,000 × 0.75 per cent = 2,550

Total ISF = 4,970

The amount payable is reduced by 150 euros per dependant.

For those with more substantial fortunes, the tax obviously bites harder, which helps to explain why a number of wealthy French now live as tax exiles – in the UK.

Declarations are sent to the tax authorities by 15 June each year, accompanied with the payment. European residents have until 15 July to submit their declaration, while others have until 15 August.

If you believe that your net assets are just above the threshold, you should think twice before adjusting your figures downwards to avoid having to submit a declaration. If you submit a declaration and the tax authorities are unhappy with it, they can go back three years. If you do not submit a declaration and the tax authorities think that you should have done, they can go back ten years.

Capital gains tax

Impôt sur les plus values is payable on the profit realized on the sale of certain assets in France, including property, antiques, art, jewellery and stocks and shares. There is a flat rate of 26 per cent.

Your principal residence is not subject to capital gains tax, provided you have lived in the property since it was purchased or for at least five years. Should you be obliged to sell your home for family or work-related reasons, you are also exempt from capital gains tax.

Second homes are subject to capital gains tax. There is a complete exemption if you have owned the property for more than 15 years, with a 10 per cent reduction for each full year of ownership from the fifth year. Costs of restoration work are deductible. There is no indexation allowance. The tax is a flat rate of 26 per cent. You are not liable to capital gains tax on the first sale of a second home if you rent your main residence, providing, that is, you have owned the property for five years.

Capital gains tax on property is collected by the *notaire* on the sale of the property. You should agree with him or her in advance how much he or she is going to retain.

Further information is available at www.impots.gouv.fr, and also at www.vosdroits.service-public.fr.

Appendix 1:
Useful addresses

See also Chapter 2 for information relating to particular regions.

British Embassy
35 rue du Faubourg St Honoré
75383 Paris
Tel: 01 44 51 31 02

British Consulates

The British Embassy Web site: www.amb-grandebretagne.fr
Has information on living in France and links to the five consulates
between which consular services in France are divided.

Paris
18 bis rue d'Anjou
75008 Paris
Tel: 01 44 51 31 02

Bordeaux
353 boulevard du Président Wilson
33073 Bordeaux
Tel: 05 57 22 21 10

Lille
11 square Dutilleul
59800 Lille
Tel: 03 20 12 82 72

Lyon
24 rue Childebert
69002 Lyon
Tel: 04 72 77 81 70

Marseille
24 avenue du Prado
13006 Marseille
Tel: 04 91 15 72 10

British Honorary Consulates

Biarritz
7 boulevard Tauzin
64200 Biarritz
Tel: 05 59 24 21 40

Le Havre
c/o P&O European Ferries
Terminal de la Citadel
BP 439
76057 Le Havre Cedex
Tel: 02 35 19 78 88

Monaco
33 boulevard Princesse Charlotte
98005 Monaco
Tel: 00 377 93 50 99 54

Nantes
16 boulevard Gabriel Guist'hau
BP 22026
44020 Nantes
Tel: 02 51 72 72 60

Nice
4th Floor
26 avenue Notre-Dame
06000 Nice
Tel: 04 93 62 13 56

Toulouse
c/o English Enterprises
Allée du Comminge
31770 Colomiers
Tel: 05 61 11 02 22

Other embassies

Australia
4 rue Jean Rey
75015 Paris
Tel: 01 40 59 33 00

Canada
35 avenue Montaigne
75008 Paris
Tel: 01 44 43 29 00

Denmark
77 avenue Marceau
75116 Paris
Tel: 01 44 31 21 21

Germany
13–15 avenue Franklin Roosevelt
75008 Paris
Tel: 01 53 83 45 00

Ireland
41 rue Rude
75116 Paris
Tel: 01 44 17 67 00

Netherlands
7 rue Eblé
75007 Paris
Tel: 01 40 62 33 00

New Zealand
7 ter, rue Léonard de Vinci
75116 Paris
Tel: 01 45 01 43 43

Norway
28 rue Bayard
75008 Paris
Tel: 01 53 67 04 00

South Africa
59 quai d'Orsay
75343 Paris
Tel: 01 53 59 23 23

Sweden
17 rue Barbet de Jouy
75007 Paris
Tel: 01 44 18 88 00

United States of America
2 avenue Gabriel
75008 Paris
Tel: 01 43 12 22 22

General information on France

The French Embassy UK
58 Knightsbridge
London SW1X 7JT
Tel: 020 7073 1000, 020 7201 1000
Web site: www.ambafrance.org.uk
See the Embassy's Web site for general information.

L'Institut Français
Queensberry Place
London SW7 2DT
Tel: 020 7581 2701
Web site: www.institut-francais.org.uk
Provides cinema, book and multimedia library, newspapers, restaurant and language facilities. Telephone classes are available. There is a children's library nearby (tel: 020 7838 2144) and a number of French shops, including the French Bookshop (020 7584 2840).

Centre Français de Londres
61–69 Chepstow Place
London W2 4TR
Tel: 020 7221 8134
There are also French cultural centres in Bath, Bristol, Cambridge, Exeter, Glasgow, Jersey, Milton Keynes, Manchester, Oxford, and York.

The British Council
Web site: www.britishcouncil.fr
Has information on education and equivalence of qualifications.

French Tourist Office
Web site: www.franceguide.com

FranceKeys
Web site: www.francekeys.com

Life in France
Web site: www.lifeinfrance.free.fr/pages/links.htm
Provides information on various aspects of life in France, including education, employment, healthcare, residency permits and so on. Links to the UK Embassy in Paris, the French Embassy in London, Rentals France, NorthernFrance.com (a site relating to property), *The Languedoc Page*, Americans in France, France Newcomers Directory, Anglo Info (a site relating to the Riviera).

Maville
Web site: www.maville.com
Find news, small ads, practical information, shopping, cinema, sport in the main cities in France.

Yellow Pages
Web site: www.pagesjaunes.fr
The *White Pages* can be accessed at this site too.

English Yellow Pages
Tel: 08 92 68 83 97 (0.34 euros per minute)
Web site: www.englishyellowpages.fr
A detailed list of English-speaking businesses and professionals in France is currently in preparation. Details of English-speaking doctors and dentists are available on the above telephone number.

For tax information see www.vosdroits.service-public.fr and www.impots.gouv.fr.

Banks

Abbey National
Web site: www.abbey-national.fr

Barclays
Tel: 01 44 95 13 80
Has over 120 branches in France.

Citibank
Tel: 01 53 23 33 60

Woolwich
Web site: www.banquewoolwich.fr

Business

APCE (Agence Pour la Création d'Enterprise)
Web site: www.apce.com
Detailed and plentiful information for those wishing to start a business.

Entreprendre en France
Web site: www.entreprendre-en-france.fr
Organization to assist in obtaining business finance and subsidies.

Franco-British Chamber of Commerce and Industry
31 rue Boissy d'Anglas
75008 Paris
Tel: 01 53 30 81 30

Churches

Details of the numerous Anglican churches throughout France, and the smaller numbers of other churches (English-speaking Roman Catholic, Scots Kirk, Baptist and so on), are available from the British Consulates. For Anglican churches, you could also contact St Michael's Church, 5 rue d'Aguesseau, 75008 Paris, tel: 01 47 42 70 88, which holds services in English. A full list of all Anglican churches and chaplancies is to be found at www.anglicansonline.org.uk. Go to 'Europe', then 'Diocese in Europe', then 'Chaplancies Location', then 'France'.

Computer services

Computers4Brits
Tel: 02 33 90 42 64
Web site: www.4brits.net

Employment

APCE (Agence Pour la Création d'Enterprises)
Web site: www.apce.com
Detailed and plentiful information for those wishing to start a business.

Apec
Web site: www.apec.fr
For the employment of managers.

EURES CV-search
Web site: www.eurescv-search.com

English bookshops

Village Voice
6 rue Princesse
75006 Paris
Tel: 01 46 33 36 47

The Abbey Bookshop
29 rue de la Parcheminerie
75005 Paris
Tel: 01 46 33 16 24

Bradley's Bookshop
8 cours d'Albret
33000 Bordeaux
Tel: 05 56 52 10 57

Appendix 1: Useful Addresses

Books & Mermaides
3 rue Mirepoix
31000 Toulouse

The Bookshop
17 rue Lakanal
Toulouse
Tel: 05 61 22 99 92

The English Bookshop
Rue de la Mairie
Montolieu (near Carcasonne)

Chimera
Faubourg St Privat
46800 Montcuq
Tel: 05 65 22 97 01

The English Bookshop and Internet Coffee Shop
25 rue St Julien
Domfront (61)
Tel: 02 33 37 13 02

The Bookworm
3 rue de Pâques
67000 Strasbourg
Tel: 03 88 32 26 99

Internet
Web site: www.amazon.co.uk

WH Smith
248 rue de Rivoli
75001 Paris

Other areas

For Nice, Monaco, Cannes, Antibes and Valbonne, see the section on Alpes Maritimes in Chapter 2.

A list of bookshops in France selling English-language books is to be found at www.wfi.fr/volterre/bookshop.html, and another at www.geocities.com/evelynkeeper/eu-fr.

English-language newspapers and journals

Living France
www.livingfrance.com

France Magazine
www.francemag.com

Connection Côte d'Azur
256 route de Nice
06 600 Antibes
Tel: 04 92 98 66 69
E-mail: info@connectioncotedazur.com
Web site: www.connectioncotedazur.com

France–USA Contacts
3 rue Larochelle
75014 Paris

Free Voice
65 quai d'Orsay
75007 Paris

French Property News
6 Burgess Mews
Wimbledon
London SW19 1UF
Web site: www.french-property-news.com
Monthly property paper.

The News
Sarl Brussac
225 Route d'Angoulême
24004 Périgueux
Tel: 05 53 06 84 40
Monthly newspaper and quarterly magazine.

The Riviera Gazette
738 route Notre Dame
Cidex 47
06330 Roquefort les Pins
Tel: 04 93 09 66 43
Web site: www.TheRivieraGazette.com

The Riviera Reporter
56 chemin de Provence
F-06250 Mougins
Tel: 04 93 45 77 19
Web site: www.riviera-reporter.com

The Riviera Times
8 avenue Jean Moulin
F-06340 Drap/Nice
Tel: 04 93 27 60 00
Web site: www.rivieratimes.com

English libraries

There are several English-language libraries in Paris, and a number in the regions (see Chapter 2). There is also a Paris-based English Language Library for the Blind that operates a service to the regions. A catalogue is available (tel: 01 42 93 47 57).

Estate agents

Numerous estate agents have Web sites that are easily accessible, including via a number of information Web sites such as French-news.com and The Languedoc Page listed below:

Coast Country
Web site: www.coast-country.com
Focuses on the Riviera.

French-news.com
Web site: www.french-news.com

French Property News
Web site: www.french-property-news.com

Internet French Property
Web site: www.french-property.com

Focus on France
Web site: www.outboundpublishing.com

The Languedoc Page
Web site: http://tlp.netfirms.com/livelinks.htm

Expatriate Web sites

There are very many such sites, some of which are listed (with links) at the Back in Blighty Web site under 'Expat Links'.

Back in Blighty
Web site: www.backinblighty.com

Financial advice

Anthony & Cie
Tel: 04 93 65 32 23
Web site: www.antco.com

Blevins Franks International
Tel: 05 53 52 09 75
Web site: www.blevinsfranks.com

Crédit Agricole Britline
Tel: 02 31 55 67 89
Web site: www.britline.com

French Mortgage Advice
Tel: 01425 653408
Web site: www.french-mortgage-connection.co.uk

Siddalls International FR
Tel: 05 56 34 75 51
e-mail: siddalls.bordeaux@wanadoo.fr

French – learning the language

Alliance Française
Tel: 01 45 44 38 28
Web site: www.alliancefr.org and www.alliancefrancaise.org.uk
Offers courses throughout France.

Europa Pages
Web site: www.europa-pages.co.uk/france/
It has a directory of schools, colleges and universities offering French language tuition in France.

People Going Global
Web site: www.peoplegoingglobal.com

It also has a directory of universities and other establishments where one can study French in France, and access to the Newcomers Club Directory for France.

French administration

Taxes
Web site: www.impots.gouv.fr

Legal contacts

Riddell Croft & Co
27 St. Helens Street
Ipswich IP4 1HH
Tel: 01473 384870
E-mail: Contact Keith Croft: kjc@riddellcroft
Web site: www.riddledroft.com

John Howell & Co
17 Maiden Lane, Covent Garden
London WC2E 7NL
Tel: 020 7420 0400
E-mail: france@europelaw.com
Web site: www.europelaw.com

Stephen Smith (France) Ltd
161 Cemetery Road
Ipswich
IP4 2HL
Tel: 01473 437186
E-mail: stephen@stephensmithfranceltd.com
Web site: www.stephensmithfranceltd.com

Sean O'Connor
2 River Walk
Tonbridge
Kent TN9 1DT
Tel: 01732 365378
E-mail: Seanoconnor@aol.com
Website: www.seanoconnor.co.uk

Annie J Digby, Guellec-Digby & Co
Milton Court
Milton Malsor
Northampton
NN7 3AX
Tel: 01604 878961
E-mail: annie.digby@virgin.net

Kingsfords
5/7 Bank Street
Ashford
Kent
Tel: 01233 665544
Contact Virginie Delplace: e-mail: vxd@kingsford.net

Prettys
Elm House
25 Elm Street
Ipswich IP1 2AD
Tel: 01473 232121
E-mail: mcameron@prettys.co.uk; mail prettys.co.uk
Web site: www.prettys.co.uk

Tee France
High Street
Bishop's Stortford
Herts CM23 2LU
Tel: 01279 755200
Fax: 01279 758400
Contact Cathy Izard: e-mail: cmi@stanleytee.co.uk

Turner & Co
59 Charlotte Street
St Paul's Square
Birmingham B3 1PX
Tel: 0121 2001 612
E-mail: turneranco@aol.com
Contact: Sharon Edwards

Simone Paissoni
22 ave Notre Dame
Nice 06000
Tel: 04 93 62 94 95
E-mail: spaissoni@wanadoo.fr

Property – buying and renting

Chez Nous
Web site: www.cheznous.com

French Property News
Web site: www.french-property-news.com

French Property Links
Tel: 01243 539119

Gîtes-in-France
Web site: www.gites-in-france.co.uk

Property in France
Web site: www.propertyinfrance.com

Village Magazine
Web site: www.village.tm.fr
French magazine devoted to rural life.

WebConnection
Web site: www.webconnection.co.uk

ADEME (Agence de l'Environnement et de la Maîtrise de l'Energie)
Tel: 01 47 65 20 00
Web site: www.ademe.fr
Gives advice on issues relating to pollution, how best to heat your home, and grants and subsidies available relating to renewable fuels.

ANAH (Agence Nationale pour l'Amélioration de l'Habitat)
Tel: 08 26 80 39 39
Web site: www.anah.fr
Provides advice in relation to grants and subsidies for building works.

ACDL (Association des Comités de Défense des Locataires)
1 rue de Bellefond
75009 Paris
Tel: 01 48 74 94 84
Tenant's organization.

ADVTV (Association de Défense des Victimes de Troubles du Voisinage)
11 rue du 8 mai 1945
60800 Crepy en Valoy
Tel: 03 44 87 57 17
Gives advice on disputes with neighbours.

ANIL (Association Nationale pour L'Information sur le Logement)
2 boulevard Saint-Martin
75010 Paris
Tel: 01 42 02 05 50
Web site: www.anil.org

CAPEB (Conféderation de l'Artisanat et des Petites Entreprises de Bâtiment)
46 avenue d'Ivry
75013 Paris
Tel: 01 44 24 59 59
Provides lists of contractors for renovation work and can help in cases of disputes relating to building work.

Relocation agencies
Insitu
17av Didier Daurat
BP 5131702
Blagnac
Cedex
e-mail: heather.hughes@insitu-centre.com

Removal firms

Allied Arthur Pierre (France)
Tel: 33 1 34 75 92 92
Web site: www.alliedarthurpierre.com

Allied Pickfords (UK)
Tel: 0800 289 229

Britannia Bradshaw International
Tel: 0161 946 0809
Web site: www.bradshawinternational.com

Grospiron International
Tel: 33 1 48 14 42 42
Web site: www.grospiron.com

Overs International
Tel: 0800 243433
Web site: www.overs.co.uk

Tooth Removals (Riviera)
Tel: 33 4 93 77 90 15
Web site: www.tooth.co.uk

World Wide Shipping & Airfreight Co.
Tel: 02380 633 660
Web site: www.worldfreight.co.uk

Satellite installers

Digibox France
Web site: www.digiboxfr.com

Big Dish Satellite
Tel: 05 55 78 72 98
Web site: www.bigdishsat.com

European Satellite Installations
Tel: 02 96 86 65 93

Susat
Tel: 0845 451 3133
Web site: www.susat.co.uk

Schools

AngloINFO
Web site: www.angloinfo.com
Has details of the main schools on the Riviera.

British Council
Web site: www.britishcouncil.fr
Click on 'Education' for details of the French education system.

Centre Nationale de Documentation sur l'Enseignement Privé
20 rue Fabert
75007 Paris
Tel: 01 47 05 32 68

English Language Schools Association
86 rue de la Tour
75116 Paris
Tel: 01 45 04 48 52

Francegate.com
Web site: http://ydelta.free.fr/school.htm
Contains helpful information and a list of schools with brief information on each of them, including contact details.

French Ministry of Education
Web site: www.education.gouv.fr
Information on schooling.

See also Chapters 2 and 11.

Support services

Accueil des Villes Françaises
Tel: 01 47 70 45 85
Web site: www.avt-accueil.com
Welcomes newcomers to an area and has branches in most main towns and cities. The Web site is in French and English. The phone number given above is for the central office.

Adapt in France
Tel: 04 93 65 33 79
Web site: www.adaptinfrance.org
Based on the Riviera, this organization gives advice to newcomers to France.

Association France–Grande-Bretagne
183 avenue Daumesnil
75012 Paris
Tel: 01 55 78 71 71
Branches throughout France. Similarly, the Royal British Legion and the Royal Air Force Association have branches across the country.

British Community Committee (BCC)
Web site: www.britishinfrance.com
Produces a digest of the many British or Franco-British associations in France. This can be obtained from the British Consulate in Paris and the British Council (see earlier in this Appendix under British consulates and General information on France for contact details).

Americans in France
Web site: www.americansinfrance.net
Contains wide-ranging information, including details of American associations in Paris, the American Church, the American Library, the American University of Paris, the American School, details of the areas in Paris in which Americans live, bookshops, a Thanksgiving store, and a variety of Web links.

Wilson Development Associates
(personal and professional coaching)
Tel: 04 93 77 06 28
Web site: www.wilson-development.com

Swimming pool safety equipment

Floatron
Tel: 04 94 04 44 14
Web site: www.provence-directe.com

Pool Security Solutions
Tel: 04 94 76 98 07
Web site: www.pss-france.com

Saferpools
Tel: 01628 524702
Web site: www.saferpools.co.uk

Airlines

Air France
Tel: 0845 082 0162
Web site: www.airfrance.co.uk

Brit Air
Tel: 08 20 820 820
Web site: www.britair.fr

British Airways
Tel: 0845 773 3377
Web site: www.britishairways.com

British European
Tel: 0870 567 6676
Web site: www.flybe.com

BMI Baby
Tel: 0870 607 0555
Web site: www.flybmi.com

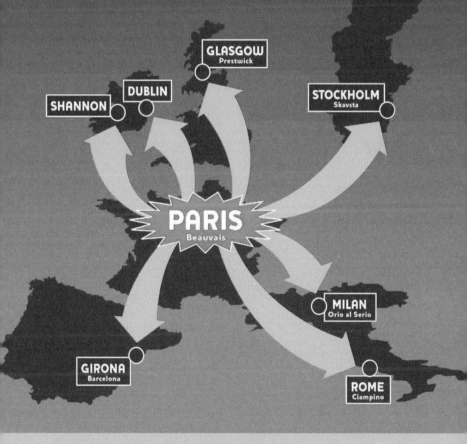

easyJet
Tel: 0870 600 0000
Web site: www.easyjet.co.uk

Flybe
Web site: www.flybe.com

Jet 2
Tel: 0870 737 8282
Web site: www.jet2.co.uk

Ryanair
Tel: 0871 246 0000
Web site: www.ryanair.com

Ferries

Brittany Ferries
Tel: 0870 556 1600
Web site: www.brittany-ferries.com

Condor
Tel: 0845 345 2000
Web site: www.condorferries.co.uk

Corsica Ferries
Tel: 0825 095 095
Web site: www.corsica-ferries.co.uk

Hoverspeed
Tel: 0870 240 8070
Web site: www.hoverspeed.com

Irish Ferries
Tel: 0870 517 1717
Web site: www.irishferries.ie

Norfolkline
Tel: 0870 870 1020
Web site: www.norfolkline.com

P&O Ferries
Tel: 0870 600 0611
Web site: www.posl.com and www.poferries.com

P&O Portsmouth
Tel: 0870 242 4999
Web site: www.poportsmouth.com

SeaFrance
Tel: 0870 571 1711
Web site: www.seafrance.com

SNCM (Société Nationale Maritime Corse Méditerranée)
Tel: 020 7491 4968
Web site: www.sncm.fr

Transmanche
Tel: 0800 9171201
Web site: www.transmancheferries.com

Rail

Eurotunnel
Tel: 0870 535 3535
Web site: www.eurotunnel.com

French Motorail
Tel: 0870 241 5415
Web site: www.frenchmotorail.com

Rail Europe
Tel: 0870 584 8848
Web site: www.raileurope.co.uk

Road and route planning

AA
Web site: www.theaa.com

Mappy
Web site: www.mappy.com

Michelin
Web site: www.michelin-travel.com

RAC
Web site: www.rac.co.uk

Yellow Pages
Web site: www.pagesjaunes.fr
The *White Pages* can be accessed at this site, too.

Appendix 2:
Direct flights from France to the UK and Ireland

Some require connections, notably via Clermont-Ferrand (C-F in the listing). The details given below will obviously be subject to change and should be checked with the operator concerned.

Airports in France accessible from the UK

Appendix 2: Direct Flights

From	To	Airline
Angers	London Gatwick	Air France (via C-F)
Angoulême	London Gatwick	Air France (via C-F)
Annecy	London Gatwick	
Basel-Mulhouse	London Heathrow	BA, Swissair
	London Gatwick	Air France (via C-F)
	Dublin	Swissair
Bergerac	London Stansted	Ryanair
	Bristol	Flybe
	Southampton	Flybe
Biarritz	London Gatwick	Air France (via C-F)
	Birmingham	Air France (via Paris)
Bordeaux	London Gatwick	BA, Air France (via C-F), Flybe
	Bristol	Flybe
	East Midlands	BMI
	Manchester	BMI
	Dublin	Air France
Brest	London Gatwick	Air France, Brit Air
	London Stansted	Ryanair
Carcassonne	London Stansted	Ryanair
Chambéry	Bournemouth	(winter only)
	Southampton	Flybe
Clermont-Ferrand	London Gatwick	Air France, Flybe
	London Stansted	Flybe
	London City	Air France
Corsica, Calvi	Birmingham	(via Munich)
Corsica, Bastia	London Gatwick	Summer charter flights
Dijon	London Gatwick	Air France (via C-F)
Dinard	London Stansted	Ryanair
Geneva	London Heathrow	BA, Swissair
	London Gatwick	easyJet, BA, Air 2000, Monarch, My Travel, Britannia
	London Luton	easyJet
	London Stansted	Ryanair (plus many charter flights)
	London City	Swissair
	Aberdeen	BMI
	Cardiff	BMI
	Guernsey	Flybe
	Jersey	Flybe
	East Midlands	BMI, easyJet

From	To	Airline
	Leeds/Bradford	Jet2
	Liverpool	easyJet
	Manchester	BMI
	Southampton	Flybe
	Teeside	BMI
	Dublin	Swissair, Aer Lingus
Le Havre	London Gatwick	British European, Air France, Brit Air
	London City	Air France, Brit Air
La Rochelle	London Stansted	Ryanair
	Southampton	Flybe
	London Gatwick	Air France (via C-F)
Le Touquet (Pas de Calais)	Biggin Hill	Lov'air
Limoges	London Stansted	Ryanair
Lille	Birmingham	Air France (via Paris)
	Southampton	Flybe
Lourdes	London Luton	
Lyon	London Heathrow	British European, Air France, BA Airways
	London Stansted	easyJet, European Airways
	London Gatwick	Air France (via C-F)
	Belfast	(charter flights)
	Dublin	Aer Lingus
Marseille	London Gatwick	BA, easyJet
	Birmingham	Maersk
	Coventry	Thomsonfly
Montpellier	London Gatwick	BA
	London Stansted	Ryanair
Nantes	London Gatwick	Air France, Brit Air, BA, Flybe
	Birmingham	(via Brussels or Paris)
Nice	London Heathrow	BA, BMI
	London Gatwick	easyJet, BA
	London Luton	easyJet
	London Stansted	easyJet
	Belfast	easyJet
	Birmingham	BA
	Bristol	easyJet, BA
	Coventry	Thomsonfly

From	To	Airline
	East Midlands	BMI
	Edinburgh	BMI
	Glasgow	BMI
	Leeds, Bradford	Jet 2, BMI
	Liverpool	easyJet
	Manchester	BA
	Newcastle	easyJet
	Teeside	BMI
Note: low-cost flights available from Nice to	Paris	easyJet
	Geneva	easyJet
	Stockholm	Sterling
	Copenhagen	Sterling
Nîmes	London Stansted	Ryanair
Paris	London Heathrow	BA, BMI, Flybe
	London Gatwick	BA
	London Luton	easyJet
	London Stansted	Buzz
	London City	Air France, Flybe
	Aberdeen	BA, Air France, Flybe, BMI
	Belfast	easyJet
	Birmingham	BA, Air France
	Bristol	Air France, Flybe
	Cardiff	BMI
	East Midlands	BMI
	Edinburgh	BA, Air France, Flybe, BMI
	Glasgow	BMI
	Leeds, Bradford	BMI
	Liverpool	easyJet
	Manchester	BA, Flybe, BMI
	Newcastle	easyJet
	Southampton	Air France, Flybe
	Cork	Aer Lingus
	Dublin	Aer Lingus
Paris (Beauvais)	Birmingham	Travelite
	Glasgow	Ryanair
	Dublin	Ryanair
	Shannon	Ryanair
Pau	Birmingham	Air France (via Paris)
	London Stansted	Ryanair
Perpignan	London Stansted	Ryanair
	Birmingham	Flybe

From	To	Airline
	Southampton	Flybe
Poitiers	London Stansted	Ryanair
	London Gatwick	Air France (via C-F)
	Birmingham	(via Paris)
Rennes	London Gatwick	Air France (via C-F)
Rodez	London Stansted	Rynair
St Etienne	London Stansted	Ryanair
Strasbourg	London Gatwick	Air France, Brit Air, Flybe
	Birmingham	(via Brussels, Frankfurt or Paris)
St Tropez	Birmingham	(via Zurich)
Toulon	London Gatwick	BA, GB Airways, Air France (via C-F)
Toulouse	London Heathrow	Air France, British European
	London Gatwick	BA, Britannia, easyJet
	Aberdeen	BMI
	Belfast	(charter flights)
	Birmingham	BA, Flybe
	Bristol	Flybe
	Cardiff	Flybe
	East Midlands	BMI Baby
	Edinburgh	Flybe, BMI
	Glasgow	Flybe, BMI
	Guernsey	Flybe
	Jersey	Flybe
	Manchester	Air 2000
	Southampton	Flybe
	Dublin	Aer Lingus
Tours	London Stansted	Ryanair
Zurich	London Heathrow	BA, Swissair
	London Gatwick	easyJet
	London Luton	easyJet
	Birmingham	Swissair
	Edinburgh	BA
	Dublin	Aer Lingus, Swissair

NB: Although not in France, the airports of Geneva and, to some extent, Zurich, provide good access to parts of eastern France.

Details of airline telephone numbers and Web sites are to be found in Appendix 1.

A comprehensive link site for French airports is www.aeroport.fr, though I have been told that this is difficult to access from the UK.

Appendix 3:
Useful French words and phrases

Conveyancing and legal terminology

un acompte	deposit
l'acquéreur	buyer
acquérir	to buy
un acte authentique	official document prepared by a *notaire* recording a transaction
un acte de vente	official document prepared by a *notaire* recording a transfer of land
un arrhes	amount paid in advance by the purchaser that is lost if he or she does not proceed
une attestation	certificate
un avocat	solicitor or barrister (primarily representing clients in court)
une clause particulière	special condition
une clause pénale	penalty clause
une clause suspensive	a conditional clause in a contract
le compromis de vente	contract for sale of land or property
constructible	land that is authorized for building on
la copropriété	property in co-ownership
la décennale	ten-year guarantee on new property
le droit de passage	right of way
les émoluments	fees
expertiser	to value a property
les frais	costs
la jouissance libre	vacant possession

le lotissement	'housing estate' – often only a few houses
le Maître	title of address for *notaire* or *avocat*
le mandat	power of attorney
un notaire	'solicitor' – for conveyancing, wills, financial advice
les parties communes	common parts of property
le permis de construire	planning permission
la remise des clefs	handing over of the keys
résilier	to cancel a contract
le testament	will
le titre de propriété	title deed
la tontine	joint ownership where on death of one joint owner the whole property passes to surviving owner
le vendeur	seller

Types of property

un appartement	apartment or flat
un appartement bourgeois	sizeable apartment, often with servant's room(s) (*chambres de bonne*) on the top floor of the block
un appartement de standing	luxury and, usually, modern apartment
le bastide	stone house
le château	large country mansion, castle or fort
la chaumière	thatched cottage
le colombage	half-timbered house (for example, in Normandy)
la commune	district or area
une demeure	a dwelling
une domaine	country estate
un duplex	an apartment or maisonette on two floors
une ferme	farm
le gentihommerie	small manor house
le logis	dwelling
la maison de campagne	country house

une maison de caractère	character house
une maison de chasse	hunting lodge
la maison de maître	family mansion
une maison jumellée	semi-detached house
une maison mitoyenne	semi-detached house
une maison témoin	showhome
le manoir	manor house
le mas	Provençal-style farmhouse
le moulin	windmill
une parcelle	plot of land
le pavillon	villa or small detached house, often on the outskirts of a town
le presbytère	vicarage
une prieuré	priory
le promoteur	property developer
la propriété	property
en ruines	in ruins
un studio	one-bedroom apartment or bedsit
le terrain à bâtir	building land
un triplex	maisonette on three floors
la vente en l'état de futur d'achèvement	sale of property before it is built
une villa	a detached house, usually modern, with a garden

Property descriptions, condition of the property and estate agents

abîmer	to deteriorate
un abri	shelter
une agence immobilière	estate agent
une alimentation	supply (such as of electricity, water)
l'amiante	asbestos
ancien	old
une antenne	aerial
une antenne parabolique	satellite dish
un appentis	a lean-to

une ardoise	slate
la baignoire	bath
un balcon	balcony
la banlieue	suburb
un bâtiment	building
le béton	concrete
le bilan	survey
le bois	wood
en bon état	in good condition
le bord de mer	by the sea
une bouche d'aération	air vent
le boulon	bolt
le bourg	small town/large village
la brique	brick
les cabinets	toilet
le cadastre	town plan registry
le cadenas	padlock
le cadre	frame
la campagne	countryside
le carrelage	tiled floor
la cave	cellar
le centre commerciale	shopping centre
le certificat d'urbanisme	certificate that property is in a residential area
la chambre (à coucher)	bedroom
la chaudière	water heater
le chauffage	heating
le chauffage collectif	shared heating (in an apartment block)
la cheminée	chimney or fireplace
le chêne	oak
une citerne à eau	water tank
le climatisation	air-conditioning
la cloison	internal wall
la clôture	fence
la commission comprise	commission included
le couloir	corridor
la cour	yard or courtyard
couvert	covered

la cuisine	kitchen
la cuisine americaine	modern fitted kitchen
la cuisinière	cooker, stove
le cuivre	copper
la cuve	tank for gas or oil
le dallage	paving
la date de livraison prévue	expected date of completion
le débarras	box room
une dépendance	outbuilding
un disjoncteur	electrical trip switch
la douche	shower
les eaux usées	waste water
l'éclairage	lighting
une écurie	stable
une entrée	hallway
l'entrien	maintenance
environ	about, approximately
épaisseur	thickness
un escalier	stair
un espace	space
un étable	stable
un étagère	shelf
étanche	waterproof, watertight
un étang	pond
une faute grave	serious defect
le ferraillage	ironwork
la fosse séptique	septic tank
le four	oven
le foyer principal	main or principal home
le guardien	caretaker
le gazon	lawn (*un gazon anglais* – a good lawn)
la gouttière	gutter
la grande surface	large supermarket
la grange	barn
le gravier	gravel
le grenier	attic
la haie	hedge
la hauteur	height

l'humidité	dampness
les installations	fittings
un interrupteur	switch
le jardin	garden
la largeur	width
le lavebo	washbasin
le liège	cork
le linteau	lintel
la longueur	length
la lucarne	dormer window or skylight
le mazout	domestic heating oil
le mètre carré	square metre
meublé	furnished
les meubles	furniture
la moquette	fitted carpet
le mur	wall
le mur mitoyen	party wall
le niveau	level
l'organisme prêteur	lender
le palier	landing
le parquet	wooden floor
la peinture	paintwork
la pelouse	lawn
le perron	flight of steps in front of a house
la pièce	room
le pierre	stone
le pilier	pillar
le pin	pine
la piscine	swimming pool
le placard	cupboard
le plafond	ceiling
le plâtre	plaster
la plomberie	plumbing
la poignée	handle
le portail	gate
le potager	kitchen garden
la poubelle	dustbin
le poutre	wooden beam

le premier étage	first floor
la prise	electric socket
le puits	well
le quartier	district of a town or city
le ramoneur	chimney sweep
les rangements	storage space
refait	restored
rénové	renovated
le rez de chaussée	ground floor
le robinet	tap
la salle	room
la salle de bains	bathroom
la salle à manger	dining room
la salle de séjour/le séjour	living room/lounge
le salon	sitting room, lounge, drawing room
le sol	ground
une source	spring
le sous-sol	basement
le terrain	ground
les toilettes	toilets
le toit	roof
la toiture en terrasse	flat roof
le tout à l'égout	mains drainage
la tuile	roof tile
le verger	orchard
le vernis	varnish
le vestibule	entrance hall
viabilisé	services laid on
la vitre	windowpane
le volet	shutter

Apartments

un ascenseur	lift or elevator
les charges (comprises)	services charges (included)
la concierge	caretaker
un immeuble	block of flats

les réglements de copropriété	rules and regulations for an apartment block or other property development

Works of renovation and repair

un agrandissement	extension
agré(e)	certified
aménageable	convertible
aménager	to convert
un artisan maçon	builder
un atelier	workshop
le bricolage	DIY
le carreleur	tiler
le chantier	work site
le clou	nail
délabré	dilapidated or tumble-down
un devis	estimate
l'échafaudage	scaffolding
une échelle	ladder
une facture	bill
la livraison	delivery
le maçon	builder
le marteau	hammer
le menuisier	joiner
le papier peint	wallpaper
une pépinière	garden centre
une perceuse	drill
le pinceau	paintbrush
le plombier	plumber
la quincaillerie	hardware shop
le ravalement	restoration
restaurer	to restore, a property
la scie	saw
la sous-couche	undercoat
le tournevis	screwdriver
la truelle	trowel
le variateur	dimmer switch

Renting

un bail	a lease
un bailleur	lessor, the owner of a tenanted property
la caution	guarantee or security deposit
la durée	duration
un état des lieux	record of condition of property at start and end of tenancy
le loyer	rent
le préavis	notice
le propriétaire	landlord
le renouvellement	renewal of lease
les travaux	building works

Utilities

un abonnement	standing charge
le compteur	meter
EDF-GDF	*Electricité de France-Gaz de France*
le gaz de ville	mains gas
la puissance	electricity power rating

Financial

un banque	bank
une caisse d'épargne	savings bank
le compte courant	current account
le comptable	accountant
constituer une societe	to form a company
un distributeur de billets	cash machine
un droit	a right
un droit de succession	inheritance tax
un emprunt	loan
le forfait	fixed amount or all in price
les frais de dossier	mortgage arrangement fee by bank

le guichet	counter
hors taxe (HT)	excluding tax
un huissier	official legal officer whose duties are like those of a bailiff in the UK
le hypothèque	mortgage
le montant	total to be paid
le plus-value	capital gain
le prélèvement	direct debit
le prêt	loan
relevé d'identité bancaire (le RIB)	bank account details
une société	company
société à responsabilité limitée (SARL)	limited company
société civile immobilière (SCI)	non-trading property company
la tacite reconduction	automatic renewal of contract
le taux d'intérêt	rate of interest
le taxe d'habitation	local tax on occupation of property
le taxe foncière	local tax on ownership of property
taxe sur la valeur ajoutée (TVA)	VAT
toutes taxes comprises (TTC)	including tax

Medical

un carnet de santé	medical record book held by patient
la carte vitale	medical card for automatic reimbursement
un médecin conventionné	doctor who works within the French health service
un médecin généraliste	GP
une ordonnance	prescription
la pharmacie de garde	duty chemist
Service d'Aide Médicale d'Urgence (le SAMU)	emergency medical service

Miscellaneous

l'accueil	reception
arrière-pays	hinterland
déménager	to move house
une fuite de gaz	gas leak
un fusable	fuse
train à grande vitesse (TGV)	high-speed train

Dealings with the authorities

une carte de séjour	residence permit
la carte grise	car registration document
le commissariat de police	police station
le constat amiable	accident report form to be signed by both parties
l'hôtel des impôts	tax office
un impôt	tax
la mairie	town hall

Internet

l'adresse e-mail	e-mail address
un annexe	attachment
l'arabas (the 's' is pronounced)	name for @ symbol
l'écran	screen
un e-mail	e-mail
un fichier joint	attachment
un lien	link
la mot de passe	password
la moteur de recherche	search engine
le point-com	dotcom
précédent	previous, back
quitter	exit

rédiger un courrier	to send an e-mail
le réseau	network
le site internet	Web site
suivant	next
télécharger	to download
le tiret	hyphen

Appendix 4:
Abbreviations and phrases used in property details

Note: French property is described by the number of rooms (*pièces*), excluding kitchen, toilet and bathrooms.

T3, F3	three rooms (not counting kitchen, hall, bathroom, toilet)
4p	*quatre pièces* = four rooms
3e ét	*troisième étage* = third floor
à ne pas rater	not to be missed
appt	*appartment* = apartment
à saisir	a must
à voir	must been seen
biblio	*bibilothèque* = library
bur	*bureau* = study
cave	cellar
chem	*cheminée* = with a fireplace
chs	*chambres* = bedrooms
climat	*climatisation* = air-conditioning
cuis éq	*cuisine équipée* = fitted kitchen
gd standing	*grand standing* = prestigious
gge	*garage* = garage
grd séj	*grand séjour* = large living room
hab	*habitable* = habitable
hon	*honoraires* = fees
nid d'amour	love nest

pisc	*piscine* = pool
proche écoles et commerces	near to schools and shops
rdc	*rez de chausée* = ground floor
rés fermée	enclosed residence
SàM	*salle à manger* = dining room
SdB	*salle de bain* = bathroom
séj	*le sejour* = living room/lounge
s/sol	*sous-sol* = basement
sur 2 niv	*sur deux niveaux* = on two levels
vue dégagée	a clear view

See also Appendix 3.

Appendix 5:
Pet travel scheme – approved routes and carriers

By sea

Caen to Portsmouth	Brittany Ferries
Calais to Dover	Hoverspeed, P&O Ferries, Sea France
Cherbourg to Plymouth	Brittany Ferries
Cherbourg to Poole	Brittany Ferries
Cherbourg to Portsmouth	P&O
Dieppe to Newhaven	Hoverspeed (summer only)
Roscoff to Plymouth	Brittany Ferries
St Malo to Plymouth	Brittany Ferries (winter only)
St Malo to Poole	Condor Ferries
Santander to Portsmouth	Brittany Ferries (winter only)
Santander to Plymouth	Brittany Ferries (summer only)

By rail

Brussels, Lille, Paris to London Waterloo	Eurostar (guide dogs only)
Calais (Coquelles) to Folkstone (Cheriton)	Eurotunnel Shuttle Service (but not Eurostar)

By air

Brussels to London Heathrow	BMI British Midland
Montpellier to London Gatwick	GB Airways
Nantes to London Gatwick	GB Airways
Nice to London Heathrow	BMI British Midland, KLM Cargo (via Amsterdam)
Paris (CDG) to London Heathrow	BMI British Midland (guide and hearing dogs only – must be in cabin), KLM Cargo (via Amsterdam)
Toulon-Hyères to London Gatwick	GB Airways
Toulouse to London Heathrow	Air France (guide dogs only)
Barcelona to London Gatwick	British Airways
Barcelona to London Heathrow	KLM Cargo (via Amsterdam)

Approved charter companies

NB: The plane must be booked, not just the ticket. Also, the following information is subject to variation, so you should check before making your travel plans. Pets travel as cargo unless stated otherwise.

Avignon to London Heathrow	Jet Aviation
Cannes to London Heathrow	Net-Jets-Transportes Aereos SA
Marseille to London Heathrow	Net-Jets-Transportes Aereos SA
Nice to London Heathrow	Jet Aviation, Net-Jets-Transportes Aereos SA, Tag Aviation
Paris CDG to London Heathrow	Net-Jets-Transportes Aereos SA
Paris Le Bourget to London Heathrow	Net-Jets-Transportes Aereos SA
Geneva to London Heathrow	Net-Jets-Transportes Aereos SA, Tag Aviation
Zurich to London Heathrow	Jet Aviation, Net-Jets-Transportes Aereos SA

Information

Pets helpline
Tel: 0870 241 1710 (Monday–Friday, 8.30 am to 5.00 pm, UK time)
Website: www.defra.gov.uk
e-mail: helpline@defra.gsi.gov.uk

Appendix 6: Public holidays

1 January
Easter Sunday and Monday
1 May
8 May
Ascension Day (sixth Thursday after Easter)
Pentecost (second Monday after Ascension)
14 July, Bastille Day
15 August
1 November
11 November
25 December

Appendix 7:
Further reading

Biggins, Alan (2002) *Selling French Dreams*, Kirkdale Books, Great Horwood, Buckinghamshire

Brame, Geneviève (2004) *Chez vous en France: Living and Working in France, third edition,* Kogan Page, London

Burch Donald, Elsie (1995) *The French Farmhouse*, Little, Brown & Co, London

Dyson, Henry (1991) *French Real Property and Succession Law*, Robert Hale, London

Everett, David (1999) *Buying and Restoring Old Properties in France*, Robert Hale, London

Hampshire, David (1993) *Living and Working in France*, Survival Books, Fleet

Hampshire, David (1996) *Buying a Home in France*, Survival Books, Fleet

Hart, Alan (1998) *Living and Working in France*, How to Books, Oxford

Hunt, Deborah (2003) *Starting and Running a B&B in France*, How to Books, Oxford

Laredo, Joe (2003) *Renovating and Restoring French Property*, Survival Books, Fleet

Mayle, Peter (2000) *A Year in Provence*, Penguin, London

Pastour, Ludovic, and Williams, Jennifer (1991) *Setting up a small business in France*, French Chamber of Commerce, London

Platt, Polly (1994) *French or Foe?*, Culture Crossings Limited, London

Index

Index of advertisers